LSD: Personality and Experience
*by Harriet Linton Barr, Robert J. Langs, Robert R. Holt,
Leo Goldberger, and George S. Klein*

Treatment of the Borderline Adolescent: A Developmental Approach
by James F. Masterson

Psychopathology: Contributions from the Biological, Behavioral, and Social Sciences
edited by Muriel Hammer, Kurt Salzinger, and Samuel Sutton

Abnormal Children and Youth: Therapy and Research
by Anthony Davids

Principles of Psychotherapy with Children
by John M. Reisman

Aversive Maternal Control: A Theory of Schizophrenic Development
by Alfred B. Heilbrun, Jr.

Individual Differences in Children
edited by Jack C. Westman

Ego Functions in Schizophrenics, Neurotics, and Normals: A Systematic Study of
Conceptual, Diagnostic, and Therapeutic Aspects
by Leopold Bellak, Marvin Hurvich, and Helen A. Gediman

Innovative Treatment Methods in Psychopathology
edited by Karen S. Calhoun, Henry E. Adams, and Kevin M. Mitchell

The Changing School Scene: Challenge to Psychology
by Leah Gold Fein

Troubled Children: Their Families, Schools, and Treatments
by Leonore R. Love and Jaques W. Kaswan

Research Strategies in Psychotherapy
by Edward S. Bordin

RESEARCH STRATEGIES IN PSYCHOTHERAPY

RESEARCH STRATEGIES IN PSYCHOTHERAPY

EDWARD S. BORDIN
University of Michigan

A WILEY-INTERSCIENCE PUBLICATION

JOHN WILEY & SONS   New York • London • Sydney • Toronto

Library of Congress Cataloging in Publication Data

Bordin, Edward S.
Research strategies in psychotherapy.

(Wiley series on personality processes)
"A Wiley-Interscience publication."
Bibliography: p.
1. Psychiatric research. 2. Psychotherapy.
I. Title. [DNLM: 1. Psychotherapy. WM420 B729r]

RC337.B67   616.8'914   74-11272
ISBN 0-471-08885-4

Printed in the United States of America

10 9 8 7 6 5 4 3 2 1

Series Preface

This series of books is addressed to behavioral scientists interested in the nature of human personality. Its scope should prove pertinent to personality theorists and researchers as well as to clinicians concerned with applying an understanding of personality processes to the amelioration of emotional difficulties in living. To this end, the series provides a scholarly integration of theoretical formulations, empirical data, and practical recommendations.

Six major aspects of studying and learning about human personality can be designated: personality therapy, personality structure and dynamics, personality development, personality assessment, personality change, and personality adjustment. In exploring these aspects of personality, the books in the series discuss a number of distinct but related subject areas: the nature and implications of various theories of personality; personality characteristics that account for consistencies and variations in human behavior; the emergence of personality processes in children and adolescents; the use of interviewing and testing procedures to evaluate individual differences in personality; efforts to modify personality styles through psychotherapy, counseling, behavior therapy, and other methods of influence; and patterns of abnormal personality functioning that impair individual competence.

IRVING B. WEINER

Case Western Reserve University
Cleveland, Ohio

v

Preface

This book was almost a decade in the writing. This was so partly because of the imperatives of a full schedule of teaching, other scholarly activities, and of practice, but also because I was frightened by the ambitiousness of my intent. I wanted to inspire the graduate student or the young research worker—to awaken him to the needs and possibilities for research in psychotherapy. I wished to help him combine his clinical experience and his natural curiosity to generalize beyond the specific person he was seeking to help. I wanted to portray the tension that arises when conviction founded in a set of clinical experience confronts contradictory convictions founded on other sets of clinical experiences. I was conscious of the number of pitfalls in research; I wanted to chart ways to avoid such mistakes as drifting away from important questions into trivialities, or using methods or research designs that are inconsistent with underlying assumptions.

There are two main parts to this book. The first four chapters are devoted to the main methodological issues: where to look for the important questions to be addressed; the strategies of evaluations; process analysis; and the use of simplifications and other analogues. The second part addresses the question of what we now know. The superficially simple question, "Does psychotherapy work?", is bypassed. Instead, I confront what we know about different processes and parts of processes in the hands of different kinds of therapists with different persons. Here I hope to help identify what the next steps should be and where they might lead.

I try to offer a comprehensive coverage of the literature. I confine myself to treatment by psychological means as distinct from biochemical, surgical or other physiological treatments. Although group and *in vivo* treatments are considered, the center of attention is the treatment situation where a person in psychological distress seeks the aid of a mental health practitioner and where the treatment process is based on their interaction.

The scholarly literature on psychotherapy is widely scattered and highly variable in quality. I am certain that my search did not uncover all of the relevant material. Given the enormity of the task, I regret but do not apologize for the gaps.

I owe the usual intellectual debts to the friends, colleagues, and students who were and are part of my life. I must make special mention of Harold Raush and Allen Dittmann, who joined with me about 25 years ago on a research program, from whom I learned a great deal. Former students, Albert Cain and Edward Ryan, and a current one, Sue Lehrke, read parts of the manuscript and provided useful criticism. Former student and Wiley Series Editor Irving Weiner offered encouragement and insightful suggestions regarding the whole.

As always, I profited from discussions with my wife, Ruth, who gave me an opportunity to see a historian's perspective. Moreover, she made specific contributions in the form of editorial suggestions and writing the index.

I am indebted to Wenda Ulmer for the patience and energy with which she labored through the typing of the various revisions.

Finally, there are the permissions to quote. The lives of all authors are made simpler by the American Psychological Association's blanket permission to quote from its journals. The officers of the journals, *Psychiatry* and the *Bulletin of Menninger Clinic,* gave permission for specific quotes. This courtesy was also granted by the following publishers: Aldine Publishing Company, International Universities Press, Julian Press, Macmillan Publishing Company, McGraw-Hill Book Company, and Plenum Publishing Corporation.

EDWARD S. BORDIN

August 1974
Ann Arbor, Michigan

Contents

RESEARCH STRATEGIES IN PSYCHOTHERAPY

CHAPTER 1

The Sources of Research in Psychotherapy

Students of psychotherapy, whether clinical psychologists, psychiatrists, or representatives of other related disciplines, are subject to conflicting orientations and motivations as they confront the problem of understanding psychotherapy and of verifying this understanding. By its very nature, psychotherapy concerns itself with some of the most complex and, therefore, most baffling aspects of human phenomena, encountered, moreover, under conditions of human suffering. A psychological treatment process places the helper-healer in a personal encounter unaccompanied by the impersonalizing and objectifying effects of biochemical treatments or of surgical interventions. His interventions are of a personal nature; the specific therapeutic agent is his reaction to the patient. These conditions force him to seek simultaneously the subjectivity and empathy needed in the service of sensitivity to another person and the objectivity appropriate to professional responsibility. When he steps back from the action role to that of observer and scientist, the psychotherapist retains this conflict. Having acquired faith in a particular mode of alleviating the patient's pain and of removing its source, his subjectivity and empathy block experimentation and suppress his doubts. The imperatives of action to offer immediate succor prohibit much attention to doubt, especially of the scientific variety, which requires time-consuming diversions of energies into laboratory experiments and other processes required for verification. Such activities postpone attention to the needs of the present patient in favor of a search for a more certain treatment to be offered at a future time for the benefit of some as yet unidentified sufferer.[1]

This perspective on the motivations of psychotherapists will make understandable the course that research efforts have taken and will add depth to discussion of designs of research. This first chapter starts with a brief overview of the history of research in psychotherapy, followed by a discussion of where the prime questions for investigation are to be found.

---

[1] For a fuller discussion of the problems of reconciling the motivations of healer and scientist in training programs, see Bordin (1966a).

A BRIEF HISTORY

The first stage of research might be called the healer-dominated one. The healer insisted that the interests of science must in no way intrude upon the treatment relationship; in this view, no person other than the therapist (and, of course, his patient) can have direct access to the events of psychotherapy. The only medium that fitted these requirements was the case study, usually reported some time after treatment was completed and, of course, with every effort to conceal the identity of the patient. These case studies were designed to describe the condition of the individual as he came to treatment, the nature of the treatment process, and the outcome. As Bolgar (1965, p. 28) has pointed out, "The case study method is the traditional approach of all clinical research. It is essentially exploratory in nature; it focuses on the individual, and it aims primarily at discovering and generating hypotheses." In addition to coinciding with the psychotherapist's ethical and emotional commitment to his patient, the case study fits the requirement that insightful observation and description precede more radical experimentation.

For a long time, up to 1920 (Paul, 1968), this was *the* method of research. Many articles in current psychiatric journals are of this character. It is interesting to note that even those who associate themselves with the laboratory and sophisticated science, when they turn to their own work, resort to the case report (Wolpe, 1958). The limitations of this way of gathering data are so obvious that it is easy to overlook the contributions of the case method. The American compulsively pragmatic stance predisposes us to view the case study only with regard to its usefulness for evaluating the effects of psychotherapy. Freud, the product of another culture, was more concerned with it as a vehicle for gratifying his epistemic curiosity. His case studies (1949b) are monuments to his drive to understand the wellsprings underlying the behavior and experience reported to him and exhibited during the course of his interviews with patients. He sought for a conception of human personality organization and development that would give coherence to these observations.

When attention was directed toward evaluating the effects of psychotherapy, many chose to examine the more limited question of how many persons benefited to what degree. In effect, this approach represents an accumulating of case reports to draw up a balance sheet of gains and losses. Many hospitals, clinics, or groupings of private practitioners by theoretical orientation published such compilations. In reviewing a great number of these reports, Eysenck (1952) called attention to the inadequacies of such data as a basis for deciding whether psychotherapy can bring about certain changes in behavior and experience and, if so, under what conditions this is possible. At the same time, he performed the disservice of fostering the conclusion that he had demonstrated that psychotherapy exerted no effect beyond that of time and general care.[2] As Kiesler (1966) has specified so well, adequate studies must take into account individual differences, even within diagnostic categories; must specify treatment procedures beyond the simple designation of theoretical orientation; and must be incisive regarding the changes sought.

Eventually, psychotherapists began to depart from a superficial view of their ethical responsibilities to their patients. Although the pressures of human suffering require whatever efforts our crude and perhaps mistaken understanding dictates, our commitments to improving our methods and insuring their effectiveness demand a balancing concern with research. Furthermore, psychotherapists began to discover that it was they rather than their patients who reacted to more intrusive modes of study. Intrusion can be minimized when therapeutic interviews are tape recorded. Even under the more intrusive conditions of sound filmed psychotherapy, Bergman (1966) concluded "that filmed psychotherapy is possible, and that in all essentials, for better or worse, such therapy does not differ much from psychotherapy in other settings" (p. 49). He found that his patient's awareness of the cameraman and of the research staff became the special avenue through which she expressed her pathologically dictated transference and distance needs. Bergman's remarkably candid report illustrates the pressures of the research procedure on the therapist, while showing that these pressures are similar to those that exist in the absence of research. He reports that some of his major anxieties involved exposing himself to the criticism of his peers, present or future, and the kinds of verbal commitments, implied or actual, he felt bound by and frustrated about when predicted events did not appear. The vividness and permanence of the record aside, therapists do make this kind of commitment to others (e.g., in staff conferences) or to themselves, which means to an implied other, even in the absence of research and are subject to the same kinds of potentially interfering anxieties.

To Rogers (1942, 1951), his students, and his coworkers must go the credit for the big breakthrough of introducing magnetic tape recording of psychotherapeutic interviews as a systematic method for making the events of psychotherapy available to an independent observer. Beginning in the early 1940s, increasing numbers of workers have extended this method. Although the early set of this line of research was directed

---

[2] Meltzoff and Kornreich (1970) criticized Eysenck for not distinguishing between adequate and inadequate studies and offered a revised tally which showed 48 of 57 studies, classified as adequate, demonstrating positive effects for psychotherapy.

toward answering the question of whether some broad orientation toward psychotherapy was empirically tenable, its major effect has been to focus attention at a more sophisticated level. Research workers began to address themselves to much more specific questions regarding the influence of one person on another. Giving additional impetus to this general trend was the great attention to sequences of behavior at the minute level that psychotherapists applying learning theory to psychotherapy bring to their task (Krasner & Ullmann, 1965). During the last two decades enough research accumulated to stimulate a periodic series of conferences on research (Rubinstein & Parloff, 1959; Strupp & Luborsky, 1962; Shlien, 1968). The most recent conference saw much less concern with broad theoretical orientations and much greater concentration on selected phenomena, for example, the characteristics of periods of peak therapeutic activity, the influence of ambiguity in therapeutic relationships, and the establishment of basic speech and other primitive social behavior in schizophrenic children.

TARGETS FOR RESEARCH

Once one discovers that to ask whether psychotherapy is effective or useful is to place a simplistic cover on a complex volume of questions, it becomes vital to examine the process of formulating targets for research. The troubled person seeking psychotherapy carries with him a complex accumulation of experiences with a wide variety of individuals at varying degrees of intimacy. In addition to his direct experience with the therapist, he can think, dream, fantasize, and even read about him. The period of treatment can stretch into years. Is it any wonder that a survey of research on psychotherapy leaves us in confusion because of the apparent lack of connection between the efforts of different investigators? If research is to achieve one of its important aims of creating a meaningful dialogue among investigators, that is, if investigators are to speak to each other through their research, each investigator must give special attention to addressing his studies to the questions which lie at the heart of the problem. Out of the mass of questions that might be asked about psychotherapy, which are the central ones? Where might answering them lead?

There are three basic sources of research questions: clinical experience and common sense, theories of human behavior and of psychotherapy, and the juncture points between competing theories. We shall here be concerned with identifying the questions inherent in clinical lore or theory and shall leave for later chapters the problem of developing the further definitions, modes of observation, and measurements necessary to securing the empirical answers. The main aim is to illustrate the process of identifying where and how the vital researchable questions are to be found.

Clinical Experience and Common Sense

An investigator does not have to be committed to a particular view of human behavior; he need only be curious and driven to satisfy that curiosity. The foremost very practical question is, of course, how useful the experience of psychotherapy has been. Did the patient change in the manner expected and desired? No special theory is required to formulate the question, though theoretical decisions, either implicitly or, it is hoped, explicitly made, will be forced on the investigator when he devises his methodology for the study. This question of effectiveness and many similar ones arise out of the very activity of psychotherapy. The interacting hopes and expectations of patients and therapists dictate them. The more general question of whether psychotherapy achieves its aims spawns a whole series of derivative questions.

Method-oriented questions: Which method produces the most results in the shortest time? Can methods be combined to produce greater results?

Patient-oriented questions: Can certain kinds of persons be helped more than others? Does the patient's view of his therapy and his therapist vary according to his personality? What are his retrospective views as contrasted with his concurrent views? Can one predict duration and/or premature withdrawal? How does a patient's attitude (expectancy) toward therapy influence its effect?

Therapist-oriented questions: Does the personality of the therapist influence the outcome? Does the therapist's attitude (expectancy) influence the outcome or duration? Do therapists have preferences and other attitudes regarding patients, goals, or methods? What is the therapist's concurrent, as compared to retrospective, view of the patient and the therapy?

Environmentally oriented questions: How do family structure, work structure, season, climate, general social events, and other external conditions influence the treatment process, its duration, and its outcome?

Interactions: Is the comparative effectiveness of a particular method of psychotherapy dependent on the personality of the patient? On that of the therapist? On environmental conditions? What are the interacting influences of all three? How do the expectations of patient and therapist interact? How do their concurrent and retrospective views of psychotherapy relate?

Theory as a Source of Research Questions

Curiosity provokes examination of that which is hidden from us or is not easily discerned or understood. Questions which are initially directed toward externals of events eventually turn attention to underlying principles and processes. Thereupon theory is born. Even our brief survey of the questions that can be asked from a purely empirical standpoint suggests that the investigator who approaches psychotherapy without recourse to theories faces a discouragingly vast array of data available for analysis. Two persons meet for a period or periods of time, 50 minutes or whatever, each bearing the residues of varieties of physiological and cultural events, of intrapersonal and interpersonal experiences. Each emits sounds, expressive movements, and the like which have an impact on the other. Surrounding these events, which are bounded by their comings and goings, are concurrent experiences taking place with other associates or their products in other settings. Does one take a highly sophisticated computer and devise a program comprehensive enough to process *all* these data for all possible relations?

As yet, no such computer or program is available. Even if it were, the past history of science does not encourage the belief that great advances are made by such undiscriminating scoopings of data. There is, of course, a place for the careful, searchingly descriptive analyses of events that are a necessary prelude to theoretical formulation, and these might include large-scale surveys of proportions inviting machine methods of data reduction. In the long run, however, a sustained investigation of psychotherapeutic phenomena through a series of studies must rest upon some thoughtful formulation about how the events of psychotherapy are to be understood.

We turn, then, to an examination of the various theories of psychotherapy and the kinds of empirically verifiable questions they raise. In the long run the search for verification seeks to pit alternative explanations against each other. After examining each theory for the internally generated empirical questions it contains, we shall seek to expose the juncture points between theories which can bring about their empirical confrontations. Before proceeding, however, it would be best to delimit the task. Any theory of psychotherapy must ultimately either embody a theory of personality development and psychopathology or be embodied in such a theory. Thus the tenability of the theory will rest on initial observations of personality development and psychopathology apart from psychotherapy as well as directly relevant to it. For the purposes of this book we shall adhere closely to the aspects of theory that speak directly to psychotherapy and to the efforts made to verify them.

ORTHODOX PSYCHOANALYTIC THEORY[3]

Any subdivision within the sprawling mass of what can be included within psychoanalytic theories is necessarily arbitrary. Various deviations and additions developed in response to Freud's basic formulations. Of these, some developed within the basic framework, and others, sometimes starting inside the framework, sometimes not, grew outside the boundaries of basic psychoanalytic thinking. To complicate matters further, some of those that were outside subsequently were reabsorbed into the psychoanalytic framework. Furthermore, some of the deviations represent alternative ways of viewing personality organization and dynamics without pointing to new ways of instigating change. In this section we shall adhere as faithfully as possible to the formulations of Freud and his closest followers.

Free Association   Psychoanalysis as a method of psychotherapy is marked by the application of the "basic rule" of free association, which requires that the patient be instructed to say whatever comes to his mind without selection, whether to avoid embarrassment, to make sense, or to be realistic. As evolved by Freud, the basic rule was accompanied by the conditions of lying supine on a couch with the analyst seated out of the patient's line of vision and, at least initially, relatively silent. As a centralist theory of personality, psychoanalysis sees the important determinants of behavior as being centered about native and acquired drives and motives which are organized into cognitive, affective, and action systems. The intent of the basic rule and the accompanying conditions is to provide a situation maximally conducive to laying bare these internally organized systems by minimizing the influence of external (situational) determinants.

Much of psychoanalytic theory contains, both implicitly and explicitly, hypotheses regarding the relations between individual differences and the nature of the response to the basic task.[4] Bellak (1961) in his very thorough review of the role of free association points out that the instruction to say whatever comes to mind without selection is an invitation to relax these functions (perceiving, reasoning, etc.) that we exercise in adapting to reality. This is an invitation to regress to a primary process mode of experiencing. Yet this regression, while sharing many of the

---

[3] In discussing each theory I will strive to treat it from "the inside," from its inner logic and attitudes.

[4] Italics will be used to call attention to assertions that raise reasonably explicit research questions. Often, as in this paragraph, the italicized sentence will be the most general statement and will be surrounded by many more specific ones.

same characteristics, is not identical with the regression exhibited, for example, in schizophrenic thinking, in that the best working analytic patient is "able to oscillate between reduction and increased adaptive functions while exercising the synthetic functioning and thereby producing new insights, working through and reintegrating previous apperceptive distortions" (p. 14). Bellak goes on to elaborate how the oscillating function of the ego in free association leads to the expectation of differential reactions. Some kinds of patients—hysteric and schizophrenic—are better able to respond in the regressive phases, whereas obsessives are better able to adapt and synthesize. The latter group finds it difficult to give up cognitive vigilance in order to regress to preconscious levels. Presumably, hysterics can be differentiated from schizophrenics by their greater ability to adapt and synthesize.

In his concept of the autonomy of the ego of inner and outer environments, Rapaport (1958) introduces ideas that point toward an understanding of how personality organization can influence response to the associative task. In essence he underlines the fact that psychic structures useful for memory storage, inhibition and delay, and reasoning evolving out of native sensory-motor-corticoneural equipment are interposed between the individual and the pressures from drives and external stimuli. Since complete independence of either drives or external reality is inconceivable, Rapaport speaks of the relative autonomy of the ego. A necessary condition to effective functioning is the organism's capacity to maintain this relative autonomy and thus escape slavery either to drives or to external stimulation. He points out that sudden intensification of drives (e.g., in puberty) or conditions of curtailed stimulation and information (e.g., sensory deprivation), especially when coupled with humiliating, degrading, and guilt-arousing information, as in brain washing, will diminish ego autonomy. Again, we find obsessive-compulsives used as the example. Rapaport emphasizes the increased elaboration of the secondary process in this condition which makes for the substitution of intensified observation and logical analysis for affective and ideational signals. "Obsessive-compulsive defense thus maximizes the ego's autonomy from the id, but it does so at the cost of ever increasing impairment of the ego's autonomy from the environment: the suppression of affective and ideational cues of drive origin renders the ego's judgments and decisions increasingly dependent upon external cues" (p. 23). Conversely, borderline and psychotic patients are seen as instances in which reduction of the ego's autonomy of drives results in loss of touch with reality. *Thus we can arrive at a general formulation that the balance of personality organization between autonomy of drives and external stimulation will predict how an individual will respond to the task of free association.*

Speculation regarding the influence of character structure on response to free association has, of course, influenced ideas regarding the adaptations in psychoanalysis necessary to the successful treatment of varieties of patients. Awareness of the consequences of the schizophrenic patient's impaired capacities to respond realistically and adaptively led to the suggestions that schizophrenic and other psychotic patients not be encouraged to free associate and that their capacities for reacting to realistic events be supported and enhanced (Federn, 1952; Fromm-Reichmann, 1950; Eissler, 1952).

It has also been suggested that psychoanalytic theory makes the implicit assumption that persons free of pathology will be able to free associate more readily (Bordin, 1964). The argument runs that, in setting the basic rule, the psychoanalyst expects that defenses and other characterological structures which are part of the pathology will become obstacles toward carrying out the task. The psychoanalytic treatment model requires that the patient's inability to comply fully with the basic task be expressed as transference resistances, the analysis of which set in motion a reorganization and redistribution of energy and its psychic structuring. This, in turn, will bring about a state in which the person is able to experience a free flow of ideas accompanied by rich affect, all of which are available for expression, are subject to observation, and are reacted to. In short, he associates freely. Thus those who have been freed of pathology through treatment or through benign conditions of development will be able to associate more readily.

As was seen in the foregoing reviews of Bellak's and Rapaport's statements, personality (diagnosis and character) will not only influence the adequacy of response to free association but also the style of response, for example, the modes of resistance exhibited. The interaction of genetic and topographic formulations leads to expectations that the contents of free association will exhibit predictable ordering based on the particular genetic and topographic organization; that is, the affects and associated experiences which are least subject to repression and which are part of the individual's ongoing experience will appear first, and those that are most intimately bound to earliest and most conflict-laden and deeply repressed experiences will appear last, presumably after the processes of repression have been analyzed.

Although many adherents of psychoanalysis have introduced modifications in the basic psychoanalytic situation, there has been relatively little systematic effort to specify the principles which might govern such modifications. Alexander and his collaborators (Alexander & French, 1946) explored thoroughly various modifications of the basic conditions (i.e., lying on a couch vs. sitting up, frequency of interviews, use of therapist's real characteristics, etc.) but considered the effects chiefly in larger terms than the specifics of free association. Braatøy (1954) was more specific in considering the influence of the supine position and its relation to general states of muscular tension and relaxation. Bordin (1955) analyzed the situation from a perceptual point of view which highlights the ambiguity inherent in the basic rule and the accompanying opaqueness of the therapist due to his abstention from expressing or offering advice or opinions, his position out of the patient's line of vision, and the general sparseness of his communications. *How much modification of the basic situation will cause a significant difference in such effects as the ease with which different persons can comply with the task and relative readiness to regress or form transference is little specified and certainly has not been investigated in any systematic fashion.*

Interpretation and Resistance   As has already been pointed out, the analyst expects that sooner or later the patient's necessary response to the task of free association is resistance. Resistance is defined as interference with the work of therapy which is most centrally expressed in circumvention of the basic rule. It is assumed that sooner or later the facilitation of regression inherent in the basic conditions leads the patient's thought and affects to those impulses which are surrounded by conflict, and this, in turn, provokes anxiety and activates customary modes of reducing anxiety (defenses) which consist of ways to interrupt the experience by blocking off awareness of the ideas or the affects or both. The logic of this position and its grounding in what has come to be subsumed under the rubric of "ego psychology" culminate in the explanation of the process of change which is central to the theory of psychoanalytic treatment (Greenson, 1967, especially Chap. 2). *The patient's distortions and maladaptive responses which are enduring portions of his personality organization are sooner or later injected into his efforts to comply with the basic rule and are expressed as resistance.* Resistance in psychotherapy is the equivalent of the modes of responding that are the patient's "symptoms" —what it is that he must change to seek the end product of a fuller, more satisfying, and more productive life. The therapist's interpretive activity is designed to disclose to the patient his internally induced susceptibilities to anxiety and his accustomed self-defeating modes of combating this anxiety. The patient enters psychoanalysis with the faith and hope that by complying with the rule he will be able to achieve the desired change. He discovers through the therapist's interpretive activity the specific ways that he has of avoiding the task. Possessing the necessary capacity (perhaps intelligence, ego strength, motivation to change, or even all of these), he struggles and succeeds in overcoming each successive obstacle toward free associating. Gradually, he unlearns these self-defeating modes of dealing with the anxieties associated with certain of his impulses and learns to respond realistically and differentially. Since it is his stance toward his impulses that has been modified, little effort is required to transfer the change to his daily functioning.

This formulation gives central importance to the interpretation of resistance, the failure to comply with the task. The fact *that most of the critical interpretations of resistance are also interpretations of transference grows out of the assumption that conflicted impulses are centered around parental objects and are fixed at early periods in the patient's life. Moreover, since the modes of defense are grounded in this interpersonal context, they are interpersonal in character, creating the situation that most resistances will take a transference form* (Freud, 1949a; Greenson, 1967; pp. 182-190). Despite this emphasis on the interpretation of resistance, one finds in the writings of psychoanalysts much attention and reference to interpretations of transference and defensive reactions without regard to whether they are at that time being used in the service of resistance.

Psychoanalytic concepts of interpretive activity prescribe pacing. How much of the core conflicts is disclosed at a particular point (depth) is a function of the current state of the patient (timing). Fenichel's (1941) dictum, "at the surface and a little bit more," specifies that interpretive activity is attuned to the increasing awareness by the patient of his own reactions, whether responses or affects. Psychoanalytic concepts of developmental periods and their characteristic crises provide a basis for an absolute scale of depth of material. *These developmental assumptions underlie the layering scheme of personality organization whereby certain experiences and modes of responding are lodged behind others, which must be released before the next layer "approaches the surface" and comes wthin reach of awareness.* What is often obscured is that the instruction "at the surface and a little bit more" insures that depth of interpretation is ideally gauged to the same level of awareness. When depth is used in the sense of its relation to awareness, it is the range of the patient's awareness that changes with time in therapy, not the depth of interpretation.

Transference and Countertransference The terms transference and countertransference have been stretched to encompass all emotional reactions. Particularly in the case of the former, loss of specificity does violence to the theory. The significance of transference as a concept is that it represents the patient's conversion of the present into the past, expressed as his inability to respond to the present significance of the persons he encounters and of their actions toward him. To define as transference a patient's friendly or deeper affective response to the therapist's actual nurturing is to blur a vital distinction.

The basic patterns of personality are, in the psychoanalytic view, laid down during the first 6 years in the context of the primary family group with parents as the central figures. It follows that infantile-like responses to the analyst will be blended with the early reactions to the real or fancied characteristics of these figures. *The vicissitudes of the various stages of psychosexual development and the form taken by the individual's resolution, incomplete though it may be, of the oedipal conflict are mirrored in the kinds of distortions he introduces into his perceptions and actions toward the therapist.*

The analyst listening to the flow of his patient's communications, their contents, including references to past and present persons, their order, and the affects and bodily movements that accompany them forms an integrated sketch of the person's personality organization, dynamics, and their genesis which convinces him of the transference determinants of his patient's behavior even under circumstances when his own behavior might have been sufficient provocation for the responses observed. The technical specifications of the psychoanalytic situation—the analyst's position out of the direct line of vision, the frugality of his verbal communications, and the ambiguity of the task he assigns—provide "the blank screen" which is supposed to obviate recourse to the principle of multiple determination to account for transference. The phenomenon of transference is clearly etched, whether for the resisting patient or the skeptical outsider, when patient responses to the therapist are in nowise justified by his actions. Alexander (Alexander & French, 1946) went a step further in suggesting that the therapist should highlight the unrealistic quality of the transference by responding to the patient in a fashion just *opposite* to his transference-determined expectations. Alexander hoped, thereby, to speed up the process of the patient's becoming aware of the influence of transference on his perceptions and conduct.

Apart from the conservative factors which keep psychoanalysts bound to the conditions laid down by Freud, the reluctance of most others to follow this lead can be based on theoretical grounds or at least on uncertainties in the theory. *There are insufficient grounds for specifying how far one can depart from the basic conditions without impairing the individual's readiness to form transference responses.* An individual's response to another is a combination of infantile predispositions and the other person's realistic impact on him. The fully matured person reacts differently and adaptively, in response to his impulses and to circumstances. He can respond passionately to his wife, tenderly to his children, and warmly to his friends. He fights furiously in the extreme, speaks firmly and frankly, and converts his anger into extended constructive effort as the occasion demands. Psychoanalytic theory does not seem to contain an ideal of the person who is fully free of infantile modes of responding. The realm of the unconscious is infinite, and the fully mature person may, through "regression in the service of the ego," dip into it in acts of creativity. *The less fully matured (i.e., the more stunted) the individual's development, the more prone he is to regression, including that of the transference variety, and the less within his control this mode of responding is.* Conversely, the less severely malformed personality is less likely to exhibit transference phenomena except under conditions that facilitate regression. Thus, assuming that the orthodox more passive, less self-defining approach is more facilitating of regression and transference, we arrive at the point that the response to Alexander's challenge involves a balancing of the effects of highlighting versus facilitating transference.

There can be no absolutely blank screen. Even the most unrelentingly literal conformity to this specification cannot completely efface partial cues to the person of the analyst. The patient, usually starved for cues to the analyst's personality, notes his taste in decor, his books and periodicals, his ways of walking and talking, his inflections, the timing of rustling sounds connoting shifts in body position, and, of course, his physical appearance. *To the extent that transference and dream phenomena represent primary process phenomena, one might expect that these realistic cues regarding the analyst are woven into his patient's transferences in the same way that realistic occurrences are woven into the patient's dreams in the form of "day residue." This expectation that certain characteristics of the therapist, fragmentary though they be, will play a part in the patient's responses in psychotherapy has been extended (Greenson, 1697; Braatøy, 1954; Stone, 1961) to suggest that the real personal characteristics of the analyst are an important ingredient in his therapeutic effect.*

In regard to countertransference, as in the case of transference, we must cope with an accretion of meanings of the term. In its original use, it referred to the unconscious reactions of the analyst to the emerging infantalized impulses of his patient. His personal analysis was designed to resolve his conflicts and make potentially unconscious reactions accessible to him so that they could be brought within his control. *In this context countertransference represented neurotic residuals which might arise to interfere with the reality of the therapist's perceptions and the therapeutic usefulness of his responses.* His perceptions and responses might be used in the service of his own defenses rather than to advance therapeutic progress. This strictly negative version of countertransference has been modified in response to subsequent ideas regarding the role of the unconscious in constructive and creative functioning. *Countertransference may be therapeutically useful as a source of increased sensitivity and even as a source of spontaneously offered therapeutically effective response* (e.g., Reik, 1949). Finally, the term is extended to include other realistically emotional and affective responsiveness subsumed under a therapist's "warmth" (Braatøy, 1954; Stone, 1961), which is given weight as an important therapeutic ingredient. Here we lack the precision achieved with regard to the roles of free association, transference, resistance, and interpretation. "Warmth" is variously described as the gratification which binds the patient to the therapist (Freud, 1949a), the nutrient for the growth of the patient (Money-Kyrle, 1956; Braatøy, 1954), and the support that enables the patient to come to identify with the therapist and to utilize the "rational ego" against his defensive ego (Sterba, 1934).

CLIENT-CENTERED THEORY

For a long time, the client-centered views offered the major alternatives to psychoanalysis. Despite changes in terminology over time and additional elaboration, client-centered theory has remained consistent in its underlying commitments (Rogers, 1942, 1951, 1959a). The individual's distorted behavior and experience stem from his incorporation of the unaccepting attitudes of others into a nuclear self-rejecting attitude. This attitude is expressed in an evaluative stance toward one's self and the expectation of a similar response from others (conditions of worth). *As in all other situations, the client[5] will reveal his self-rejecting attitudes in psychotherapy by presupposing that he must respond in certain ways to obtain the therapist's approval (conditional positive regard).* He expects that the therapist will respond to him from the therapist's frame of reference, will respond evaluatively, and will seek to impose this evaluation upon the client. *When the client encounters instead a commitment to understand his own (internal) frame of reference and to accept it and the reactions that reflect it as intrinsically worthwhile (unconditional positive regard), he is able gradually to relinquish the distortions and denials of experience to awareness which have been built up and maintained in an effort to construct a framework consistent with self-esteem.*

In the beginning, Rogers and his collaborators (Porter, 1943a, 1943b;

---

[5] In discussing each theory, I will adhere to its terms. Among psychologists there is an increasing trend away from calling those served "patients" because of growing disenchantment with the application of medical analogies to problems of functioning arising from personality.

Snyder, 1945; Seeman, 1949) concentrated on the specific modes of communicating acceptance. Listening, acknowledging, and using agreeing responses and responses that restated or clarified the feelings being expressed were the ways whereby the therapist communicated his acceptance of the intrinsic worth of the individual and the absence of a desire to impose change. The converse of an unconditional acceptance of the individual and a desire to impose change on him is conveyed in interpretive activity, that is, active efforts to reveal to him feelings and other responses of which he is unaware, direct suggestions, or other actions which constitute taking the initiative away from the client. With time, emphasis shifted from specific therapeutic interventions to the more general question of the therapist's attitudes toward a specific client or toward persons in general.

There have been corresponding shifts in specifications regarding the client. At first, the specific self-evaluative responses that he exhibited during the course of psychotherapy were considered (Raimy, 1948); focus then shifted to the more generalized state of the individual's self-esteem (Rogers & Dymond, 1954). Current attention has returned to observations available during therapy of changes in the evaluative and experiencing behavior of the client (Rogers, 1959b; Gendlin, 1961). *In successful therapy the client is expected to become more fluid, more immediate, and more comfortable in his experiencing, more self-aware and more congruent, more undefensively communicative, and more flexible in his self-constructions.*

At the same time renewed attention has been directed toward therapist behavior. In addition to the earlier defined variables of empathy and acceptance, a new one called congruence, transparence, or genuineness has been added (Rogers et al., 1967; Truax & Carkhuff, 1967). Although these variables are called "attitudes," only acceptance fits that concept. Both of the others seem to be actions of the therapist in conveying his understanding of "deeply felt meanings" experienced by his client (accurate empathy) and his actual reactions to his client without inhibition or dissembling (genuineness). These are thought to be the ingredients of the therapeutic effect of relationships.

Client-centered theory denies the therapeutic relevance of client personality differences. These differences presumably arise from particular vicissitudes of the experience of conditional regard from others. The formula for change remains the same, the experiencing of unconditional positive regard accompanied by empathy and genuineness. The one concession to individual differences is that long-standing and comprehensive holds of conditions of worth, which are presumably to be found in severely disturbed persons, call for a longer, more pitfall-riddled process (Shlien, 1961; Rogers et al., 1967).

NEOANALYTIC THEORIES

Many of the ideas of the associates of Freud who broke away from him were later reabsorbed into psychoanalytic theory. Many aspects of Adler's and, especially, of Rank's notions fitted in with the developing ego psychology. Furthermore, many later ideas, mainly regarding personality development and organization, seem rooted in the psychoanalytic framework of therapeutic process and influence only how the therapist thinks about his patient; they do not influence his treatment process per se. Perhaps it would be more accurate to say that the writings of such theorists as Fromm, Horney, Sullivan, and the more recent existentialists either contain little about the process of change or, where the subject is discussed, seem to assume the basic framework of psychoanalytic treatment. This may account for the scarcity of studies aimed at testing the tenability of these theories as theories of psychotherapy.

Two of the neoanalytic theories, those of Adler and Rank, do seem to have some discernibly different propositions to offer regarding psychotherapy, and a third, that of Sullivan, provides not so much a new proposition as a contrasting emphasis. Let us consider Adler (1924, 1964) first. His technique of asking for earliest memories and the significance he attached to birth order for personality patterns have broadened clinical understanding. The key idea, however, is that the individual, in defense of his self-esteem, develops "arrangements," ways of distorting his perceptions and relating to others which are designed to conceal his real or fancied inferiorities. This is essentially a focusing on the power aspects of relationships, one which started by looking at instances of organic inferiority but eventually moved to the more universal circumstance that all of us pass through the period of infancy, when we are in fact virtually powerless and dependent on the resources of others. *The change process in Adler's view is a relatively straightforward one of disclosing to the patient the nature of his style of life, the arrangements through which he seeks to maintain his superiority and to deny his underlying feelings of inferiority.* The therapist must take care to avoid enmeshing the therapeutic relationship in this neurotic superior-inferior preoccupation, and he does this by seeking to establish a partnership of equals. He and his patient interact as colleagues. From the Adlerian point of view, the therapeutic process need not be prolonged. With proper safeguards, such as those mentioned above, the therapist, having discerned the patient's life style—and Adlerians pride themselves on the rapidity with which they can do this—proceeds to disclose to the patient the arrangements he has developed and the purposes they serve. The patient then develops and expresses more fully his "social interest," which replaces his preoccupation with power as a key motivation in his relations with others.

From the foregoing, it can be seen that Adler's ideas give primary emphasis to the influence of processes of thought and reasoning introduced to one person by another in a more or less didactic fashion. The therapist makes the basic discovery and transmits it to the patient by means of a disclosure. Reasoning with the patient and explaining to him are prominent processes. Dreikurs (1961) provides a clear statement of this stance when he says:

> He (the patient) needs our help to see what he is doing and to free himself from his false assumptions. In other words, our treatment is not directed toward a change in emotions, but a clarification of cognitive processes, of concepts. We do not attempt primarily to change behavior patterns or remove symptoms (p. 79).

Ellis (1962) has, of course, sharpened this point of view in his "rational" psychotherapy.

Rank (1945), like Adler, gives central emphasis to the early experience of the infant; in fact, his ideas stemmed from his initial thought that neurosis was founded in the traumatic experiences of the separation from the mother at birth. It is sometimes overlooked that in the more developed form of his theory birth is the biological separating event which sets in motion a longer enduring process of psychological separation which must be successfully completed to avoid neurosis. The individual's difficulties arise because he cannot reconcile his continuing needs for oneness (Allen, 1942, calls it "integration") with those impulses which are expressions of his uniqueness (Allen's "differentiation"). He deals with the threat of separation by projecting his differentiating wishes onto the other person. *This capacity to project one's wishes onto another and then to combat them as though they were being imposed from outside represents the individual's ability to change and his readiness to make use of psychotherapy.* This is the source of Rank's use of the term counterwill and his conception of "resistance" as a positive characteristic. Counterwill is the expression of the patient's capacity to will, activated by his entering into a relationship which has his (the patient's) change as a goal.

Allen, more clearly than Rank, states the assumption that difficulties in differentiation arise out of the unwillingness of parents to offer the infant the love and direction which provide the necessary security and haven from which he can venture forth into the exploration of his growing potentials for self-expression. These difficulties reside also in the unwillingness of parents to acknowledge the increasing disparity between their wishes and that of the growing individual and, where necessary, to enforce their desires while at the same time offering him the haven and the degree of support he still needs in his struggle for a mature interrelation with others. In psychotherapy, the patient is given the opportunity in this new relationship to break the stalemate that has arisen in his efforts to differentiate himself. *He has an opportunity to experience a relationship in which his need to emphasize his own weakness and to feel the strength of another is accepted and permitted. Yet the therapist demonstrates through his use of limits that this acceptance is not incompatible with a self-definition by the therapist as having wishes separate from those of his patient and correspondingly with the fact that the patient has wishes separate from those of the therapist. The patient learns that a meaningful and mutually satisfying pattern of relationship can be developed which includes both individuality and communality.* The seemingly incompatible patterns of dependence can be welded into a single pattern of interdependence.

As was true of so many psychotherapists following Freud, Sullivan concentrated attention on the therapeutic relationship as a particular social system. He attended to the specific ways in which anxiety was communicated as a person interacted with another, mainly through nonlinguistic accompaniments of formal communication, and the ways in which this anxiety served to interfere with persons understanding each other. Psychotherapy is a process of achieving fuller communication, undistorted by the effects of anxiety. Thus it was possible for Sullivan to suggest that the chumship period, when the individual achieves that almost ideal fullness of communication with another, can provide a basis for the attenuation or correction of the effects of previously incapacitating experience (Sullivan, 1953). Sullivan's great interest in the detailed analysis of an ongoing relationship and his conviction that the therapist as a participant lost some reliability as an observer led him into the examination of tape-recorded sessions and a proposal to photograph them. To this extent, then, Sullivan offers not so much a distinct set of hypotheses about psychotherapy as an emphasis on process analysis as the preferred medium for testing them.

The views of Gestalt therapy sponsored by Perls (Perls, Hefferline, & Goodman, 1951) profess to be an improvement on psychoanalytic treatment. As is suggested by its name, this therapy concentrates on a field-theoretical approach grounded in Gestalt principles of awareness and perception. Neurosis is seen as a set of habits acquired out of fear or deprivation which interrupt the completion of experiences. The method of therapy is "to train the ego, the various identifications and alienations, by experiments of deliberate awareness of one's various functions, until the sense is spontaneously revived that it is I who am thinking, perceiving, feeling and doing this" (Perls et al. p. 235). Though Perls finds much to agree with in psychoanalytic theory in so far as it is concerned with obstacles to experiencing, for the couch and the free associative rules *he substitutes the posing of certain tasks (experiments), some more basic, for example, feeling the actual (in the here and now), sensing opposing forces, shifting figure-ground relations in attention, and others more derivative and self-grounded, for example, retroflection (redirecting activity inward and substituting self for environment as the target of behavior)*. These ideas have been merging with the mushrooming varieties of group activities involving sensitivity and self-awareness training, confrontations, and marathons. Not only are therapists more actively assigning tasks, but also they are diminishing the differentiation between patient and therapist roles with regard to self-revelation and confiding. Most of the rationale is too loosely stated to provide hypotheses susceptible to empirical test. The Gestalt "experiments" seems susceptible to more extended and more systematic descriptive observation than has been made. Such efforts might then lead to more definitive formulations.

LEARNING THEORIES

Theories of learning have been a source both of more explicit statements of certain aspects of other theories of psychotherapy (e.g., Dollard & Miller, 1950) and of new statements as to how behavior change is to be understood and effected (Wolpe, 1958). As an example of the former, Dollard and Miller specify that resistance phenomena will conform to Miller's formula for approach and avoidance conflicts and that transference phenomena will reflect generalization principles. Wolpe is representative of the group who have come to refer to themselves as behavior therapists. Characteristically, they concentrate on a specific response system, claiming to apply "learning theory" to the task of modifying it. One difficulty with this group is that its members have often extended the term behavior therapy to apply to all efforts to instigate and modify behavior such as are involved in the socialization processes engaged in by parents or teachers and the management of behavior in schools, prisons, and hospitals. Most of the other approaches to psychotherapy with which we are concerned have addressed themselves to the individual whose behavior and experience are problems to him and who wishes, therefore, to achieve changes in them. Moreover, there is no single learning theory, and applications may vary in how faithful to a given theory they remain in their extrapolations to specific human problems (Breger & McGaugh, 1965). Yet it seems apt to propose that one implicit theoretical assumption is *that it makes no difference whether or not the person involved is specifically motivated toward the change and has asked for it.*

Although the abstract level sought by learning theories tends to shed concern with therapeutic relationships per se and with psychic mediating events, such factors are not completely eliminated in the treatment processes that have evolved from these orientations. One finds two basic formulations of the therapeutic situation arising from the application of learning theories. Wolpe, whose desensitization approach represents one of these two, concerns himself particularly with feelings of anxiety and their modifications. The therapeutic relationship is not the center of attention. The therapist functions primarily as the off-stage director of the experiences that the patient goes through. Relying mainly on the principles of reciprocal inhibition, in which deep relaxation is most frequently the countervailing state, the therapist arranges for the patient to experience, usually in imagination, successive events arranged in hierarchy of their anxiety-evoking potential. The timing and number of exposures to each event in the hierarchy are geared to maintaining the primacy of the relaxed feeling over the anxious ones. Thus, from the Wolpean point of view, the main ingredient of the change process is to be found in the maintenance of the primacy of the countervailing experience or action, with the further assumption that *there is a functional link in the hierarchically arranged events such that the strength of the most powerfully anxiety-evoking ones is somehow diminished by the experience of calm in the face of the less powerfully evoking events from lower positions in the hierarchy.* This hypothesis seems required by the procedures of timing and repetitions of exposures designed to prevent the anxiety-evoking event from being more potent than the relaxed state. It is apparent from case descriptions that a great deal more occurs in desensitization,[6] but behavior therapists aver that the core of the change process is lodged in the establishing of the potency of relaxation or of certain approach or consumatory responses as substitutes for the anxious or avoidance ones. In contrast to desensitization treatment of fears is the reliance on simple extinction proposed in implosive therapy (Stampfl & Levis, 1967). The patient is exposed to the most anxiety- and fear-provoking conditions in his hierarchy from the very beginning. Moreover, the therapist exerts his ingenuity and an almost macabre imagination in concocting newer, more horrible versions of them.

The other general treatment approach is oriented toward control of reinforcements, either positive or negative. The former, as used in operant conditioning (Krasner, 1962), is by far the more widely applied. All of the learning theory applications are similar in their concentration on specific responses or response systems and in their conviction of their inde-

[6] For an account by non-behavior-oriented therapists of observations of Wolpe and his associates see Klein et al. (1969).

pendence of each other. Those who use operant conditioning are concerned with the therapist because they are likely to see him as the source of reinforcement. The argument runs that the therapist can shape his patient's behavior by emitting cues to his approval or disapproval, by expressing or withholding affection or attention according to whether the patient is emitting the desired behavior or the behavior to be eliminated The personality of the therapist and the personality of the patient enter in so far as they influence the reinforcing qualities of the therapist (Eysenck, 1965a).

Thus behavior therapists believe that all of the difficulties presented by patients can be understood and dealt with in terms of specific responses or response systems. Their intense devotion to parsimony makes them unreceptive, even overtly rejecting, of efforts at offering unifying constructs, as exemplified by personality theories. Although the constructs on which learning theories draw do not rely on central or mediating processes to bind or organize separate response systems, we shall see in reviewing relevant research that some investigators and therapists have begun to turn to mediating conceptions, particularly as they turn to modeling and self-control of reinforcements.

The Juncture Points Between Theories

A theory represents an effort to fit a series of events into a single group or related groups of coherent explanations. Theory offers propositions from which the events are derivable and, to be more fruitful, provides the opportunity to turn to new events not yet examined by the theory and to demonstrate that these events are also derivable. A good deal of research can be carried on within the framework of a single theory, but sooner or later alternative theories address themselves to the same universe of phenomena, and the critical step in the empirical evaluation of theories is faced, namely, the confrontation between alternative theories. In this confrontation are to be found the critical studies which go beyond the question of how well a given theory corresponds to observation. These investigations turn to the question of which explanation corresponds better to observation. This entails identifying the differences in expectations derivable from the various competing theories.

A choice between competing theories of psychotherapy becomes possible when we identify differences in their specifications for how changes are effected, the sequence in the change process, and the consequences following on it. When propositions are uniquivocally stated, for example, in mathematical form, the identification of contradictory predictions is easy.

Unfortunately, psychotherapy propositions are generally so far at the other extreme that sometimes they are hardly worthy of the name. At this stage the research worker must immerse himself deeply in the theoretical view so as to be able to restate it with greater clarity and thus to bring out the propositions implicit in it. When this has been done, the points of confrontation between theories will be exposed.

I turn, then, to an examination of the aspects of psychotherapy about which two or more theories offer contradictory propositions. This examination will focus on concepts of the basic therapeutic situation, the role of therapeutic interventions, the sequence of therapeutic change, the role of the patient's personality, and the role of the therapist's personality.

THE BASIC THERAPEUTIC SITUATION

For the most part, neoanalytic and nonanalytic theories of psychotherapy reject the utility of the task of free association and the specifications surrounding it, principally the "blank screen." In some instances it is difficult to decide whether this rejection entails a contradictory proposition. For example, Sullivan's unenthusiastic attitude toward free association was conditioned by the circumstance that the patients whose therapy he discusses were severely disturbed obsessive neurotics or outright psychotics. But psychoanalytic theory also suggests that free association is inappropriate for such patients. The most recent formulations of client-centered theory, emphasizing genuineness or transparency, would seem to provide the most direct contradiction to psychoanalysis. This is particularly true when the nuance of transparency is the one stressed. There is no indication that psychoanalytic theory requires the analyst to deny or falsify his feelings. The requirement of the "blank screen" only pressures him to be reserved in expressing his thoughts and feelings—all this, of course, in the service of releasing and highlighting inner, unconscious determinants of the patient's responses. But current psychoanalytic theory also stresses the role of certain real and presumably expressed characteristics of the therapist, subsumed under the general category of warmth, that serve to establish the patient's alliance with the therapist, which in turn provides the fulcrum for therapeutic effort.

Rank and Adler, in addition to Rogers and Perls, manifest the general conviction that free association, couch, and "blank screen" are detrimental to effective therapeutic collaboration. Consequently, they advocate working relationships less removed from the usual situation. All four appear to subscribe to the principle that the individual's neurotic patterns will be manifested in his interactions with the psychotherapist as they are in all other relationships. But modern psychoanalytic theory, with its emphasis on character and defense, contains the same commitments. The main difference seems to lie in conceptions of the nature of the unconscious and the ways whereby its realm can be diminished. For the moment we shall consider the difference in intrapsychic terms, leaving for later a discussion of the differences in the role of therapist interventions.

It is clear that Freud's elaborate, complex, and sometimes obscure analysis of the personality, with it topographical postulates of id, ego, and superego and the constituent apparatuses of the latter two sustained by countercathexes, was not to the liking of the other personality theorists. Each showed a tendency to introduce simplifying assumptions. Although Adler's concept of life style with its fictions and arrangements are reminiscent of character and defense, he seems to have rejected the notion of repression and to have treated the phenomenon of unawareness as a purely cognitive one resulting from the selective attention created by life style. If the individual's goal shifts from seeking to overcome his feelings of inferiority to implementing social interest, the lost experiences become available. Both Rank and Rogers see the individual's difficulties in accepting himself as the obstacle to awareness, but there are differences in their views of self-acceptance. Where Rogers concentrates on the more specific influence of the evaluative attitude toward the self, Rank turns his attention to the more complex processes, which he treats in terms of differentiation. Here Rank holds that the real characteristics of the therapist have an important function in therapy beyond that of aiding to establish the therapeutic alliance. The major processes of change, he insists, revolve around the patient's learning that he and the therapist can build a solid relationship, despite conflict of wills, and that such a solid relationship, while containing many elements of unity between partners, need not require the surrender of the basic feeling of individuality. Thus attention becomes focused on the real characteristics of the therapist and of his wishes, rather than on the patient's inner-determined fabrications of the therapist with which he seeks to fill the vacuum created by the psychoanalyst's unexpressive stance. But even here the contradiction is not very sharp because the Rankian still is much concerned with inner determinants and their manifestation as transference, except that he is likely to speak of them in terms of the patient's projection of his will onto the therapist and, as a result of therapy, his ability to accept as inner what he had treated as outer.

With the exception of such psychoanalytic learning theorists as Miller and Dollard, the group relying solely on learning theory is likely to adopt an even more simplified conception of personality organization than the neoanalytic group. Beyond the patterns invoked in the direct expression of biological drives, there is no normative patterning of motives and behavior potential. Patterns are dictated by the specific history of the individual. Other than the influence of such principles as stimulus generalization and radiation of effect, the learning theorists see no organizing principles to be added to the specific accidents of the individual's history which pair particular stimuli and responses. The collaborative relationship which accompanies this view is likely to emphasize the role of the expert, with a more or less passive collaborator. In some cases it may approach that of the animal trainer and his subject.

From the foregoing, it follows that the psychoanalyst is likely to doubt that the methods of these other therapists will lead to any basic changes in the range of repression, though he might concede that some modifications in modes of defense may occur, particularly in mildly neurotic individuals. As we shall see in later chapters, the difficulties in testing these theoretical differences lie in the fact that not all will agree as to the kinds of observations to use as criteria.

Summarizing the confrontations among theories with regard to the basic treatment situation, we are able to identify a general tendency for psychoanalytic theory to lean toward a less expressive stance for the therapist than the various ego-analytic positions. To test the relative tenability of these alternative positions, it would be necessary to relate this feature of the working relationship to the readiness with which the patient can experience feelings accompanying distorted perceptions in present interpersonal relationships which are heavily laden with perceptions and feelings carried over from the past. Learning and behavior theory-oriented approaches to psychotherapy generally stand apart from this issue. They emphasize a technical relationship, but generally tend to give greatest weight to the therapist as an arranger of situations. Their emphasis is upon certain behavior resultants rather than upon feelings and perceptions that might accompany behaviors. Thus one way to bring about a confrontation between psychodynamic theories, whether psychoanalytic, neoanalytic, or nonpsychoanalytic, would be to conduct a study of the conditions surrounding the experience of the feelings accompanying distorted perceptions, including the relation of other behaviors to perception and feeling.

THERAPEUTIC INTERVENTIONS

As might be expected, the various theories of psychotherapy collide most directly in their views of the effects of various kinds of interventions. Unlike the other positions, psychoanalytic and Adlerian theories emphasize the role of the therapist as one who calls the patient's attention to overlooked and denied elements in the behavior he emits or the affects he expresses. The Freudian discloses to the patient his modes of avoiding anxiety. This is conceived of as a sequential process of exposing, first, anxieties (and avoidances) about impulses toward the therapist, then their sources in still active, unintegrated impulses toward father and mother figures, and, ultimately, the primitive nature of these libidinal and aggressive impulses. Correspondingly, the Adlerian discloses to his patient the arrangements and fictions which play such prominent parts in his style of life and the feelings of inferiority and the compensatory strivings toward superiority.

In addition to differing in the content of their disclosures, Freudians and Adlerians differ in the specificity with which they stipulate the conditions that will make a disclosure useful to the patient. As is well known, Freud and those who followed him developed very careful specifications in which it was assumed that the way for disclosure is prepared by such factors as the developing of an alliance with the therapist in which the patient is ready to observe himself (Sterba's "ego-splitting"); by the encouragement toward regression implicit in the conditions of free association which relaxes the grip of the set to adapt and permits more of the infantile forms of impulses to come close to awareness; and by the preliminary disclosure of the more peripheral modes of resistance, which leads to their being dropped and paves the way for awareness of the more basic patterns. All of this participates in and is accompanied by a pacing in the rate of disclosure in which what is disclosed is already close to awareness. as exemplified by the increasing appearance of close derivatives of it in the patient's associations and his noting of parts of it in periods when he is reflecting on his own productions. All of this, Fenichel summarizes in the expression "at the surface and a little bit more."

Adler was much less specific. He did suggest that the patient's experience of being treated as a partner and of being respected and accepted in such a role was important. Furthermore, he anticipated that the process of disclosure would start with the specific arrangements and fictions, and that important forms of it would be demonstrated in his patient's modes of relating to him. But one is still left with the impression that the process of disclosure was seen in a much more straightforward light than by the Freudians and that the latter's elaborate preparations were viewed as examples of preciousness or deviousness.

Disclosure is no particular concern of either the Rankian or the Rogerian. In fact, though Rankians have at times responded interpretively, neither group find this very congenial, and would be specially adverse to the term intervention. They stipulate that what is learned comes out of the experience of the relationship to the psychotherapist. What is learned is contained, not in the content of his interpretations, but in the current meaning of his responses. For the Rankian the significant actions of the therapist lie in his willingness to accept the patient's projections onto him of the patient's own willing. For Rank will was more than the Freudian impulse, an energy which provided the driving force for the various psychic apparatuses. It combined the characteristics of libidinal energy and executive powers into a more independent, more powerful ego which was seen as the source of creativity. Much of this is also contained in the conceptions of ego which have developed out of the contributions of Hartman, Kris, and Erikson.

The neurotic conflict resides in the patient's inability to accept his own impulses. He still retains his capacity to will, but expresses it as counter-will directed toward his projections of his own will onto others. Thus, though the patient as the first move in a process of change takes the step of seeking the therapist's help, his fear of growth, which to the Rankian means differentiation, and his fear of loss of self in too close a collaboration with the therapist combine to stimulate him to project onto the therapist his desire to change. He can then test his own strength and individuality against the strength of this expert who seeks to change him. The therapist understands this process and allows the patient to test his strength without in fact trying to change him. Yet the therapist also shows that he can stand firm on the issues which structure their relationship, time, the use of materials, and the inviolability of the person of the therapist. In this context, the Rankian therapist offers interpretations, but they are expressions of his understanding of his patient's struggles with the dilemma of whether one can have an intimate relationship with another without losing one's individuality. By words and actions he attempts to demonstrate that each can assert himself without this action destroying their basic relationship and that the patient can use the therapist's strength without losing the capacity or the right to self-assertion. The Rankian therapist's interpretations are directed toward the meaning of what is going on for his relationship with the patient. Sometimes he comments regarding some persistent mode of reacting. For example, George, a 5-year-old patient, puts clay in the paint, an action which is not allowed. When he tries to dilute the force of this being "bad" by saying, "It's only a joke for boys and girls to be bad," the therapist points out that it is a joke he likes to play (Allen, 1942, p. 81).

The client in client-centered psychotherapy, through his experience of the therapeutic relationship, discovers that another can value him irrespective of specific actions. From a process of attempting to implement a self-concept which is not necessarily congruent with his true self, he turns toward responding more fully to his experience of himself and toward building a set of values based on himself and his relationships to others. Earlier Rogers stipulated that the client-centered therapist sought to understand the internal frame of reference of his client and to test that understanding through reflecting and clarifying statements. Although the latter dictum is now dismissed as a matter of technique which may be irrelevant, the emphasis on understanding remains and tends to be accompanied by efforts to test it. Since the individual is being understood from his frame of reference, the communications are confined to matters within his awareness. The difference between such communications and those directed at "the surface and a little bit more," however, becomes problematical when one seeks to escape the banal. Presumably the client-centered therapist seeks to understand the most subtle, newly forming experiences rather than the obvious surface elements and to communicate that understanding. As a result he escapes a banal parroting back of a client's verbal statements, but his communications may be indistinguishable with regard to depth from those dictated by Fenichel.

Thus the client-centered and psychoanalytic positions may not be so far apart when it comes to the relation of their communications to the patient's awareness. The big difference may lie in their concepts of the relation of these communications to what is going on in the client. The psychoanalyst assumes that his communications come at a point of struggle within the individual between his desire for change, epitomized in his commitment to follow the basic rule, and his desire to avoid the discomfort entailed in allowing his conflictual impulses to rise to awareness. The analyst's interpretation illumines that struggle and aids the patient to use his forces for constructive action. Thus psychoanalytic theory stipulates a specific influence of interpretation on resistance. Client-centured theory proposes no such specific effect of the therapist's communications. To the client-centered therapist his communications form part of the tissue of an accepting relationship within which the client discovers a new attitude toward himself and a new way of relating to others. Resistance is not a required phenomenon, as it is in both psychoanalytic and Rankian and Adlerian therapy; it comes in response to the therapist's efforts to impose an external frame of reference.

This seems to be the best point at which to clarify the Rankian and Adlerian positions regarding resistance, implied in the preceding assertion. If we employ the psychoanalytic meaning of the term resistance—working against change and, more specifically, failure to comply with the task— then it is clear that the Rankian expects his patient to exhibit such behavior. The difference is that, unlike the Freudian, he does not see it as "bad," something to be overcome. Instead he views it as a capacity for individuation and for creativity, to be converted from its negative expression as counterwill to a positive affirmation of self. Yet both the Freudian and the Rankian see in these phenomena a "moment of truth," a point at which the individual comes to grips with vital issues within himself and at which the therapist plays a part through his communications. The major difference, then, seems to lie in the Rankian's confining himself to communications directed toward immediate events and affects in the relationship, and the Freudian's moving beyond these to communications about other relationships, past and present, and the feelings and impulses involved. In the case of the Adlerian, resistance is also inevitable as an expression of the patient's all-pervasive search for superiority. It is inevitable that the patient respond to the feelings of inferiority engendered by his step of seeking the therapist's help by seeking to establish some form of superiority, which usually involves efforts to deny the significance of the therapist's disclosures. More importantly, exposures of particular arrangements and fictions are likely to be responded to by the substitution of other processes designed to preserve the life style, until the whole pattern is revealed and the critical struggle between the defense of self-esteem and social interest is joined.

Neither "resistance" nor "interpretation" has any place in the lexicon of the behavior therapist. "Resistance" connotes too much of the flavor of intrapsychic processes, which are foreign to his system of thought. A patient has a particular mode of reacting, his symptom, which he wishes to change. He persists in it because of the influence of learning, and new modes of responding are to be learned. That is all there is to it. The therapist arranges for the kinds of experiences that will lead to the required learning. In the Wolpean approach the therapist interrogates the patient, securing his cooperation by explaining the general formula for understanding the problem. Obtaining the patient's cooperation should not be particularly difficult, since the Wolpean seems to promise much more for much less effort than do personality-oriented psychotherapists. On the basis of his understanding of the behavior in question, the therapist then prescribes a series of tasks for the patient or, more often, arranges a series of experiences in his office designed to desensitize and to open the way for the substitution of alternative responses. Sometimes this is done through the use of hypnosis, sometimes by suggested fantasying of situations, and sometimes by the use of physical acts or relaxing drugs.

For the most part the behavior therapists who apply Skinner's notions of operant conditioning have worked in some institutional setting in which the therapeutic experience is grafted onto some regular program. Thus the child's behavior is influenced by instructing his nursery school teachers when and how to offer him a particular schedule of social reinforcements, or the behavior therapist works with a mute schizophrenic to shape vocalizing behavior into speech. There is no specific eliciting of the "patient's" cooperation. He usually does not ask to be changed, and the therapist acts on him. Recent developments in programming activities to be carried out by the individual, even including self-administered reinforcements, give the patient a much more active role (Salzinger, 1969).

Cognition, thinking, and other central mediating processes play no assigned or acknowledged part in the behavior therapist's conception of the change process. This in itself rules out processes of interpretation or any other form of disclosure.

Behavior theory makes one prediction regarding the phenomena to be observed during the course of the "talking therapies," namely, that where behavior change has occurred, this change will have been accompanied and shaped by a consciously or unconsciously emitted schedule of verbal or nonverbal reinforcements selectively applied.

The confrontations among psychodynamic views regarding therapeutic interventions can be summarized as centering more on the content than on the depth of interpretations. There appears to be a convergence on the importance of staying close to, but not right on, the patient's current level of awareness. Differences arise in the psychoanalytic emphasis primarily on resistance as the object of interpretation, in contrast to the more generalized client-centered concern with feelings and the Rankian emphasis on self versus other as the source of feelings. The latter emphasis may also be representative of the Gestalt position. It would be possible to compare the alternative interventions in terms of subsequent increases in richness of self-experience. It would be difficult, however, to bring behavior theory into this confrontation because its proponents would profess disinterest in such a target as "richness of self-experience." They would, no doubt, be interested in participating in a debunking role by seeking to demonstrate that the verbal behavior from which "richness of experience" is inferred can be manipulated through control of contingencies of reinforcement.

THE ROLE OF THE PATIENT'S PERSONALITY

In contrast with psychoanalytic theory's rather differentiated conception of the treatment of various kinds of persons, most of the other methods pay little attention to the questions of their applicability. Client-centered theory, in fact, affirms the universality of the method. Rogers' most recent efforts were directed toward demonstrating the applicability of client-centered thinking to psychotics. As we have seen, psychoanalytic theory specifies the inapplicability of free association to psychotics and predicts how they and other kinds of persons will respond in such a task situation. Although Rogers' most recent statements (e.g., 1959a) have specified the necessary conditions for client-centered therapy, there is little in these stipulations about the client's personality, other than that there is a discrepancy between perceived self and actual experience (incongruence), and that the individual is unaware of this discrepancy, making him vulnerable to anxiety or actually anxious.

Behavior therapists who emphasize the therapist as the reinforcer and the social element in his reinforcements have taken the logical next step of assuming that dependency will play an important role in the therapeutic process. In this view, the dependent personality will be more responsive (will learn more readily) than the independent personality. Although Ullmann and Krasner (1969) differentiate patient groups, it is clear that they are offering a perfunctory bow to clinical tradition. The behavior treatment methods offered are not differentiated by pathology, except that specific cases are not cited in connection with depressions and obsessive-compulsive disorders.

THE ROLE OF THE THERAPIST'S PERSONALITY

One way to pose this question of the role of personality is to ask whether therapists are taught or are born equipped for this vocation. Of course, a nativistic conception of personality is not necessarily at issue. Usually the questioner is wondering whether therapists have to be taught to respond in a therapeutic manner or whether therapy is primarily a natural phenomenon arising from the particular native and acquired modes of responding of certain individuals. The less specification of method, the greater is the tendency to downgrade the importance of training. Rogers considers vital to therapy the therapist's attitude of unconditional positive regard, his experiencing of an empathic understanding of the client's internal frame of reference, and his full awareness of his own experience in the relationship, which makes it possible for him to be genuine.

Psychoanalytic theory, with its emphasis on specific conditions of therapeutic work and specific activity of the therapist, tended to place less emphasis on the therapist's personality as a positive factor, Indeed, the emphasis on the "blank screen" appeared to rule it out. The therapist's personality seemed to enter in only as countertransference which interfered with his ability to carry out his task. Later, as mentioned in foregoing discussions, awareness of countertransference reactions was given a positive role as a sensitizer to deeper understanding. The warmth of the therapist was also assigned some role (Sterba, 1934; Braatøy, 1954), primarily that of providing an additional motivation for therapeutic work and a stimulus toward the patient's identifying with the therapist. Neither Rank nor Adler nor the behavior therapists have anything systematic to say regarding the role of the therapist's personality. The former two often appear to be accepting the psychoanalytic version of the role of transference. To the latter, the therapist and his theory seem inseparable, and most questions about the therapist's personality disappear in considering the mechanics of the application of the theory.

Vital though it may be, the step of identifying significant goals for research, as stated in the crude terms used in this chapter, brings us only slightly closer to the production of studies which provide definitive answers to our questions about psychotherapy and are productive of new insights. There must intervene the kind of further examination of the questions and relevant theories that permits ready conversion to the observables in psychotherapy. It is to this intervening process that most of this volume will be addressed.

The next three chapters will be devoted to sketching an overview of strategies and processes about which research workers must make decisions and with which they must become conversant. In chapter 2, we shall consider the problems of choosing criteria for evaluating the effects of psychotherapy and appropriate research design. Chapter 3 will be concerned with the requirements and strategies in the development of process measures. Finally, we will give attention in chapter 4 to the role of simplification in designing research.

CHAPTER 2

Outcome or Process?

The methodological questions that press hardest on any would-be investigator of psychotherapy are those surrounding its evaluation. "Was it worthwhile?" is such a practical question and cries for an immediate answer. At first glance, it appears to be a question susceptible to a direct reply. A person seeks psychotherapy because he is in pain. Therefore the continuance or disappearance of the pain after psychotherapy will give us the answer to our question. But even a rudimentary understanding of the principles of research design or just plain commonsense tells us that many other considerations intervene between such a simple question and an uncomplicated answer. First, there is the pain itself. Human beings are subject to many varieties of psychic pain which push them into psychotherapy. How are these varieties best classified and sampled? How do we best classify the varieties of treatment? How do we rule out alternative explanations that relate the change to self-limitation, which requires only the passage of time, or to the many concurrent influences experienced during the treatment period?

As our examination of the history of psychotherapeutic research suggested, serious investigators were soon at work on many aspects of these and related questions, particularly those associated with defining the alternative treatment influences and delineating the process of treatment. Participants in the first conference on research in psychotherapy (Rubinstein & Parloff, 1959) took sides in an outcome versus process controversy, and others have since joined the fray. Some have suggested that the avoidance of simple, direct evaluative studies was a form of functional autonomy[1] of the psychotherapy enterprise (Astin, 1961), and others have warned of the development of a state of functional autonomy[1] of the psychotherapy research (Goldstein, Heller, & Sechrest, 1966).

But nature is not confined to "either-ors." Any curious clinician who is not frightened by his uncertainties will want to see whether his patient

---

[1] That is, that psychotherapy and psychotherapy research have become ends in themselves rather than being responsive to evidence of effectiveness or lack of it.

appears to have changed. And we shall not accuse him of defensiveness when he is aware of the limitations of such observations. Similarly, we shall need to distinguish between the sophisticated investigator's awareness that unequivocal demonstration of the *planned* effects of psychotherapy will require a marriage of process and evaluation studies and the escapist, Penelope-like work of doing and undoing. Sargent (1961) says it well:

Since "process" is a series of emergent outcomes, and since "outcome" stops process at a point in time, understanding of process without reference to its outcomes is hardly conceivable; likewise, outcome studies which contribute nothing to knowledge of determinants would consist only in statistical summaries of judgments on gross change. The distinction appears, therefore, quite artificial unless certain semantic confusions and overdetermining values are considered. . . . More broadly, process research may be conceived of as concerned with the *how* of change, while outcome research attempts to identify *what* changes (p. 97).

In summary, evaluation and process research are different sides of the same coin, which can be separated only to obtain incomplete or spurious answers, sometimes to questions that are themselves incomplete or spurious.

In the following discussion, I propose to examine in detail the problem of measuring change in persons undergoing psychotherapy, the ways in which various investigators have endeavored to solve it, and the relations of their solutions to their implicit or explicit views of human behavior. In the second half of the chapter, I will give brief consideration to the requirements of experimental design in evaluative studies.

THE PROBLEM OF CRITERIA

When Mahrer (1967) solicited statements of their goals from psychotherapists, it was not surprising that he asked all of them to start with their views of man. This was true whether the writer was a self-proclaimed foe of psychodynamic theories (Wolpe), a rationalist (Ellis), a proponent of client-centered views (Gendlin), or an advocate of psychoanalytic views (Saul). Naturally, all agree that the experience of stress drives a person to psychotherapy. As clinicians acquainted with the raw stuff of human living, they tend to agree on the same elaborations of the central areas in which persons experience stress and well-being: (1) symptoms, involuntary actions, and experiences which are disturbing to the person and to others; (2) pleasure and intimacy of interpersonal relations; (3) the special intimacy and pleasure which is found in the sexual relationship; (4) productive and creative activity; and (5) reactions to self. The difficulty is that our understanding of the interrelations among these areas of stress and of their sources is incomplete, often vaguely formulated, even self-contradictory, and certainly unverified. The fact that these uncertainties and ambiguities, which apply equally to our understandings of human difficulties and to our efforts at remedying them, are anchored in the realities of human suffering insures that the effort is worthwhile and must continue.

Classes of Criteria

To enrich our understanding of the alternative decisions that confront the research worker when he seeks to determine what changes have occurred during the period of psychotherapy, it will be useful to formulate categories into which these efforts may be placed. As has already been suggested, one class of measures of change will encompass those which seek direct descriptions of the patient's stress before and after psychotherapy. This class of measures might be called *intrinsic* criteria because their meaningfulness is directly apprehended; it does not rest on the acceptance of any further assumptions. We learn, however, that even here the mode of observation is not always simple and direct. The presence of disturbing symptoms is usually obtained most simply, either through direct observation or patient reports (Parloff, Kelman, & Frank, 1954). But even here we need to be careful to obtain observations from a disinterested observer rather than from either the patient or the therapist, each of whose observations will be biased by his or her investment in the therapy. When we turn to the nature of the patient's interpersonal and sexual relationships, his effectiveness in productive activity, and his reactions to self, we face more complex problems. Many of these depend on self-report, yet involve conditions of self-report most subject to distortion from the social demands of the particular situation (the "hello-goodbye" phenomenon cited by Hathaway, 1948) and the general influence of response sets such as social desirability. If the investigator takes psychodynamic assumptions seriously, he will not be satisfied that self-report is unbiased by largely unconscious defense mechanisms. Given the willingness of patients, these difficulties can be minimized in a study funded adequately to make use of interviews conducted by experienced clinicians with significant family members, friends, and fellow workers and of independent direct observations of the patient.[2]

At this point we must introduce a further caveat: although temporary

[2] The Menninger Foundation study (Robbins & Wallerstein, 1959) approached this ideal.

relief may be welcomed by a sorely beset patient, both he and his therapist seek more enduring changes. Hence we need to know what observations will tell us when changes are *temporary* and when they are *enduring*. This might be ascertained by continuing observation over time, but we might hope to reach a level of knowledge of personality that would permit us to define the state of the person which is an enduring one.[3] We seek this greater specificity because we want to know how these difficulties arose so that we can more effectively prevent or erase them. Furthermore, such knowledge makes it easier to estimate when a more enduring change has been produced. Thus, although we would find criteria which have been empirically demonstrated to forecast an enduring change in the patient, we want also to formulate and validate theories of personality and psychopathology which incorporate these empirically derived criteria.

Even though the two are so closely interwoven, it is important to keep in mind this distinction between *empirical* and *theoretical* criteria. It highlights the intimate relation between evaluation of psychotherapy and progress in interrelated activities directed toward sharpening our formulations of personality theory through improving and empirically validating our methods of personality measurement and firming up the data base on which they rest. Some of the measures used in evaluation are almost wholly empirical, such as the Minnesota Multiphasic (Schofield, 1966), whereas others are almost entirely theoretical, for example, self-ideal discrepancy in Q sorts (Rogers & Dymond, 1954). The ideal measure would be one that has theoretical coherence and has been thoroughly validated as a measure of personality organization relevant to psychopathology and effectiveness of function. It is unrealistic, however, to expect to end up with an all-purpose single measure. One measure might concentrate on providing an analysis of personality structure and dynamics, another might take as its target an analysis of interpersonal relations, past and present, and a third might concentrate on assessing degree and form of pathology.

Finally, we will want to distinguish between *mediating* and *ultimate* criteria. *Ultimate* criteria are those that either directly or indirectly reflect the desired end state. Direct observations of the desired end state will, of course, fit our earlier definition of *intrinsic* criteria and will, for most clinicians, be supported by theoretically and/or empirically based predictions of an enduring condition. Similarly, indirect indicators of ultimate criteria

[3] There is, of course, the troublesome question of how long a period will qualify a change as an enduring one. The definitive answer can come only from that level of knowledge which permits us to specify the conditions giving rise to each undesired condition so that we can state with confidence under what circumstances recurrences of old conditions or the development of new ones will occur.

will correspond to both previously defined theoretical and empirically based criteria which have established deductively and/or empirically demonstrated predictive relations to desired end states. *Mediating* criteria, by contrast, are those observations of intervening processes which are thought and/or have been empirically demonstrated to be a necessary part of the road to be traversed on the way to achieving the goal condition. For example, psychoanalytic theory supposes that the analysis of a resistance phase of patient response will give rise to greater awareness of the specifics of his defensive feelings and behavior and the effective heightening of his motives toward change, so that there will ensue an interruption in the defensive response and a substitution of freer, more spontaneous reactions. This reduction in resistance, then, is an indicator, at least to the psychoanalyst, that the process is working and that the patient is on his way to the desired goal. There should be no misunderstanding that theoretically based ultimate or mediating criteria will be of interest as criteria only to those who espouse the theory until their relationship to intrinsic criteria has been empirically verified. Mediating criteria, it should be clear, are centrally involved in any effort ot establish why and how change takes place.

Our distinctions regarding criteria are summarized in the accompanying table.

The "Temporary" column of the table is shown with a (?) to indicate the existence of a question that, in the absence of empirical contradiction, might be raised about any criterion which professes to refer to an enduring change. Entered in this column are examples of *intrinsic, empirical,* and *theoretical* criteria readily subject to doubt about their enduring quality.

Reference has already been made to the possible influence of situational and social set factors in self-report, which is included in the *intrinsic* cell. Beyond these, the sincere attention and concern of another which the patient experiences with unusual vividness in psychotherapy seems likely to comfort and distract him from his pain, so that, at least momentarily, he is likely to feel better.[4] Symptom removal is, of course, included because of the controversy over whether treatment that is solely concerned with symptoms will result in either temporary change (i.e., the symptoms will return) or symptom substitution.

The *temporary-empirical* cell shows the Discomfort-Relief Quotient, which was devised by Dollard and Mowrer (1947). Since they derived it from learning theory, some might have been inclined to place it in the *temporary-theoretical cell.* However, since the index consists essentially in

---

[4] Schofield (1964) has even contended that psychotherapy is no more than an artificial device for obtaining friendship.

Relationships Among Different Kinds of Criteria Using Illustrative Examples

	Temporary (?)	Enduring	Mediating
INTRINSIC	Self-report of relief Symptom removal	Report by self and others on effectiveness of functioning Health-Sickness Rating	
EMPIRICAL	Discomfort-Relief Quotient	MMPI Speech Anxiety	Premature termination Number of interviews Quality of communication Liking therapist
THEORETICAL	Transference cure Q sort	Quality of free associating Level of experiencing Rorschach Q sort	Interpretation-resistance sequences Empathy–self-experiencing sequences Movement up the desensitization hierarchy

the recording of all instances of expressions of either discomfort or relief by the patient during the course of his interviews, its derivation does not seem to depend on the theoretical dispositions of its creators. Its placement in the "Temporary" column reflects my opinion that the doubts expressed regarding patient reports apply to this particular systematic method of analyzing them.

In the case of transference cure, which appears in the *temporary-theoretical cell*, we have an example of a criterion of change which is *expected* to be temporary. The other entry in the same cell, Q sort, is much more questionable. This criterion, which involves the correlation between self and ideal, has generally been treated by Rogers and others as an index of an enduring change. They argue that this correlation reflects an enduring state of self-acceptance or nonacceptance which has consequences for general functioning. It can also be (and has been) viewed as a measure of self-satisfaction which may be transitory (Block & Thomas, 1955). An inferred example of this is buried in one of the thorough evaluative studies of client-centered therapy (Rogers & Dymond, 1954). One of the control groups in the research design was asked to defer treatment for a 60-day period. Eight members of this group declined therapy when the wait period was concluded and were not considered in the basic evaluation (Chapter III). From Chapters V and XIV, however, one finds that this group showed a .28 increase in self-ideal correlation during that period, which is not greatly different from the change of .35 displayed by the treated group from pre- to post-treatment, or even from the .42 displayed by the subgroup within the treated group which was rated as improved. One possible interpretation is that in the intervening period of time the members of this group had achieved a momentary state of relief from their psychological difficulties which in turn was reflected in their self-ideal correlations.

Turning to the "enduring" column, we find entered in the *intrinsic* cell two forms of a full evaluation of the patient. One is a generalized statement of evidence obtained from the patient as well as others and from clinical observation; the other refers to a particular systematization of the same kind of evidence which was developed as part of the Menninger project (Luborsky, 1962). Although the Health-Sickness Rating is basically atheoretical, it contains some aspects that are specifically derived from psychoanalytic theory and might be accepted as intrinsically important only by clinicians of this theoretical persuasion.

The Minnesota Multiphasic Inventory (MMPI) clearly belongs in the *empirical* cell. Since Speech Anxiety refers to a measure developed by Paul (1966), it is listed in the *empirical* rather than the *intrinsic* cell.

The *theoretical* cell in the "Enduring" column lists quality of free associating, level of experiencing. Rorschach, and *Q* sort. The last one has already been mentioned in several connections, all of which brought out its grounding in client-centered theory. The Rorschach has clearer theoretical than empirical underpinnings as a comprehensive appraisal of personality appropriate for evaluating the effects of psychotherapy (Beck, 1966). The job of evaluating the massive accumulation of research on the Rorschach to pinpoint how tenable are the varied and complex hypotheses underlying it is yet to be done. In its absence there occurs polarization between those who wholly reject it and those who wholly accept it. Level of experiencing (Rogers, 1959) and quality of free associating (Bordin, 1966c) are process-oriented, theoretically based measures which can serve as either enduring or mediating criteria. When Rogers (1959b) presented his seven strands of the process of personality change during psychotherapy, which I am designating by the collective title "level of experiencing," he suggested the possibility that this measure would not only "give us knowledge of where he [the individual] stands on the continuum of psychotherapy . . ." but would also indicate "the even more general continuum of personality development . . ." (p. 106). Gendlin (1968) has followed this lead by developing and seeking to validate a general measure of level of experiencing which he calls "focusing ability." In somewhat parallel terms, I have argued that the process measure of ability to free associate taken in a sufficient sample will prove to be a measure of personality suitable as an enduring criterion (Bordin, 1964). It is of interest, incidentally, that the descriptions of these two measures, one derived from client-centered theory and the other from psychoanalytic theory, suggest that they might well be measuring similar or highly correlated human phenomena. Furthermore, both measures appear to speak to many of the concerns of the existentially oriented psychotherapists (Bugental, 1965; Perls et al., 1951).

By definition, *mediating* and *intrinsic* criteria are mutually exclusive; therefore there can be no cell representing them in the "Mediating" column. The *empirical-mediating* criteria are those parts of the process of psychotherapy that are inherent to it and therefore do not depend on a particular theoretical commitment. It is not easy to identify unequivocal examples of such criteria. Probably the least controversial would be premature termination. If the patient decides to give up the quest for change or withdraws, using as an excuse an obviously fabricated semblance of change at a point where there plainly has been little opportunity for change to occur, then such events, it is primitively clear, must be studied to understand how and why they occur and how they can be prevented. Virtually all psychotherapies require open channels of communication and a tie between therapist and patient. Using these qualities as criteria for examining what influences them, then, becomes a contributory process to evaluating and improving psychotherapy. The relevance of number of interviews to adequacy of treatment depends on what kind of curve this relationship is presumed to generate. If we assume that it follows a learning curve with an asymptote, number of interviews can be thought to reflect differential success only up to that point. Many studies have used this criterion, but too often, as Lorr (1962) has rightly pointed out, with a confounding of intensity (number of times per week) of treatment.

When a theory of psychotherapy becomes sufficiently articulated to specify the sequences which will characterize the process of change and the necessary aspects of this process, a comprehensive evaluation of that theory becomes possible and will include the utilization of criteria of the sort listed in the *theoretical* cell of the "mediating" column. Three examples, drawn from psychoanalytic, client-centered, Wolpean desensitization theories are entered. The psychoanalytic example refers to the expectation that certain levels of interpretation will be most effective for dissolving resistance (Speisman, 1959). Similarly, self-exploration and self-disclosure, which are seen as part of the process of self-acceptance, will be furthered, according to client-centered theory, by empathic therapist responses (Truax

& Carkhuff, 1965a). Wolpe's (1958) formulations regarding the role of reciprocal inhibition in behavior change require that experiences of imagining events low on the patient's anxiety hierarchy while in a state of relaxation will bring events that are somewhat higher in his set of anxieties within the desensitizing powers of relaxation. As far as I know, none of the investigations of this approach to phobias has provided detailed statistical analyses of the desensitization trials to demonstrate the central role of the expected sequences, but such studies seem possible.

Theoretical and Measurement Problems

Having reviewed the sources and purposes of criteria, we will again traverse the same ground, this time to consider the theoretical and technical decisions involved in selecting particular measures. Since mediating criteria fall into the more general class of problems in process studies, I postpone consideration of them until the next chapter.

Once more I sound the recurring theme that our solutions to the problems of selecting criteria for evaluating psychotherapy are embedded in the state of theory and measurement of personality and psychopathology. Most clinicians and researchers who are grounded in clinical experience lean toward a humanistic view, with little tolerance for analytic models which segment, simplify, and provide an incomplete picture of man. This predisposition to wholistic formulations cannot be disposed of solely by terming it a symptom of unscientific and sentimental involvement. The fact is that the clinician encounters persons whose complex reactions in thought, imagination, and feeling make demands on him over and above their socially directed actions. He is impressed by continuities and themes in persons' lives. He seeks for ways to comprehend these complexities and is not satisfied with more limited and segmented formulations.

These should not be matters of taste. The tenability of constructions about man and his behavior must rest ultimately on their consistency with observation. We must speak, then, of an entire network of confirmed propositions which provide a basis for deeper understanding. This understanding should permit us to improve the validity of our methods of assessing personality; it should yield specifications about the conditions that foretell endurance in behavior and experience and those that presage change. It should even tell us when our personality measures are to be trusted and when they are not to be relied upon. The argument, then, is that evaluative measures will be only as effective as the level of knowledge permits and that improvement in these measures will depend, in the long run, on progress in personality theory and measurement. This is not to say that evaluative studies ought to be held in abeyance. On the contrary, the greatest progress in theory and measurement can come from just such studies, providing the need to contribute to such progress is accepted as part of the end.

Let us examine what this means in terms of some specific criterion measures. One place to start is with measures that seek global estimates. Here we are indebted to Angyal (1941) for the distinction between analyzing the person through a series of abstracted variables or traits and analyzing into a structured aritculation. In the latter method, one starts with a conception of the whole and asks how is it put together. Any element is defined in terms of its relations to other elements and to the whole. Most psychodynamic theories strive for such a formulation of personality. But when it comes to developing formal measures, even those who subscribe most fully to a psychoanalytic formulation turn to the former method (Luborsky, 1962). There are at least two reasons for this: first, comprehensive theories are still both so complexly and so vaguely, and even so self-contradictorily, stated that they defy formal methods; second, research workers strive for outcome measures which will be acceptable to those of different theoretical persuasions.

The two most carefully worked out general clinical assessments of the mental health status of the individual are those developed at the Menninger and Phipps Clinics. Both were designed to replace the often used crude and frequently misleading rating of improvement by the therapist himself or an outside judge. For purposes of evaluating short-term group therapy, Frank and his associates (Parloff, Kelman, & Frank, 1954) evolved a three-part criterion consisting of measures of (1) comfort-discomfort, relying on patient report regarding a list of distressing symptoms; (2) effectiveness-ineffectiveness, defined by 15 types of behavior generally recognized as socially ineffective, rated by interviewers on the basis of information obtained from the patient and an informant; and (3) self-awareness, based on a comparison of self-ratings with interviewers' ratings based on observations of the patient. These measures were studied for internal consistency and agreement between independent raters and for their relations to each other and to repeated application with therapy intervening. For some reason not fully explained, only the discomfort and ineffectiveness measures were used in the major series of studies which will be discussed in the section on research design.

As part of an ambitious effort to evaluate long-term psychotherapy conducted from a psychoanalytic orientation, the Menninger Clinic group employed a (mental) Health-Sickness Rating (HSR) defined by seven criteria: (1) ability to function autonomously, (2) severity of symptoms, (3) degree of discomfort, (4) effect on the environment, (5) utilization of abilities, (6) quality of interpersonal relationships, and (7) breadth and depth of inter~sts. An independent judge, after reviewing all of the initial data, including psychological tests, decides approximately where the patient would fall within a ranked standard series of sample patients and assigns a single rating from 0 to 100 (Luborsky, 1962). Very high correlations between independent raters are obtained. By definition, HSR seems reasonably independent of the specifics of psychoanalytic theory. Yet when it was correlated with ratings of a series of specific characteristics made by other judges using the same data, two of the three variables correlating highest with it, .84 and .81, respectively, were patterning of defenses and ego strength, which are psychoanalytic constructs.[5] This raises the possibility that judges who were not psychoanalytically oriented might not have rated the patients similarly, a question which could be put to empirical test.

Self-perception and self-evaluation are, of course, central to client-centered theory. Initially, client-centered investigators coded client self-referent responses made during psychotherapy in terms of negative, positive, and neutral (Raimy, 1948). Later, seeking methods offering greater potential for statistical manipulation and, it was hoped, providing more incisive observations, they turned to the Q sort, in which the client is asked to arrange a general series of self-descriptive statements, phrases, or even adjectives in order of self-relevance according to a fixed distribution. Typically, he is asked to do this twice, once as he sees himself and once in accordance with his ideal self. This correlation of self with ideal is taken as an index of the state of his self-esteem, which in the context of the theory refers to whether his locus of evaluation is self or other based. Pathological states are thought to arise from the denial to awareness of certain experiences of self which are in conflict with the evaluation reactions of others. This basing of self-evaluation in the reactions of others will be reflected in low or even negative self-ideal correlations. The desired state of evaluating self in organismic terms leads to self-acceptance and high positive self-ideal correlations.[6]

Underlying all this is, of course, the general theory of self as a construct in personality and behavior. This is a construct which, despite varied operational expressions and many ambiguities, continues to enjoy a robust existence (Wylie, 1961). The Q sort for self represents only a slight technical variation on the personality inventory. In fact, Dymond (1954) used it to derive a measure of adjustment. Yet the particular set of self-

---

[5] The third variable of the three, severity of symptoms, which is not a theoretically based one, showed an expected −.84 correlation.
[6] Shlien and Zimring (1966) offer an excellent summary of the evolution of criteria in client-centered theory and research.

descriptive items that has been the base for most Q-sort studies (Butler & Haigh, 1954) has not been subjected to the varied validity studies that have characterized the background for using other established inventories. The more specific index, self-ideal correlation, raises particular questions. It would appear to be one means by which an individual expresses a current state of dissatisfaction with himself. Shlien (1962) has presented evidence to show that one can obtain a comparable expression no matter what content one provides the individual for sorting, or even if one provides him with two Plexiglas circles or squares, one representing self and the other ideal, to manipulate to show self-ideal relation. If we are safe in assuming that the Q-sort procedure using self-ideal correlation is a means for permitting an individual to communicate his currently felt dissatisfaction with himself, it becomes relevant to ask how this expression of dissatisfaction is to be understood. How likely is it that a person will express dissatisfaction without there being realistic reasons for it? It does not seem probable, but one can conceive of conditions that might stimulate exaggeration of such expression. Any time that a client feels called upon to justify his search for psychotherapy, either to himself or to others, it seems likely that he will be motivated to accentuate his dissatisfaction with himself. Conversely, when he is trying to justify not seeking psychotherapy or prematurely terminating it, he will be prone to emphasize his satisfaction with himeslf through high self-ideal correlations.[7] The increase in self-ideal correlation over a 3-month waiting period for those who refused therapy or dropped out of it in the Chicago study has already been mentioned as one example of possible exaggerated expression. In another example, Lesser (1961) found that prematurely terminating clients showed greater increase in correlation than those continuing without regard to length of treatment.

It seems likely that the most frequent accompaniment of low or negative self-denial correlations is an enduring state of dissatisfaction, reflecting psychic malfunctioning. Conversely, high correlations reflect satisfaction and effective psychic functioning. Although this will be the common significance, we have seen that there is reason to believe that special circumstances may alter these meanings. The work of Chordorkoff (1954a, 1954b) showing that persons with high self-ideal correlations above a certain level tend to be more rather than less maladjusted suggests that, in addition to situational factors, structural personality factors affect the significance of this correlation. It has been observed, for example, that paranoid persons are likely to present a high self-ideal correlation.

Gaylin's (1966) study, which was directed toward clarifying the use of the Rorschach as a criterion, provides further data suggestive of the limita-

[7] Snyder (1962) has made a similar point.

tion of the self-ideal correlation as a criterion of the effects of psychotherapy. Seeking the sources of contradictory results obtained with the Rorschach, Gaylin distinguished between conventionally used indices of pathology, which he terms "structure scores," and indices of creative life style, such as originality, organizational ability (Beck's Z-W), and organizational complexity, which he terms "function scores." Using therapists ratings and self-ideal correlations as criteria, he formed four groups: I, pure success; II, pure failure; III, success defined by therapist, but failure defined by S-I correlation; and IV, success defined by S-I correlation, but failure defined by therapist. As he expected, Gaylin found that function scores differentiated group I from the rest, whereas structure scores did not. He also found that, where individual function indices did differentiate, with only one exception it was from group IV. In the case of non-$F\%$, which is taken as an index of affective complexity, group I and group III exceeded group IV in change scores. These data suggest that the Rorschach function score and the therapist's evaluation of progress are responsive to more similar changes than is the S-I correlation, despite the fact that the therapists were client centered in orientation.

The use of target symptoms as a criterion for evaluating psychotherapy would appear to be relatively uncomplicated. Pascal and Zax (1956), reviewing files of psychotherapeutic cases, simply identified behavior that was considered deviant by the patient or (usually in the case of child patients) someone else who gave the history. Their list, which includes such items as "unable to work," "not completely toilet trained" (for a 5-year-old), "several attempts at suicide," "excessive drinking," is heavily weighted with intrinsically significant behavior items. Their further procedure consisted of reading the case summaries, progress reports, or statements of the patient for evidence on which to base a judgment as to whether or not the behaviors previously noted had changed in the desired direction. There are, however, questions about the accuracy of the reports because of biases of whoever wrote the record, the intangibles underlying the patient's "good" reports, and the like. This study represents the selection of target symptoms within an ongoing clinical program, sampling a full range of persons seeking help, with more than one target symptom possible for any given patient (two and three were tied as the modal number of symptoms). Quasi-clinical studies such as those by Paul (1966) and Lang and Lazovik (1963) select a sample with only a single target symptom. In both of these investigations the individuals treated had been recruited on the basis of their volunteering the fact of possessing the given symptom—in the case of Paul, speech anxiety; in the study of Lang and Lazovik, snake phobia.

Without recourse to theoretical polemic, but solely on empirical grounds, one must be skeptical about these seemingly direct and simple indices. For example, Novick (1966) demonstrated that the effects of symptomatic treatment of enuresis in children differed depending on whether the symptons have persisted since birth or have been acquired after a period of continence. Similarly, Marks and Gelder (1966) have distinguished between simple and complex phobias, reporting experience that the former are successfully treated by behavior therapy methods, concentrating on the target symptom, whereas the latter are more effectively treated by psychodynamic methods. Thus, in using this approach, we would, at a minimum, want to know a great deal about the anatomy of the target symptom, the range of conditions under which it appears, and the varieties of its natural course.

Somewhat similar questions arise in the special instances where the investigator seeks to use psychophysiological indicators of psychological malfunctioning. Measurements of muscle potentials, skin resistance, respiratory rate, heart rate, and finger volume are among the indices that have been used with the intention of obtaining not only evidence of moment-to-moment shifts correlatable with discussion of specific conflict-laden content but also proof of more general change. Lacey's (1959) lively and definitive review of such research underlined complexities similar to those cited in discussing the strategy of using target symptoms. One cannot be certain how these measures are to be interpreted without taking into account individual differences in physiological response systems and both general and therapeutic contextual factors.

Desirability of Multiple Vantage Points

The very crude state of personality theory and measurement dictates a strategy of assessing personality change in psychotherapy from the vantage points of the patient, therapist, and independent observers and, in so far as possible, the choice of instruments and targets that reflect multiple theories of behavior and personality (Ryan, 1970). Hence an investigator might look to various techniques for obtaining direct reports or self-ratings from the patient. These might be selected from among the Symptom Checklist (Lipman et al., 1969), the Q sort (Butler & Haigh, 1954), and the Psychiatric Outpatient Mood Scales (McNair & Lorr, 1964b). In place of or in addition to direct self-reports, the investigator might choose one of several personality inventories, such as the California Personality Inventory or the Minnesota Multiphasic. In the sphere of target symptoms, he would probably choose an ad hoc instrument tailored to a particular population or to individual patients. For the special case of phobias, various versions of Fear Survey Schedules are available (e.g., Lang & Lazovik, 1963). In seeking the therapist's evaluation, the investigator might utilize the Health-Sickness Rating Scale (Luborsky, 1962), the Interpersonal Behavior Inventory (Lorr & McNair, 1963), or the aforementioned target complaints. A rarely used vantage point is that of significant others. One of the few formal instruments for obtaining such reports is the Katz Adjustment Scales (Katz & Lyerly, 1963). Finally, there is the vantage point of the clinical evaluator. The Psychiatric Status Schedule, in addition to providing a vehicle for obtaining patient self-reports, can also serve as a basis for clinical evaluations. The Health-Sickness Rating Scale, similarly, provides a common base for ratings by therapist and clinical evaluator. Finally, there is of course the possibility of using clinical evaluations based on a battery of projective tests.

A representative array of such measures makes possible an examination of the interrelations of data obtained from different vantage points of observation and from different frames of reference. Campbell and Fiske (1959) have discussed the theory and technique of analyzing such a matrix to identify the different sources of variation involved in generating it, and Cartwright, Kirtner, and Fiske (1963) have illustrated its applicability.

RESEARCH DESIGN IN EVALUATIVE STUDIES

Our understanding of the technical problems to be solved in planning an evaluative experiment is far more advanced than our solutions to the problem of criteria. In his now classic paper, Campbell (1957) points out that any experiment, whether naturalistic or laboratory, if it is to merit the title, must involve a minimum of one formal comparison and therefore observations at least at two points in time. In psychotherapy research such comparison is represented by observations—tests, clinical interviews, situational observations, and so forth—before and after the intervening treatment. Though one cannot help inferring that his aim was to undermine the dominant psychodynamic psychotherapies, Eysenck (1952, 1954, 1955a, 1955b, 1961, 1964) professed to be demonstrating the inadequacies of this minimum research design for eliminating alternatives to the conclusion that treatment was the factor accounting for the differences between observations taken before and after it. He argued that a minimum control required comparison of the rate of change (improvement) after therapy with that obtained under conditions of no or minimal treatment. To establish this base rate of improvement, he drew on two studies, one by Landis (1937) of the amelioration rate in state mental hospitals for patients diagnosed under the heading of psychoneurosis, and the other by Denker (1947) on 500 disability insurance claims made by persons reportedly ill of a neurosis for at least 3 months before submitting their claims. Eysenck analyzed the data from these two studies to show that both exhibited an improvement rate of two-thirds and used this yardstick to demonstrate that various studies of then practiced psychotherapies had failed to prove their effectiveness.

Kiesler (1966) has well summarized the countercriticisms which have spelled out the shoddiness of this demonstration. Yet Eysenck must be given part of the credit for provoking a series of examinations of the issues of research design, of which Kiesler's was an important example; these include papers by Frank (1959) and Breedlove and Krause (1966), added to the early contribution by Edwards and Cronbach (1952). It may be most instructive to examine first the five general classes of extraneous variables requiring control, as spelled out by Campbell: history, maturation, the effects of observation, instrument decay, and statistical regression. Then I will examine issues specific to psychotherapy connected with defining treatment and the populations of patients and therapists to which it is possible to generalize.

History

During the time span represented by psychotherapy the patient experiences many other influences as well, and any change may be due to any or all of these. The straightforward strategy for controlling for this factor is the use of an untreated control group, either matched to the experimental group or obtained by random assignment to experimental or control out of the pool of possible patients. The former method offers imposing problems because the poverty of our knowledge of which are the important patient variables makes selection difficult and urges us toward matching on large numbers of variables, vastly increasing the size of the pool needed to produce an adequate match. The Wisconsin study (Rogers et al., 1967) matching for six factors (sex, age, level of schooling and culture, similarity of diagnosis within schizophrenia, history of hospitalization, and degree of disturbance) drew on a hospital population of 800 patients and still encountered delays while waiting for new patients to provide the matches necessary to fill each cell. Random assignment avoids the difficulties created by our ignorance and can be adapted to any size sample, but presents its own difficulties, especially when the study involves the naturalistic conditions of clinical practice. Under these conditions it is difficult to avoid intentional and unintentional bias in assignment. Thus the integrity of the "wait" control group in the Rogers and Dymond study (1954) was compromised by the tendency to place clients greatly in need of help in the experimental group. It is easiest to apply this method in experimental studies where subjects are recruited for a single target symptom, as Paul (1966) did in his study of the treatment of speech anxiety.

Apart from questions of ethics, it goes against the grain for clinicians to withhold treatment or to offer minimal contact, as control for the effect of time and accompanying intervening events requires. In some instances (Rogers & Dymond, 1954; Breedlove & Krause, 1966) the strategy of asking the patient to wait before undertaking treatment provides a no-treatment period to compare with treatment. Wherever waiting lists are already in operation, a situation which applies to most facilities, it is no departure to use this kind of control. The difficulty in keeping biasing factors out of the assignment has already been mentioned. Another difficulty is that many other experiences which change the individual can occur during the waiting period, changes that have sometimes been termed "spontaneous remission." Bergin (1971) has well discussed the misleading nature of this term. An equal difficulty is that of having the waiting period match the calendar time in the treatment sample, a factor which blurred the results obtained in the Rogers and Dymond project (Calvin, 1954). The client-centered group tried to compensate for this defect by including a normal control, a sample of persons not seeking psychotherapy, but it is doubtful that this sample, in no way comparable, could serve any purpose, even that of testing the stability of the criterion measurements, because this characteristic may vary between normal and pathological samples.

Maturation

During the course of psychotherapy the patient not only experiences many concurrent events that may influence him but also grows older and experiences other systematic changes which come under the heading of maturation. The need for accounting for this factor is obvious in the evaluation of psychotherapy with children or adolescents, but may be important also with adults. Later developmental experiences in marriage and vocation, instead of exacerbating a problem, may have an ameliorating effect. If our knowledge of development were such that base rates for changes under various conditions could be established, these base rates would offer a control against which to test the effects of psychotherapy. Since such precise knowledge seems almost unattainable, some variant of the strategy applied to control for history will have to be employed.

Effects of Observation

Whenever the patient knows he is under research observation, this can have an effect on the observations obtained. Most often clinicians have feared that the effect will be adverse as a reaction to invasion of privacy.

But such knowledge may also have the effect of stimulating reactions designed to display oneself or one's therapist favorably. Furthermore, some observations or interactions with the observer may in themselves have influencing effects, either by providing practice in certain responses or by directing attention toward certain issues and thereby stimulating new trends of thought. Incidentally, the effects of observation need not only influence the patient directly; they may also operate indirectly through their influence on the therapist. In fact, Breedlove and Krause (1966) propose a control group consisting of patients and therapists, with precautions taken to keep both unaware that they were participating in a study. Neither patients nor therapists would, therefore, participate in providing research data at the beginning or during treatment. After treatment, outcome measurements would be taken. Such a control group would be meaningful only in a complex research design which included other controls for the influence of repeated observations and for the passage of time. Not only are there direct effects of observations on therapists, but also there are indirect effects, either positive or negative, through influencing morale. If the study or preparation for it included discussions among the group of therapists and other exchanges designed to clarify treatment or other issues, it could result in heightened morale, which would influence their therapy and might be communicated to the patient as a special effect beyond that produced by the technical methods of treatment under study.

Instrument Decay

In nonpsychological research, this alternative source of change might be exemplified by the fatiguing of a spring scale or the condensation of water vapor in a cloud chamber. In psychotherapy research, changes in observation before and after treatments may be due to raters becoming more experienced, more fatigued, or even bored, or from their having learned the purpose of the experiment. Only prior studies designed to establish the interchangeability of raters and the effects of various conditions on their observations can provide a basis for estimating and controlling these effects. More will be said about this topic in the next chapter.

Statistical Regression

Concern with this factor was originally rooted in the fallibility of tests or other forms of measurement (McNemar, 1940). An unreliable measure means that the sampling of observations is such that even with no change a second set will be expected to yield a slightly different result, reflecting chance fluctuations. These fluctuations have been demonstrated both mathematically and empirically to exhibit the phenomenon of regressing toward the mean; that is, the more the initial observation deviates above or below the mean of the population distribution, the more the second set of observations, even on the absence of any true change, will move in the direction of the mean. Although this phenomenon is typically thought of in terms of the unreliability (i.e., internal inconsistency) of a test, it applies also to random fluctuation in individuals (i.e., inconsistency of the individual). For example, if one is concerned with mood states, which are subject to variation over relatively brief periods of time, such as days, selects a subset of individuals all of whom display an extreme mood at one point in time, and observes them at a second point in time, it is predictable that the average for this group will be less extreme at the second point.

The applicability of this factor to evaluation of psychotherapy should be clear. Persons who seek psychotherapy are inevitably those who will exhibit extreme scores on the kinds of measures that are likely to constitute the criterion. Usually the tests have been developed with just this aim in mind. Furthermore, a person is most likely to submit to the time, expense, and discomfort entailed only when he is experiencing extremes of pain and discomfort. At some later point in time, perhaps because of fluctuations in external stresses or other factors, he may not feel the pain so greatly. Any sets of observations which are influenced by such temporary fluctuations will then reflect these changes, which may be very different from the ones sought.

These phenomena provide another reason for requiring an untreated control group. Where enough data exist, it may be possible to substitute statistical estimates of the effects of regression toward the mean.

Defining Treatment

Any experiment involves evaluation of the effects of exposing an individual or group to some event. In the case of psychotherapy the experimental variable is an extremely complex series of events extending over lengthy periods of time, often calibrated in years. Without further documentation, reliance on the therapist's designation of his treatment represents insufficient control of the treatment factor. Even the step of asking the therapist to describe his treatment seems insufficient. Where strong theoretical traditions have been established, therapists who are part of that tradition develop a culture which conditions how they talk about their therapeutic efforts but need not be a direct translation of their activities. One of the major deficiencies in the ambitious Menninger project (Robbins & Wallerstein, 1959) is that its data on treatment are written summaries by the therapists rather than direct observations. The fact that supervisors' reports were also included does not solve the problem. The supervisor may correct for personality-dictated biases in the therapist's observations, but he himself is subject to theory-dictated observational biases. One of the basic aims of the painstaking methods we call science is to free observations from the influence of the experimenter's beliefs. At its core, freed of the influences of greed and self-aggrandizement to which scientists, being human, are no less subject than other men, scientific method is directed toward making it possible for the scientist to learn which of his beliefs are distortions and therefore untenable.

The client-centered group has pioneered in controlling the treatment factor by introducing direct observation of the therapist. Even this step, unfortunately, does not resolve the question of treatment. The difficulty is that any designation of treatment (e.g., client-centered, psychoanalytic, behavioral) selects for observation only a relatively limited aspect of the behavior of the therapist during the treatment process, often as expressed in the content of his communications with his patient. But there are also facial expressions, gestures, other bodily movements, and body positions, as well as paralinguistic cues, which may turn out to be the important events. To be sure, such uncertainties may apply also to simpler laboratory experiments—for example, the subject may react to the click which turns on the colored light rather than to the color itself—but the range of alternatives is much more manageable. This, then, is one of the factors which makes process research such an important part of developing definitive evaluating studies.

Another way of looking at the complexity of the treatment variable is to say that it is difficult to separate the treatment from the psychotherapist who is its source. One can concentrate on the technical specifications, such as they are, contained in the treatment method. But the effective ingredient may turn out to be some personal characteristic, ranging from whether the therapist likes the patient or is spontaneous in expressing himself to such factors as his expertness, which in itself may be a carrier of the concealed ingredient not defined by technical specifications. In fact, several research workers have produced data to demonstrate that results showing little or no effects of psychotherapy may conceal the positive effects of expert or otherwise appropriate work canceled by the negative effects of an inexpert or inappropriate version of psychotherapy (Bergin, 1963; Cartwright, 1956; Rogers et al., 1967).

Defining Populations

The minimum amount of knowledge gained by a study of a particular sample of patients, clients, or subjects is the conclusion about the influence of the experimental variable on them. We are then in a position to say that this person or set of persons changed this much as a result of this treatment. Although such an answer serves patient and therapist as a justification of their efforts, most investigators seek more than this: they seek to generalize to some wider sample and context. In order to do this, assuming that the kinds of controls discussed above are present, the persons involved in the study must be identifiable as a sample of some more general population. The population might be the kinds of persons who seek the service of clinic X, in which the study was done, a very limited generalizing group. If the population were definable as all persons seeking service from outpatient clinics in the United States, this would be an impressively general population. To be able to say that, we would of course need data on the essential parameters of the population of outpatients and a demonstration that the persons in our study fitted such parameters reasonably well.

The question of the sample is important not only for generalizing but also for achieving greater precision. A particular treatment may not be effective for all kinds of persons, a truism which is demonstrated by the absence of treatment studies displaying universal or nearly universal improvement rates. By refining our definitions of the personal characteristics of patients and the nature of their personal difficulties, we pave the way to studies which will lead to more differentiated successful treatment. Novick's (1966) earlier cited study showing differential success for symptomatic treatment for enuresis, depending on whether continence had previously been established, is an example of the direction that studies must take to achieve greater precision in our knowledge of treatment.

The various factors to be considered suggest that, to be meaningful, complex research designs will be required. Not only will the multiple group designs described by Campbell (1957) and Breedlove and Krause (1966) be necessary, but also we must see the factorial analyses advocated by Edwards and Cronbach (1952) to partition out variances due to varieties of treatments and to varieties of patients and to their interactions. We should however, avoid the trap of imagining that one definitive study will prove, once and for all, the effectiveness of psychotherapy and define the process by which it works. The complexities cited in this chapter point to Kiesler's (1966) conclusion that there is an "infinitesimal probability that any one-shot research attempt will ever significantly advance our knowledge in this area" (p. 127). We join Kiesler in agreeing with Seeman (1961) that the pattern of research required is "one of plugging away at small bits of knowledge which, only after an appreciable period of time, might attain a higher order of significance" (p. 190).[8]

CHAPTER 3

Tactics in Process Studies

In Chapter 2 I discussed the intimate connections between process and outcome. Outcome may be seen as the process of change taken at a particular point in time. Furthermore, an examination of the events of therapy is required to understand and to demonstrate how changes are brought about. Hence we are interested not only in the course of changes occurring in the patient but also in the interactions between him and the therapist which are the sources of these changes. A full research program will have to be concerned with the nature of the psychotherapeutic relationship, seeking to discern those features of it which are the necessary ingredients of change. This chapter will consider the various decisions and problems which surround such ventures.

THE INNER VERSUS OUTER VIEW OF PROCESS

How shall we observe the process of psychotherapy? We could rely on our own observations or those of fellow therapists. We could secure concurrent and retrospective accounts from patients. Or, via film and sound recording, we could seek a full recording of the events. Each of these approaches provides certain gains, but also incurs certain losses. For those who insist that thinking and feeling are important human events which cannot be adequately observed when introspective reports are excluded, the third vantage point will not be complete without the other two. Ultimately the mode of observation deemed necessary will depend on the particular aspects of the process chosen for study. Later in this chapter we will give further attention to this question and the susceptibility of certain aspects of it to empirical answers. At this point I will concentrate on the complexities and ambiguities created by treating patient and therapist views of the process as the primary data.

A full understanding of process requires that we be able to separate influences from their effects and from preconceptions about their relationships. The therapist and patient as observers are conditioned by a number of cultures. Some of these cultures provide the necessary context for understanding action and expression, for example, the significance of para-linguistic (intonation patterns, stresses, junctures, etc.) and kinetic (facial and bodily movements) cues. But others represent sets that can rearrange and distort perceptions of the order of events. One of these is the culture of psychotherapists. Here I refer to the whole set of influences exerted by communication among therapists, but more particularly by the allegiances to particular theoretical constructions that each therapist develops. Such constructions are themselves the product of the experience of psychothera-peutic events. Most scientific constructions, especially at more primitive stages of development, are founded in naturalistic observation. If our purpose is to study how psychotherapists think about psychotherapy, then therapists' reports will be a prime source of data. But if we are seeking to verify a particular construction or to pit it against a rival one, we need some means of disentangling the events from the observer's expectations. We must assume that psychoanalytic, client-centered, and behavior thera-pists (I choose a few examples from many) have all founded their con-structions of the nature of psychotherapy in their experiences. Thus it seems inevitable that the psychoanalytic therapist will concentrate his report on transference, resistance, and interpretive sequences; the client-centered therapist, on therapist attitude-patient experiencing sequences, and the behavior therapist on schedules of reinforcement geared to emis-sion of particular classes of behavior. The same can be said when the therapist is asked to endorse statements descriptive of his behavior or of other events in psychotherapy. Therapists have acquired or been taught certain principles and can recognize these in the statements offered.

Psychotherapists' attitudes and beliefs about psychotherapy and their reports of their practices have been studied by a number of investigators who examined to what extent views were shared by all therapists or defined subgroups, composed on the basis of doctrine espoused, profes-sional affiliation, and experience. In one of the early studies, Fiedler (1950b) found a common culture among a small sample of therapists of psychoanalytic, Adlerian, and client-centered pursuasions. Differences were obtained only between experienced and beginning therapists. His items contained three major variables, labeled "communication," "emo-tional distance," and "status role." In a later study, Sundland and Barker (1962), sampling a much larger group but one composed only of psychol-ogists, constructed a questionnaire covering these three variables, but including also many additional scales and selected items which maximized the variance among therapists, particularly by orientation. With such an instrument they found a single general (second-order) factor which they tentatively defined in bipolar terms as analytic versus experiential, but which might also be described as objective versus subjective, cerebral versus visceral, impersonal versus personal, or planned observer versus unplanned participant. All of these represent familiar language in the dialogues among therapists. In view of their methods of selecting items, it is no surprise that Sundland and Barker, contrary to Fiedler, found the main source of variance to be theoretical orientation rather than experience.

McNair and Lorr (1964a), feeling that at least three independent dimensions: (A) psychoanalytically oriented techniques, (I) impersonal versus personal approaches to patient, and (D) directive, active therapeutic methods, were necessary to characterize therapeutic techniques, constructed a new questionnaire based on the somewhat modified Sundland-Barker collection but with a few items drawn from Fey (1958) and some original ones. Their sample of psychotherapists employed in Veterans Administration Mental hygiene clinics was numerous and heterogeneous with regard to professional affiliation, with substantial representations of psychiatrists, psychologists, and social workers. Since their three factors are slight variants of Sundland's and Barker's polar definitions, and factor analysis is more of a descriptive than a hypothesis testing statistic, no very definitive statements can be made about the differences between the two studies in this regard. McNair and Lorr did find technique and profession related to patterns of belief, but replicated the lack of differentiation by experience.

Using a set of items almost purely descriptive of therapist behavior, Wallach and Strupp (1964) found, once again, no differences for experience but differences according to theoretical orientation. Since they used only 17 items, the six factors they extracted stretched the capacity of their item pool. Four of the six seemed identifiable as (1) maintaining personal distance, (2) preference for intensive therapy, (3) keeping verbal interventions at a minimum, and (4) seeing psychotherapy as art rather than science. Although orthodox Freudians and psychoanalytically oriented therapists had higher scores than Sullivanian or client-centered therapists, the differences only approached statistical significance. Comparable differences were significant for preference for intensive therapy. Therapists professing adherence to Sullivan reported the least tendency to keep verbal intervention at a minimum, with orthodox Freudians reporting the most. Client-centered therapists were most prone to endorse psychotherapy as art.

Most of the statements included in such studies refer to behavioral predilections, for example, whether the therapist is willing to see the patient's family, or how planful or spontaneous he is. Less frequently they refer to beliefs, such as the importance of unconscious motives in behavior. In so far as they center on behavior, one may assume that therapists' reports are responsive to the realities of their own behavior. Furthermore, reports obtained from running notes such as those in the Menninger study (Robbins & Wallerstein, 1959) probably reflect these realities more fully. Strupp's (1960) technique of asking therapists to respond to a filmed therapeutic interview at selected juncture points as they would in their own therapy seems to come much closer to the actual events. In the next chapter the role and limitations of Strupp's and other simplifications and analogues will be discussed more fully. Returning to the question of the accuracy of therapists' reports, we find that the results of a number of studies are relevant. In some of the earliest work, Covner (1944a, 1944b) compared running notes with sound recordings of the same interviews, finding that, although the materials included were 75 to 90% accurate, 70% or more of the actual interview was omitted. He concluded that not only unimportant but also important material was omitted, and that these omissions often resulted in a rather distorted picture of the interview.

Knapp, Mushatt, and Nemetz (1966) illustrated the discrepancy between an analyst's process notes on the first 10 minutes of an hour and the transcript of a sound recording of the same period. Much that was essential was preserved by the notes, and certain relevant information was added, such as the significant fact that the analyst was 12 minutes late for the session. However, the notes completely obscure the fact that the therapist replied to the patient's question about when he was *leaving for* his vacation by giving the date that he was *returning*. This bore on the issue of separation, which was bypassed at the moment. Knapp et al. comment on the prophetic nature of the analyst's slip in that the patient left therapy on approximately the day in question. Mention has already been made of the influence of theoretical orientation on both attention and memory. As part of a study of countertransference, Cutler (1958) found the therapist's conflicts in interpersonal behavior to be reflected in distorted reports of his interactions with his patients. In somewhat the same vein, Kiesler, Mathieu, and Klein (in Rogers et al., 1967) and Burstein and Carkhuff (1968) found that process ratings by independent observers of empathy, regard, genuineness, concreteness, and self-disclosure did not correspond to self-ratings by therapists. If anything (in the latter study), there was an inverse relationship for the experienced therapists. Since this relationship was insignificant, it may not need explanation, but it is difficult to understand. Since other studies by the Truax-Carkhuff group have offered evidence that independent ratings of the above characteristics of therapist behavior are associated with patient progress, these results suggest that it is appropriate to use such ratings as criteria of the usefulness of therapists' self-ratings. On the other hand, in the 1968 study the therapists were participating with subjects simulating clients and were observed for only a brief interview, raising questions about the transferability of the results to psychotherapy. Furthermore, the briefness of the report leaves the conditions of the study and the data obscure. The above reservations do not apply to the results obtained by Kiesler et al.

To summarize, there seems to be ample evidence to suggest that any effort to use the therapist's view of the events of psychotherapy must take into account the biasing effects on his observations of his theoretical orientation and of his personal conflicts. In any case, caution is in order because of evidence that these reports are less than accurate.

The patient's view of the process of psychotherapy, in addition to aforementioned cultural factors, would appear to be influenced by context and character style. Inevitably, the culture of psychotherapists is transmitted to patients. Much of this transmission is independent of the events of primary interest. The prominence given to psychology, psychiatry, and various change processes (i.e., psychotherapy, personal development, expanding personal openness, etc.) in the mass media testifies to the pervasiveness of ideas and vicarious experience regarding patienthood for large numbers of potential patients. So important are these sets deemed to be that some have argued that, combined with therapist sets, they may be the main source of changes observed in psychotherapy (Frank, 1961).

Evidence obtained by Begley and Liberman (1970) suggests that, although patients do come to therapy with well established sets, these are not identical with those of therapists. These investigators, using an adaptation of McNair's and Lorr's (1964a) questionnaire, found that prospective patients, when queried about their expectations, viewed therapy from a frame of reference different from that of therapists. Items that in responses of therapists reflected the same factor, when responded to by patients, did not correlate any more closely than items supposed to reflect other factors. The major orientation of the patient's responses revolved around personal involvement with the therapist.

Context and character style can be assumed to influence the patient's report on his therapy. As Hathaway (1948) pointed out, the condition under which a patient experiences considerable effort by the therapist to help him sets up pressures to give favorable responses toward these efforts to show his gratitude and to reassure himself that his and the therapist's sacrifices have not been in vain. A cross-cutting factor would be the patient's character style, which, depending on the particular individual, might lead him to emphasize the therapist's activity or inactivity and such qualities of the activity as its assertiveness, friendliness, or criticalness.

If we assume that the therapist's report may be biased by his personal conflicts, it is natural to raise the same question about the patient. The supporting data are by no means clear cut. Barrett-Lennard (1962) and Kiesler, Mathieu, and Klein (Rogers et al., 1967) find appreciable correspondence between patient reports on process variables and ratings by independent judges based on examination of segmented samples of interview protocols. Although Truax (1966a) finds some correspondence here, patient reports are less closely related to criterion measures of outcome than ratings by independent judges. Furthermore, other investigators (Burstein & Carkhuff, 1968; Bozarth & Grace, 1970) report little or no relationship between patient reports and independent ratings. All of the last three investigations cited are so briefly reported as to make it difficult to resolve methodological questions. For example, Truax carried out his study under therapeutic conditions comparable to those of Kiesler et al., but seems to have combined, without justifying explanation, outcome measures differently derived for state hospital patients and juvenile delinquents in computing correlations. The Bozarth and Grace study involved ratings based on the fifth interview in counseling with no indications as to the nature of the clients; (that of Burstein and Carkhuff) involved a single undergraduate, role-playing a client.

It should be clear that lack of correspondence between a patient process report and the report of either the therapist or an independent observer does not in itself undermine faith in the veridicality of the patient's report. It is possible that the patient is giving us realistic views of aspects of the process not accessible from other positions. It would take much more subtle and searching evidence to demonstrate that the patient's report is a superimposition of some set or other psychic process rather than a description of therapeutic interactions. In any case, the significance of such observations must rest on the relation to criterion measures of the effects of therapy which are independent of patient or therapist reports and are not in themselves based on direct observations of process. Apart from considerations of veridicality and validity, patient reports are of interest in themselves as products of psychotherapy. Strupp, Wallach, and Wogan (1964) have provided one of the most searching uses thus far of retrospective reports of patients. They were able to make the most use of reports on the personality and general behavior of the therapist. They found that the position assigned by the patient to his therapist on a scale ranging from the extremes of coldness, remoteness, and distance to those of warmth, nearness, and humanness was related to his therapist's rating of the intensity and depth of the therapy. The less intense the therapy, the more human and warm the therapist was seen to be. Ryan and Gizynski (1971) reported that their interviews with patients concerning recent experiences in behavior therapy gave them the impression that behavior modification techniques added little to therapy, which instead seemed to hinge on interpersonal elements involving feelings toward and attitudes about the therapist. Furthermore, ratings of the degree of use of behavior modification techniques were unrelated to outcome as rated by the patient, the therapist, or the investigators on the basis of their interviews with patients. These same ratings, however, were negatively related to experimenter judgments of degree of pathology and positively related to judgments of the therapist as disliked, incompetent, or distrustful of the patient, and to seeing the techniques as unpleasant.

CONTENT VERSUS PROCESS

In setting out to study the process by which a therapeutic relationship results in change, we must decide on the terms of such observations. Since one of the salient features of a therapeutic relationship is the words spoken during interviews, shall we concentrate on an analysis of the semantic content of the speech, as is done in many studies in the social sciences (Holsti, 1968)? Use of the explicit content has the advantage that it is fairly easy to train a coder to do the job. But many clinicians are more interested in the actions directed toward another person, of which the verbal content of speech is only a part. What a person says is usually accompanied by vocal stresses and other paralinguistic signs. His speech is part of a total body movement in which head, facial expression, trunk, arms, and legs participate. Each act is embedded in a matrix of acts by both participants. Thus one might observe that, in addition to responding to the content of the therapist's question, which was accompanied by the therapist leaning forward and increasing the intensity of his gaze, the patient first tightened his fists and became slightly rigid in his chair, speaking rapidly, then eased off, maintaining a watchful gaze.

Depending on theoretical orientation, investigators have varied from coding fairly explicit features of the content of communications to highly inferential aspects of the ongoing relationship.[1] Thus, proceeding from a client-centered view, Raimy (1948) coded references to self by the client in terms of whether they were accompanied by positive, negative, or

---

[1] For comprehensive reviews of process studies in psychotherapy see Auld and Murray (1955) and Marsden (1965, 1971).

neutrally toned modifiers. From a psychoanalytic viewpoint, Colby (1960) prepared a code to apply to references to members of the nuclear family and significant others and the tone of the modifiers surrounding them. When the categories are explicit and the rules for entry can be fully specified, it is possible to create a conceptual dictionary susceptible to computer analysis of the semantic content (Harway & Iker, 1966; Laffal, 1968). Through focusing on thematic material, some investigators have devised methods for inferring such affective states as anxiety and hostility (Mahl, 1956; Gottschalk et al., 1966). Interest in affective states naturally turns attention to the paralinguistic (Duncan, Rice, & Butler, 1968) and kinetic (Ekman & Friesen, 1968; Mahl, 1968) aspects of interactions.

An emphasis on the contextual and sequential aspects of relationships grows out of the assumption that the impact of one person on another does not reside in a single act. This leads to coding schemes which seek ways of categorizing what one person is doing to another, rather than just what he is saying (Freedman et al., 1951). In some cases, this emphasis leads to the development of highly inferential coding schemes, for example, depth of interpretation. Seeking to reflect Freudian theory, one research group (Harway et al., 1955) defined depth of interpretation not only in terms of the therapist's view of the patient's behavior, motives, and feelings conveyed in his communication (interpretation), but also by inferences about the patient's level of awareness of this characteristic of himself, derived from observations of the patient (depth). Most of all, this interactional framework leads to examinations of the sequences of actions by the two or more persons involved in the process (e.g., Auld & White, 1959; Raush, 1965).

Another reflection of the view that interest in process transcends a narrow interpretation of content is the coding of relatively content-free aspects of communication behavior. For example, one group (Matarazzo et al., 1968) has examined the length of utterances, the duration of silences, and the frequency of interruptions in controlled and psychotherapeutic interviews. Another group (Bordin, 1955) selected for attention the structuredness or ambiguity of the therapeutic situation as defined by the therapist's communications.

STRONG VERSUS WEAK APPROACHES

As we have seen, there are infinite ways (i.e., choosing aspects and levels) of selecting observations out of the events in psychotherapy. We can select what is said or how it is said, as well as the accompanying motor and postural characteristics. All of these are subject to further grouping and construction in the mind of the investigator and his observers. Coombs

(1964, p. 4) has pointed out that the scientist usually records less than the full universe of potential observations. Notice that in the listing above of possibilities there was no mention of physiological events or of the clothing worn. But even the recorded observations are not yet data in the sense that individuals, stimuli, and responses are to be identified and classified, and, finally, structure and order relations detected. Thus the investigator is imposing something of himself onto his data from the very outset of his study. The question becomes how radical this imposition will be.

As already mentioned, I will leave to the next chapter discussion of the radical impositions involved when we convert the phenomena for laboratory observation. Under the conditions of naturalistic observation, radical impositions arise at the levels both of recording and of classification. An investigator, for expedient or theoretical reason (more frequently the former), decides to dispense with sound film recording and turns to sound recording or process notes. Instead of having observers respond to sound recordings, the investigator arranges to record their reactions to typescripts. Similarly, the choice of classification systems involves implicit or explicit constructions about the phenomena under observation. The more explicit and the more elaborate the constructions, the more radically the researcher is likely to impose on his data. Obviously, the more radical the imposition, the greater is the risk of an extended excursion into a blind alley. In the end, each investigator has to choose his preferred mode of work. Some will seek to minimize their impositions in the hopes that better and deeper insights will grow out of formal empirical analyses of the broadest level of data, or will depend on insights gained from a completely unformalized immersion in the events. Others, convinced by a particular theory, will concentrate attention on features of psychotherapy highlighted by the theory or will even turn to analogues of these features. Thus one man may start his formal research by a purely exploratory examination of a low-level set of classifications (e.g., numbers of words spoken, duration of silences, grammatical forms of speech selected, gestures and facial expressions), whereas another will choose some larger, more abstracted set of observations, such as might be exemplified by concepts like transference, acceptance, empathy, or differential reinforcement.

My own preference is to find ways to cycle the strong and weak approaches to data.[2] My ideal is to let my curiosity about the underlying process and the imagination linked to it have free reign. But I want to go

---

[2] My one quarrel with Butler, Rice, and Wagstaff (1963), who emphasize minimizing imposition, is that they do not give enough attention to the cycling process in the growth of classifications.

back to fairly weak levels of data to trace in more formal terms of observation and, through the eyes of others, the path of observation and thought. I will offer illustrations in the next section. Here I will only add the comment that a very weak and therefore a thoughtless empirical approach strains even the astonishing analytic capacities of our most advanced computers and that I have no faith that computers can replace thinking and imagining.

Finally, I want to consider some features of the translation of developed theory into observation. I have spoken as if the investigator were the original source of his theory. Most of us, however, are in the position of working from and building on the creative products of our predecessors. The field of psychotherapy is well supplied with theories. In fact, empirical confirmation-disconfirmation processes lag far behind. New theories accompanied by new treatment procedures are introduced; they and older theories and procedures wax and wane on tides of fashion rather than being refined or discarded from the crucible of research. If such research is to be done, those who select a particular theory for investigation must not just borrow it, but must make it their own. By this I mean that they must become sufficiently immersed in it to arrive at classifications that are authentic representations of the terms of the theory. Rogers and his co-workers have, of course, best illustrated this process, but many behavior therapists and, with increasing frequency, psychoanalytically oriented investigators have also exemplified it.

Although examination of the internal empirical consistency of any one theoretical view is important to science building, an even more critical process, as pointed out in Chapter 1, is bringing about confrontation at the level of data between alternative positions. Now the investigator must engage in the difficult task of achieving an understanding of some other position as though it were his own. This is necessary in the primitive state of psychological knowledge where propositions are rarely fully explicit with regard to either their conditions or their contraries (Popper, 1963). One way to bring about confrontations is to fit the implications of contending theories into the classification schemes constructed. I have labeled this process the search for pantheoretical variables. A pantheoretical classification scheme seeks to construe phenomena in ways that incorporate basic elements selected by contending views. Examples of the need for doing this with regard to the basic treatment situation and specific therapeutic interventions were discussed in Chapter 1.

MEASUREMENT ISSUES AND DECISIONS

When we turn to the use of independent observers as the source of data on process and to the associated problems of instrumenting process measures, a wide range of issues and decisions confronts us. These extend from the qualifications that observers must meet to specifications about the conditions of observations. About 20 years ago, associates of the University of Michigan Psychotherapy Project sketched a blueprint of the kind of empirical proving program needed to establish sound process measurements (Bordin et al., 1954). Much has been done by that group and others in implementing such a program, and much more needs to be done. This is the painstaking, undramatic forging of tools that precedes definitive research. In the rest of this chapter I shall bring that earlier sketch up to date, summarizing what methodological answers are now available.

UNIDIMENSIONALITY AND REDUNDANCY

Our goal should be obtaining observations which most fully reflect the events being observed and are least influenced by the observer. Highest priority should go to the recording of concretely defined instances of a particular kind of behavior, with dependence on frequency or other operations to derive judgments of degree or intensity. This is well exemplified by the methods used by Gottschalk and his associates (Gottschalk et al., 1966) in coding affect. They reduced the observational process to the coding of typescript for all instances of clauses containing anxiety, hostility directed outward, hostility directed inward, and ambivalent hostility themes. Intensity differences are obtained by the assigning of weights to classes of instances and by making the assumption that frequency reflects intensity. Unfortunately, not all attributes of dyadic interactions lend themselves to such mechanical modes of differentiation. We are thrown back on asking our observer to make a qualitative discrimination or rating.

In any instance involving ratings, one matter of interest is whether we have in fact obtained discriminations of a single attribute or of a composite. Rating scales force data into unidimensional-appearing continua. It is possible, however, using psychophysical methods, such as Coombs's unfolding techniques (Coombs, 1964), to test this question by studying the discriminating responses of raters toward sets of stimuli. This was the method used by the Michigan group in studying ambiguity (Osburn, 1951) and depth of interpretation (Raush et al., 1956). In the case of ambiguity, rater discriminations fitted fairly closely the assumption of unidimensionality. On the other hand, although a major source of the variance in discriminations seems to have been accounted for by the depth of interpretation concept, two other dimensions were found, one tentatively identified as the rater's anticipation of the patient's emotional response to the therapist's communication, and the other unidentified.

A less exact[3] way of examining the dimensionality of a rated attribute is to investigate its correlates. The limitation of this kind of evidence is that it may be difficult to distinguish correlations that are reflections of functional relationships from those that reflect a composite entering into the rater's discriminations. Fisher (1956) asked raters to respond to interpretations in terms of their plausibility, given a case history and diagnostic data about a hypothetical patient. His finding of an extremely high correlation with ratings of depth might be taken as dimensional information or as validation. I will consider the latter implication later. Howe (1962a, 1962b) used the semantic differential format to obtain results suggesting that depth ratings incorporate one attribute, capacity for arousing anxiety, which includes both depth and potency, and another attribute, professional evaluation, which includes plausibility.

When we examine two or more rating schemes designed to be addressed to the behavior of the same partner in an interaction and based on potentially identical concepts, the question of redundancy certainly arises and is well tested by correlational methods. For example, Mintz, Luborsky, & Auerback (1971) demonstrated that 110 ratings of early therapeutic interviews were reducible to four factors: optimal empathic relationship, directive mode, interpretive mode with receptive patient, and patient health versus distress. When an individual or a team of investigators generates a set of attributes to be rated, their intercorrelations should and often have been examined. For example, Bordin (1966c) found a great deal of redundancy in the part attributes of patient responses to the task of free association: freedom, spontaneity, and involvement. Great variability in redundancy is found among the client-centered scales of empathy, genuineness, and regard, perhaps reflecting differences in conditions of rating. One condition of rating that is likely to overestimate redundancy is that in which the same rater is asked to respond to the same behavior with multiple ratings. This condition could unsettle the rater with regard to one or more of the attributes to be rated and lead to their fusing in his mind. When, as often is the case, raters have theoreti-

---

[3] Karl and Abeles (1969) are mistaken when they assume that rater agreement (reliability) can be taken as evidence of unidimensionality. It is true that, when raters react to different parts of a composite, the effect will be to lower the reliability. But through systematic training a rater can be taught to include all parts of a composite of attributes in his rating, thereby increasing reliability, but not necessarily making it unidimensional.

cally or commonsense-based presumptions about the relations between two attributes which are being rated simultaneously, this loss of experimental independence can lead to highly spurious results.

Less frequently investigated has been the overlap between process scales developed by different investigators. The literature is full of scales, which although given different designations appear to be directed toward similar or partly similar attributes. Two examples are (a) the Free Association Scale (Bordin, 1966c) and the Experiencing Scale (Rogers et al., 1967), and (b) Spiesman's Self-Exploration Scale (1959) and Truax's Depth of Intrapersonal Self-Exploration Scale (Truax & Carkhuff, 1967). Identification of redundancy can be useful as a way of finding simpler substitutes for more complex ratings. For example, Osburn (1951) found that the number of responses by the therapist multiplied by the mean of specificity-generality ratings of responses giving information about the patient correlated with the rating of ambiguity at a level equal to its reliability.

Conditions of Observation

The sheer extensivity and extreme complexity of the data of psychotherapeutic interaction force upon the research worker a decision as to what aspects to present to the observer. The question of whether the same observer is to be asked to rate more than one attribute to the same stimuli has already been mentioned. In addition we must be concerned with the factors of context, observation channels, unit size, and sampling.

CONTEXT

The more restricted the attribute, the less critical will be the factor of context. For example, the number of words uttered, the duration of pauses, and the expression of certain themes can all be coded without knowledge of the sequences of behavior or the background of the actor. On the other hand, interactional variables, such as accurate empathy or depth of interpretation, which require knowledge of what is being responded to, call for careful concern about how much context for his judgments the rater must be given. Where context is thought to be necessary, it would be best to put this assumption to empirical test, both because increased context augments the onerousness of the rater's job and because in some cases it bears on the validity of the rating. If we place our emphasis on accuracy in accurate empathy, evidence that the rater is uninfluenced by knowledge of the patient's behavior (i.e., his ratings are essentially the same whether or not he has this information available to him in rating the therapist's responses) casts doubt that accuracy is in fact included in the rating. Similarly, since depth of interpretation is supposed to be a distance relationship between what is communicated and the patient's level of awareness, evidence that ratings are uninfluenced by information bearing on the patient's level of awareness would cast doubt on this assumed character of the ratings.

There have been surprisingly few studies of the influence of context, and those that have been carried out have found little evidence for context effects. In its analysis of depth of interpretation, the Michigan group found that giving a rater the opportunity to hear or read the preceding interview and to either hear or read a typescript of the interview rated did not influence either the degree of agreement or the mean level of rating assigned, as compared to judgments based on either hearing or reading the therapists' responses with the patients' communications deleted (Harway et al., 1955). They did find that scrambling the order of the therapists' responses had an influence on the ratings, suggesting only slight contributions of context to the ratings. Even when the raters were highly experienced and sophisticated clinicians, no greater use of context was demonstrated (Cutler et al., 1958). These results are reminiscent of many other studies of clinical judgment and clinical prediction suggesting that raters are severely limited in their capacities to process information. There are, of course, some who would argue with some validity that in the case of depth of interpretation the critical increase in context had not been included, namely, making available to a rater-psychoanalyst all of the interactions preceding the interview rated. Truax (1966b) compared the effect of hearing the full interaction between patient and therapist with having the patient's voice deleted on ratings of accurate empathy and warmth. Deletion had no effect on empathy ratings, but there was some evidence that it deflated ratings of warmth. Howe and Pope (1961, 1962) found that deleting patient communications for judgments of therapist activity level and deleting therapist communications for judgments of the diagnostic utility of patient communication had no significant effect on ratings of these two traits from typescripts of initial interviews.

OBSERVATION CHANNELS

Previous discussion has already suggested that full observation of the psychotherapeutic interaction requires the opportunity to witness actions, sounds, and words. In a sense, observation channels can be considered part of the context. From this point of view the interaction between observation channels and context, as discussed above, has not been fully explored in that the visual aspects have been ignored. One important methodological question involves the amount of redundancy there is in information obtained from various channels of observation. Does hearing the spoken word result in an observation sufficiently different to warrant the greater cumbersomeness entailed in working from sound recordings rather than typescripts? What is the influence on ratings of the introduction of the opportunity to observe actions as well as to hear words? Does increase in channels result in a much higher noise-to-information ratio, leading to a lower consensus among observers?

Full-dress examinations of these issues are virtually nonexistent. The one attempt to examine the contribution of all three channels to judgments of affect in interviews (Shapiro, 1966) suggests that, when ratings based on audiovisual observations are taken as a criterion, the addition of a typescript component adds little to a multiple correlation, whereas both audio and visual components make significant contributions. The latter two components are virtually independent. No consistent variation in reliabilities was obtained using each modality. In a later study confined to the audio and visual channels, Shapiro (1968b) found much greater overlap between them than in his 1966 study although not quite as great as resulted for each of them when related to ratings based on simultaneous observation on both channels. This difference from his earlier results may reflect the difference in attributes rated. Where earlier affect was being rated, the second study focused on degree of client exploration and therapist genuineness, empathy, and warmth. The fact that in the later study all judges rated the same therapy or therapy-like segments under all three conditions, thereby introducing a possible memory factor, may constitute another explanation for the different findings. This latter possibility holds, in my opinion, despite Shapiro's effort to rule it out by demonstrating that agreements between audiovisual ratings and those based on audio alone, if anything, increased slightly over time intervals ranging from the same day to as much as 6 days later. Without more precise information on the shape of the forgetting curve, Shapiro's control study does not rule out the possibility of only a slight decay in memory during the first week.

Two investigations compared tape recordings and typescripts. The Michigan group found that for depth of interpretation neither clinical psychologists nor psychoanalysts were influenced by method of observation in either the mean level of rating or in degree of agreement within a single method or between the two methods of observation (Harway et al., 1955; Cutler et al., 1958). Waskow (1963) not only compared sound recording and typescript for effects on ratings of counselor attitudes of acceptance, expressiveness, judgmentalness, and interest, but also included a sound condition in which intelligibility was filtered out. Under the filtered condition only judgmentalness and expressiveness could be rated reliably; under the other two conditions only acceptance was unreliable in one (unfiltered sound) and expressiveness in the other (typescript). Judgmentalness, which could be reliably rated under all three conditions, produced similar relationships to client discussion and expression of feelings under all three conditions of rating. Filtered and transcript ratings of judgmentalness correlated .49, as compared to .73 and .74, respectively, for comparisons of unfiltered to filtered and to transcript.

Visual exposure via either movie or kinescope filming raises the question of what parts of the body to focus on for cues, an issue explored in depth by Ekman and Friesen (1968). Their work suggests that there are actor-, observer-, and affect-expressed specificities which limit the applicability of any general rule. Another group (Shapiro, Foster, & Powell, 1968) used facial and bodily cues gleaned from photographs as a basis for ratings of therapist empathy, warmth, and genuineness. Two sets of raters, one trained and the other untrained, agreed fairly well when their ratings were based on exposure to the full photographs. Almost as much agreement was obtained from exposure to the face alone (body masked), but exposure only to bodily cues resulted in virtually no agreement.

One argument for redundancy in visual, auditory, and verbal cues is to assume a mechanically determined agreement among the cues. For example, one might hold that kinetic and paralinguistic phenomena are fully consistent with rate and content of speech. Boomer and Dittmann (1964) tested this assumption for rate of speech, which has been shown to be responsive to affect arousal. They found that bodily movements and rate of filled pauses (e.g., emission of "ah" during pause) varied independently of rate of speech.

UNIT SIZE AND SAMPLING

There is quite a range of possible choices in the size of process unit to be rated. These include the sentence or "single free utterance" (Auld & Dollard, 1968; Dollard & Auld, 1959); response, defined as the speech of one person bounded by the speech of the other; natural or arbitrary time segments (e.g., 3-minute segments or whole interviews; ratio time segments (e.g., thirds of the treatment series of interviews); and units based on meaning (e.g., topic units). In some instances the choice of unit size will be guided by actual or presumed characteristics of the phenomena under study. If we assume, as many psychoanalysts would, that transference phenomena can be surely distinguished from other affectively charged interpersonal reactions only when the observer has large units of interactions available to him, we will want to use units of whole interviews or larger. Similarly, if we are interested in atmospheric or stylistic variables, which build up slowly and change slowly, we might expect to use large units. Or, if we assume that ratings of small units can give us reliable indications, we can take sample readings over large time units of the process. On the other hand, when the phenomena of interest are presumed to occur at a minute level of the interaction, small units (e.g., sentence or response) are indicated. Haggard and Isaacs (1966) became involved in minute units when they became interested in micro-momentary facial expressions such as are revealed when motion picture films are run at one-sixth their normal speed. Their preliminary exploration of changes of expression within three to five frames (equivalent to one-eighth to one-fifth of a second) led them to believe that these are indications of ego mechanisms.

The tenability of many of the judgments regarding unit size and sampling is subject to empirical tests. Too frequently, however, the required tests have not been made. The design of the Wisconsin study of client-centered therapy with schizophrenics (Rogers et al., 1967) is outstandingly expert in its examination of the conditions surrounding the rating of patient level of experiencing. One study using the Experiencing Scale (Kiesler, Mathieu, & Klein, 1964) found that time segments of 2, 4, 8, and 16 minutes resulted in comparable rates of rater agreement within a level, but that longer time segments tended to receive high ratings. Since the ratings corelated highly between levels, the main conclusion about this unit size effect is that, with regard to experiencing, one must avoid designs in which segments of different size are combined. Since similar results have been found with regard to depth of interpretation (Harway et al., 1955), amount of lead, counselor assumption of responsibility, client assumption of responsibility, and working relationship (Muthard, 1953), this may be a general effect of unit size. Another study of the Experiencing Scale turned attention to the effect of the location of the interview segment (Kiesler, Klein, and Mathieu, 1965). In addition to a result expected by the theory that schizophrenic patients were lower in experiencing level than neurotics, Kiesler et al. found two linear trend effects for neurotics, for segments within interviews and between early and late interviews. In other words, the neurotics displayed a steady progression in level of experiencing over time.

When Karl and Abeles (1969) used a similar set of segments of interviews for college students in outpatient therapy, with four client variables and seven therapist variables, they found that all but one client and one therapist variable manifested significant differences in relative frequency of occurrence by segment, but in differing patterns. For example, client dependency responses tended to be manifested most frequently in the last segment of the hour and least frequently in the middle. Conversely, client hostility statements appeared least in the first and last segments and were most manifest in the middle. Much of the variation seemed to fit common-sense conceptions of situational dynamics. For example, it seems to fit the nature of dependency reactions for the patient to feel dependency most strongly as he is about to end his hour. Similarly, the finding that therapist prescriptive responses occur predominantly in the last segment of the hour is compatible with commonsense ideas of when the therapist is most likely to seek or convey suggestions and directives. For some reason, Karl and Abeles did not examine the influence of portion of the treatment process on sampling of segments within the hour. In any case these two studies underline the fact that process within hours and over hours is by no means homogeneous and is not distributed similarly across attributes. This factor must be taken into account whenever an investigator is forced to respond to the volume of his data by sampling.

Selection and Training of Raters

Since clarity of perception and response to the behavior and feelings of others is a core concern in the theories of personality underlying modes of psychotherapy, it follows that one's stance regarding the qualifications and preparations of raters will be considerably influenced by theoretical commitments. The greater the emphasis on the psychodynamics of perception, the more likely that the investigator will be concerned with how free of conflict the observer must be. There are also concerns that the observer be well versed in psychotherapy. Conversely, therapeutic experience within a given theoretical framework might disqualify the rater as an observer of other frameworks.

In view of the prevailing imprecision of theoretical formulations and crudity of measurements, it should not be unexpected that the few efforts to gather an empirical base for such decisions have revealed relatively little effect of differences in raters with regard to either personal qualities or experience. For example, the earlier cited study by Cutler et al. (1958) found no differences between ratings of depth of interpretation obtained from clinical psychologists, many in the training stage with just beyond the minimum of 100 hours of experience as therapists, and those of psychoanalysts who were not only more experienced but presumably also more likely to be free of the distorting effects of personal conflicts on perception. Harway et al. (1955) found one kind of evidence that naive judges, undergraduates in the first course in psychology, have a concept of depth different from that of clinical psychologists. When 70 statements of therapist activity were sorted on a seven-point scale, the naive judges were significantly more variable and placed significantly more items at the deeper end of the scale than the experienced judges. Kiesler (1970) reports that naive and clinically sophisticated judges correlated in their ratings on the Experiencing Scale at a level about equal to the level of agreement found within each class of rater. Waskow and Bergman (1962) found no difference between psychoanalytic and client-centered raters in rating warmth.

Interwoven with the theme of the qualifications of the rater is the specific training given him. As a way of achieving convergence, raters are given preliminary definitions and explanations of the attribute to be rated and then undergo trials in which their ratings are compared with each other's or with a standard set of presumably correct ones. Shapiro (1968a) found that undergraduate volunteers without previous rating experience or training agreed with undergraduates specially trained and experienced in rating therapist warmth, genuineness, and empathy at a level about equal to that found among trained raters. The only qualification is that the untrained raters used, in place of the standard format, a series of adjectives embedded in a semantic differential format. In the Wisconsin project (Rogers et al., 1967), which also employed undergraduate raters, two methods of training judges for rating on the Experiencing Scale were compared. One method, designated group training, concentrated on mutual exchange of ratings as the form of feedback; the other method, called self-training, provided each rater with feedback from a standard rater. The self-training method seemed more effective in that higher reliability was achieved for the scales of experiencing and congruence, where this method was employed, than for the scales of accurate empathy and unconditional positive regard, where the group method was employed. In an effort to distinguish scale from method of training, Schoeninger, Klein, and Mathieu (1968) arranged for a comparable set of raters to receive group training for rating experiencing and obtained comparable levels of reliability. This seeming interchangeability of group training and self-training would, of course, need to be checked for other scales.

Cannon and Carkhuff (1969) examined the interaction effect of the rater's personal level of function and rating experience on his ratings of therapist level of functioning in terms of the three client-centered conditions. The method of ascertaining level of functioning was to ask the total pool of subjects to offer to a tape of 16 client statements, each of no more than 2 minutes' duration, their own best responses to client feeling and content. The sample included experienced counselors, graduate students in counseling and psychotherapy, and two sets of undergraduates, one with experience in a helping role and the other without such experience. The responses of each subject were rated by expert raters for facilitative quality, and the 10 most and the 10 least facilitating members of each group identified. These were, in turn, asked to rate four alternative responses to the same taped excerpts for the same quality. Not surprisingly, ratings of their own responses by expert raters corresponded with their degree of agreement with the experts' ratings of the responses of others because of the degree of specificity in the carryover between the two sets of conditions. It is interesting that this specific control of variances did not wipe out a variance due to experience in counseling and psychotherapy. The design of this study is clearer and more readily interpreted than the results of an earlier study (Carkhuff, Kratochvil, & Friel, 1968), in which effects of graduate training, whether or not clinical, were demonstrated.

RELIABILITY AND VALIDITY

What emerges from our examination of the problems of measurement is that thorough processes of instrumentation comparable to those employed in the development of all psychological tests are required. This means concern with reliability and validity.

In the context of coding and rating, reliability represents the usual range of concerns. One important question is how replicable the observations are, given another observer or set of observers. Even when observers share the same general frame of reference but direct their attention to broad, vaguely defined attributes, they may not be able to achieve agreement in independent observations (Seitz, 1966). Strupp, Chassan, and Ewing (1966) found a rho of .71 between rated level of inference involved in a series of rated attributes of psychotherapeutic interactions and order of interobserver agreement obtained. If Forer and his collaborators (Forer et al., 1961) had taken into account the amount of inference required in even their most direct observations, as well as the number of simultaneous attributes their observers were being required to make, they might not have been so discouraged by their failure to reach high levels of agreement.

Estimates of reliability need to be attuned to the conditions of observation. As Dittmann and Wynne (1966) have pointed out, a judgment arrived at by consensus among observers requires comparison with the consensus reached by an alternative, comparable group of observers. The agreement among two or more raters obtained for averages of ratings by each of sets of responses is not an appropriate estimate of reliability to apply when the investigator is interested in sequences of interactions which utilize ratings of individual responses. On the other hand, when

agreement between the two raters on individual responses is not sufficiently high, averaging the ratings of two or more raters is a way of
increasing reliability. It is comparable to the increase in reliability obtained for averages of ratings for a set of responses by the same rater
(Dittmann, 1958).

Rerating by the same rater, as a way of estimating reliability, has a
somewhat different significance from test-retest reliability in psychomet-
ric tests, especially when comparable forms are employed. Without comparable forms, which are precluded in the usual rerate design, successive
ratings of the same material would appear to constitute a test of the
rater's memory, in addition to or instead of a test of whether he is discriminating the stimuli in the same way on the second trial. For these
reasons, I believe that rerate reliabilities are to be treated as weaker evidence than reliabilities based on agreement among two or more independent raters.

The frame of reference for judging when an acceptable level of reliability has been achieved includes considerations of one's sense of the
precision required and of base rates. To the extent that an investigator
believes that he is dealing with gross effects, he can afford to proceed
with confidence that ratings containing a large amount of error variance
will not conceal true experimental effects. If he obtains negative results
and loses confidence only in the expected grossness of effects, he can then
turn toward trying to improve the reliability of his measures for another
attempt at demonstrating the effects he believes are there. Percentage
agreement in coding, even when accompanied by a test of significance,
will not in itself be an indication of whether a high rate of agreement has
been obtained. Even when numerous alternatives are available to be
coded, we need information on the incidence of their use by raters. If, to
simplify the point for ease of explanation, raters typically code 90% of
observations as A and 10% as B, an overall percentage of agreement
between two raters of 80% is possible with no overlap in the observations coded as B. Thus, 80% agreement would have different meanings,
depending on base rates for use of the categories offered to the rater.
Information on distributions of rater assignments and estimates of chance
agreements generated by such distributions should accompany the obtained
agreement. Conversely, tests of significance unaccompanied by some estimate of degree of agreement represent incomplete information.

The frame of reference for validity of ratings is construct validity
(Cronbach & Meehl, 1955). This means that assumptions about the nature of the attribute under observation are tested against the theory-
generated network of expectations regarding the influence of various
measurement factors on observations, and the relations concurrent and

predictive between these ratings and other ratings or other kinds of observations. Thus one part of the validation of a rated attribute can rest on empirical results regarding the process of measurement in addition to the more usual testing of theories bearing on concurrent and predictive events involving other attributes.

Let me translate the foregoing abstract statements into concrete terms. Take depth of interpretation as an example. Since this attribute of the therapist's communications is defined as the relation between his view of the patient and the patient's level of awareness, valid ratings would appear to require evidence of an effect on ratings when the rater has no access to information about the patient which would give clues to his current level of awareness. Some evidence for validity, albeit weak, is therefore adduced when it is found that ratings of therapists' responses presented in random order, with surrounding patient responses deleted (i.e., the rater has no information regarding the patient), do not correlate with ratings of the same responses presented in their actual sequence of occurrence (Harway et al., 1955). Accurate empathy, which appears to have the same requirements as depth of interpretation, has not been thoroughly validated in this respect, but, as we shall see, has been validated by other criteria. Truax (1966b) found that, as in the case of depth of interpretation, deleting the patient's communications did not affect ratings. He did not, however, test whether randomizing order would have an effect. This same study includes an illustration of validation based on directly apprehended rather than deductive expectations. In the case of warmth, it would seem that paralinguistic and kinetic features would come closest to our idea of what this characteristic represents. It is a common belief that warmth is represented not so much by what a person says in so many words as by how he says it and by other interpersonal actions. Thus when in this study, in which raters are hearing the communications, Truax finds that deleting the patient's communications influences ratings of therapist warmth, we suspect that what is actually being rated is to some degree a reflection of the idiosyncratic subjective response of the patient rather than a shared perception of the therapist. On the other hand, Shapiro (1968b) found separate audio and visual influences on ratings of warmth. Unfortunately, a fully definitive set of studies, disentangling the content and expressive style factors in judgments of warmth, is lacking.

Our illustrations thus far have dealt with validating evidence on the basis of methods of observations. Another form of validation involves concurrent relations to other variables. Continuing with depth of interpretation, we find that Fisher's (1956) study of its close relationship to the plausibility of the therapist's views of the patient offers a clarification and modification of our conception of the attribute. It suggests that, under the conditions rated, depth of interpretation may be related more closely to general than to momentary states of awareness. Howe (1962a, 1962b) offered evidence supporting the relevance of plausibility and added evidence that ratings of the anxiety-arousing properties of the communication were correlated with depth. A study by Caracena and Vicory (1969), demonstrating relationships betwen ratings of accurate empathy and the number of words per response and the proportion of words spoken by the interviewer, suggests the possibility that this rating depends more on stylistic features of the therapist's communication than on its bearing on patient communications. Thus this study combines with Truax's failure to find an effect from deleting the patient's communications to undermine confidence in whether this attribute is in fact what it is thought to be.

The network of evidence of validity can and should include support for predicted relationships derived from the theory underlying the attribute. In the case of depth of interpretation, for example, psychoanalytic theory as well as client-centered theory led to expectations, differing according to the theory, regarding the impact of this attribute on the patient. Client-centered theory holds that interpretations other than those at the shallowest level (i.e., those that go beyond the level of simple acceptance or reflections) will stimulate resistance. Although psychoanalytic theory admits that resistance, an unwillingness to proceed with the task of free association, can be stimulated by therapist responses, its central concern is with resistance arising from the personal conflicts of the patient and the way in which interpretation enables the patient to grapple with his conflicts to return to free association and achieve lasting effects. This theory leads to the expectation that moderate levels of interpretation will be followed by a reduction in resistance, which was what Speisman (1959) found, thereby offering simultaneous support for the validity of the measures and of the theory. It should be clear that such a validating study requires validity of both theory and measure. If Speisman had obtained negative results, it would not have been possible to choose among the alternatives: was it the theory, the measures, or both that were at fault?

It might be well to look at a few more examples of the predictive aspects of construct validity. Knapp, Mushatt, and Nemetz (1966) showed that their judges' ratings of sadness and hostility were related to expected concurrent biochemical changes in an asthmatic patient. Krause and Pilisuk (1961) contrasted the verbal reactions of subjects when imagining themselves in stress (disaster) with those obtained in non-stress situations. The validity of speech disruptions as measures of anxiety was supported by finding a greater number under stress conditions. A study by Townsend (1956) of ambiguity as a feature of the treatment relationship offers us another example of an experimental approach to construct validation. An ambiguous stimulus field does not readily lend itself to one interpretation. Therefore we can assume that therapists rated as being more ambiguous will be perceived with greater variability. Applying Q sort methods, Townsend asked naive observers to sort descriptive adjectives according to the degree to which they applied to the therapist after hearing a section of one of his interviews. The intercorrelations of Q sorts by 10 raters were distinctly lower when the therapist had been independently rated as behaving in a more ambiguous manner. Recorded excerpts of interviews by four different therapists yielded rankings in terms of average intercorrelations that corresponded exactly to their ranks with regard to ambiguity.

A final link in the chain of validity is forged when we can relate a process measure to some more enduring and intrinsically valuable measure of change. Tomlinson and Hart (1962) sought to relate the client-centered process scale to therapists' judgment of outcome. This example, unfortunately, illustrates a pitfall in such a study. Since the therapists were all client centered, it would be natural to expect that their estimates of the client's improvement would be greatly influenced by the degree to which he had exhibited the kinds of process changes that their theory had led them to expect. Thus we must conclude that the relationship found does not qualify as evidence of a relationship to an experimentally independent measurement of change. On the other hand, Rogers et al. (1967) did find relations between the process scale and an independently derived outcome index based on a composite of objective and projective measures.

SUMMARY

The design of process studies requires awareness of and skill in dealing with a variety of tactical problems. These include coverage of the alternative vantage points for observing therapy, the selection of the features to observe and the sense modalities to use, and the special problems of ratings in regard to unit size, context, selection and training of raters, and reliability and validity.

Each of the possible sources of observation—patient, therapist, and independent observer—has limitations and unique contributions to make. The first two vantage points are needed as a source of knowledge about the inner experience and intentions of the participants; the third is necessary to disentangle reality from myth and motivatedly modified reconstructions. Cultural and theoretically based sets have been shown to prevail among psychotherapists and patients. In addition, there is evidence that the reports of both parties are subject to the distorting effects of their conflicts and personal styles.

Process research inevitably requires selection of what is to become data. Most studies have concentrated on the verbal aspects, but not necessarily on the content. The emphasis is on the actions of therapist and patient toward each other and in response to each other. When the codings or ratings of independent judges are employed, they have usually been asked to respond either to typescripts or to sound recordings. Interest in kinetics has led to increasing investigation of the role of visual observation. Investigation of redundancy and uniqueness provided by the different sense modalities is incomplete, so that these questions are largely unanswered. If and when evidence of uniqueness is found, theoretical orientation and the particular therapeutic phenomena of interest will undoubtedly determine selection.

The same will apply to the determination of what context is needed by independent raters and the unit size to which they are exposed for making successive ratings. Thus far, evidence of the effect of sense modality has been mixed: there is little support for requiring clinically trained raters, only slight influences of context have been found, but there is consistent evidence that the larger the unit the higher the rating. Finally, the proper distribution of the parts of hours and the portions of the total treatment process sampled seems to depend at least on the kind of patient and the attribute being studied. None of the above questions has been studied thoroughly enough to provide confident generalizations, and it may turn out that the appropriate generalization is simply, "It all depends."

If dependable process research is to be done, we must go through the same painstaking processes of scaling and the establishing of reliability and validity that we require of psychological tests.

CHAPTER 4

Simplification

Chapter 3 dealt with the technical criteria which must be satisfied in the use of observations and measurements. These considerations require attention whether the events subject to study are occurring in their natural setting or under modified conditions. This chapter will be devoted to the vicissitudes of modifying and simplifying naturalistic events. Sometimes the modified conditions represent the preservation of the natural setting, but with systematic variation of certain features of the phenomena under consideration. At other times the investigator abstracts from the originally observed phenomena certain features as a means of bringing them into the laboratory for ease of observation and control. Simplification and control are inevitable processes that follow the identification of natural phenomena that arouse our curiosity, provoke our desire to understand and explain, and promise some practical uses in our daily living. In order for the dialogue of research to proceed there needs to be general agreement regarding acceptable processes of simplification as well as regarding observation and measurement. We shall consider the controversy over simplification among clinical researchers and offer a basis for resolving this disagreement. The fact that this problem is paralleled in other areas of psychological research will often take us beyond clinical psychology and psychotherapy. There is no doubt that this is a general problem, but our argument will keep its more limited focus.

A decision currently looming large in research strategy is whether to choose the naturalistic or experimental path. Let us hurriedly acknowledge the familiarity of the issue and forestall an exchange of cliches: for example, "Only when we bring phenomena under precise control as in the laboratory can true knowledge be gained," versus "Of what use is precision when it is obtained by reduction to the trivial?" This inherent readiness to assume a frozen posture is not helpful to psychology or any

---

[1] This chapter is an adaptation of an earlier published paper (Bordin, 1965a). For a similar treatment see Heller (1971).

other scientific discipline. To me it is not a question of adopting either stance. The arguments in favor of schematization, experimentation, and control are compelling, as are also the arguments against trivialization as an expense of becoming experimental. We need to specify criteria for deciding how meaningful are the more powerful experimental methods of research. As a preliminary, it is instructive to examine a representative range of efforts to simplify for research purposes. After this survey, I will offer criteria for evaluating these simplifications and apply the criteria to the examples selected.

A SURVEY OF SIMPLIFICATIONS

Over the past 15 years, there has been increasing recourse to experimental studies. One of the earliest examples was Keet's (1948) invstigation. By means of word association methods he identified words tapping conflicts in volunteer subjects and established the presence of blocks toward remembering these words during word association learning. The experiment proper consisted of a comparison of the efficacy of reflection versus interpretation in aiding the subject to overcome a memory block, with interpretation appearing superior. Subsequent failures to replicate the preliminary condition, establishing a memory block to words tapping conflicts, rendered stillborn this experimental technique (Merrill, 1952; Grummon & Butler, 1953). So great is the attractiveness of control and simplification as research strategies that this failure only spurred further efforts in this direction. We can look back and identify at least four broad types of simplifications.

The Study of Interview Phenomena

As is immediately apparent upon examination, simplification proceeds by means of a process of abstraction and generalization. "Psychotherapy" is a term used to describe, among other things, a meeting or series of meetings between two persons involving an exchange of oral communications. A number of investigators have focused on this attribute of psychotherapy by creating various kinds of interview situations. Following Chapple's lead, Saslow and Matarazzo observed the timing and duration of the interviewee's utterances when comparable characteristics of the interviewer's utterances were controlled. In a series of studies summarized during the 1958 Conference on Research in Psychotherapy (Saslow & Matarazzo, 1959), they verified that interviewers could be taught to follow a specified pattern of interventions and that persons will exhibit stable patterns of response to such interviews when conducted as much as 8 months apart. The interviews in most of their studies seemed to have been conducted for the ostensible purpose of assessment, sometimes of job applicants, sometimes of newly admitted psychiatric patients. In a few instances, these interviews were inserted at different stages of psychotherapy, the experimental interview being conducted by an interviewer other than the therapist. The general aim of these studies seemed to be the development of a criterion for personality change founded in interview behavior as a preliminary to studies of psychotherapy. A later investigation (Phillips, Matarazzo, & Saslow, 1960) showed the use of this kind of standardized interview as a means of examining process issues. In this study, one period of the interview was marked by interpretive statements for an experimental group. The controls were offered only the standard noninterpretive interventions during the comparable period. Utterances of shorter duration were found in response to the experimental variable. Mainly, however, these authors concentrated attention on the influence of the duration of interviewer utterance and silence and the frequency with which he interrupted on comparable interviewee behavior (Matarazzo et al., 1968).

Dibner (1958) provides another example of the observation of interview behavior under control conditions. He set out to test certain ideas developing out of my identification of ambiguity (Bordin, 1955) as an attribute that seems to differentiate theoretical orientations. The argument is that psychotherapists differ in the ambiguity or structuredness of the interview situation which they create for the patient. The therapist controls this attribute through the specificity or open-endedness of the task or tasks that he imposes, the degree to which he communicates his specific views of the patient and his activities, and the degree to which he defines himself as a person. It is further argued that level of ambiguity will influence the degree of discomfort the patient experiences in the interview, as well as his readiness to form transference-distorted perceptions of the therapist and to act on them. Dibner set out to test the relation between ambiguity and discomfort through diagnostic interviews conducted with psychiatric patients. He was able to train clinicians to conduct two types of interviews, differing widely in ambiguity, and obtained confirmatory evidence of greater speech disturbance in response to the more ambiguous interview. It was found that PGR indices correspond more closely to the patient's subjective impression of ambiguity than to the objective conditions. In other words, the physiological measure seemed to reflect a feedback process.

Artificial Therapist Response Situations

For both training and research purposes, artificial situations focusing on therapist response patterns have been utilized. These vary from using confederates to role-play a patient without the knowledge of the therapist to asking therapists to respond to individual patient communications presented in written form and without context. Strupp (1960) carried out an extensive series of studies which utilized a sound film of 30 minutes of an initial psychotherapeutic interview conducted by a relatively inexperienced therapist. The film was interrupted at 28 points for audiences of therapists to record the response each would have offered at that point. Differences purporting to reflect theoretical orientation, professional affiliation, experience, and the fact that the respondent himself had or had not received personal analysis were obtained. The term purporting is used because, unfortunately, there was much confounding of experience with the other variables, which, except for the analysis variable, were never fully distinguished.

Whereas Strupp tried to make the situation "real" by utilizing a real patient in actual psychotherapy and counted on the sound movies to induce therapists to identify with the actual therapist, others (e.g., Russell & Snyder, 1963; Heller, Meyers, & Kline, 1963) chose to place the therapist in what was for him a real situation but gained control by using actors to role-play patients. The major advantage of this strategy is, of course, that it permits control of patient characteristics, thus making possible investigation of the impact on therapists of hostility versus friendliness, dominance versus dependence, and so forth. Its disadvantage is that its cost makes prohibitive large-scale surveys of psychotherapists such as those by Strupp.

The Learning Paradigm and Operant Conditioning Studies

One obvious basis for simplification is that, if one interprets behavior change broadly, psychotherapy aims to bring about change in behavior, which is what theories of learning are all about. Since virtually all of the empirical basis for learning theory is lodged in laboratory experimentation, much of it using subhuman subjects, any effort to effect direct transfers of learning theory to psychotherapy involves questions about simplification. Instead of relying solely on direct transfer from general studies of learning, there have been many attempts to demonstrate that psychotherapeutic-like phenomena can be reproduced through verbal operant conditioning. The conditions of these studies are essentially similar to those prevailing in certain of the Saslow-Matarazzo investigations, which were discussed above. Typically, the subject is given the task of talking about some general topic, such as his life history, or is assigned some other task that requires verbalization. The experimenter reinforces on a set or variable schedule a preselected class of the subject's verbal behavior by carefully controlled verbal or nonverbal cues. Thus far, the degree to which this particular experimental paradigm can be generalized to feeling states, perceptions, and other complexities associated with human suffering has not been fully tested other than through the report of case studies. In a good many studies using schizophrenic patients and children and carried on in natural settings, the behavior change goals have been rather rudimentary, for example, to establish communication behavior or to shift interactions from teachers to peers.[2]

Analogues of Psychoanalysis

The task of free association is central to psychotherapy as seen by psychoanalytic theory. Several investigators (e.g., Bordin, 1966b, 1966c; Colby, 1960, 1961) have utilized an experimental analogue of the psychoanalytic situation. Paid subjects are given the task of free associating for a 30-minute period. The subject reclines on a couch, and the experimenter is seated out of his line of vision. In my study, I was interested in relations between personality measures and free association. To reduce the amount of work I started with the subject's response in a single session. Since with only a single session one needs to be concerned about the influence of prepared talk, we gave our subjects to forewarning of its nature. They had been recruited for "a study of different methods of measuring personality in which interviews such as are sometimes conducted in psychotherapy would be included." The subject was warned that his privacy would be invaded and that cooperation was vital to the purpose of the research, and was asked to consider before volunteering his willingness to cooperate. We were not satisfied with an automatic dismissal of the issue and usually elicited the natural doubts and questions raised by such a proposal. In this way we hoped to minimize some of the situational factors in free association performance (e.g., the motivation to confide), so that more of the variance would be a function of personality.

This study investigated three broad domains of personality differences: personality inventories, Rorschach, and laboratory perceptual tasks. The clearest evidence for a relation between personality and free association was found in the Rorschach. Many aspects of Rorschach performance

[2] See the behavior therapy section of Shlien (1968).

were implicated. Although some of these aspects could not be readily rationalized, there was support for a view that a personailty in which drive and organizational influences are well represented and well balanced is able to respond more effectively to the free associative task.

Taking his cue from an information theory model, Colby carried out an ingenious pair of studies of the influence of experimenter (therapist) inputs on free association. His subjects knew in advance the nature of the task, but were asked to perform in a series of sessions. In the first two studies (1960), Colby demonstrated that his presence in the room increased the number of references to males as compared to control periods when he was not in the room. In his second study (1961), he showed that more interpretive experimenter inputs were followed by response sets of longer duration.

THE PROBLEM OF SIMPLIFICATION

Having examined some representative examples of the kinds of simplifications to be found in experimental studies of psychotherapy, I turn now to the problems surrounding such enterprises. The criticisms of such studies boil down to the addition of the prefix over- to the term simplification. It is argued that, in the process of transplanting the phenomena from their natural settings to the laboratory, features important for understanding and deriving principles have been lost. Hovland (1959), for example, while pleading the importance of the experimental approach to the study of attitude change, points up the consequence of excluding the factor of the subject's control over the persuasive messages to which he is exposed. It may be recalled that this resulted in laboratory findings of much greater effects of persuasive messages than were revealed in survey studies. Similarly, Lewin (1951), in the course of his important set of essays on scientific methodology, argues for the superiority of the field-theory approach because it starts with a characterization of the situation as a whole, "instead of picking out one or another isolated element within a situation, the importance of which cannot be judged without consideration of the situation as a whole," (p. 63). Finally Rapaport (1960) offers these pungent remarks:

Yet one essential methodological task—the study of the relationship between theory and method of observation by which the data are obtained—is rarely pursued. The question is: to what extent does a theory, based on data obtained by a given method, reflect the nature of the data itself, and to what extent does it reflect the method of data gathering and its limitations? The man who shouts into an empty room is likely to hear his own echo; likewise the investigator may get back little more than what he has already built into the method, (p. 79).

All three of these men are agreed that simplification is a necessary part of the process of acquiring knowledge, but insist that there are good and bad simplifications. What, then, are the rules for achieving acceptable simplifications? The philosophers of science—Northrup, Nagel, Popper, and their fellows—offer surprisingly little help. The difficulty is that the large simplifications that are represented by transplanting the phenomena in question from their natural setting to the laboratory involve us in questions about the observational side of acquiring knowledge. How do we insure, for example, that the phenomena in the laboratory that we label "motivational" do in fact correspond to those of the natural setting to which they are intended to refer? When philosophers (Popper, 1963, for example) speak of simplification, they are referring to propositions and the characteristic which makes them testable. Now it is true that at an advanced state of knowledge such as characterizes the physical sciences the translations between laboratory and natural setting are easily established and are buttressed by a good deal of empirical verification. Unhappily, such is not the state of affairs in psychology or any of the other social sciences. When the empirical events are laboratory events, we need to recognize that the achieving of simplified propositions (i.e., propositions whose language corresponds readily to empirical events) does not in itself insure that we are going to learn more about the phenomena which first aroused our curiosity. On the contrary, it may involve us in a new set of empirical phenomena without meaningful relationship to real-life experience. The simplified observations clothed in real-life terms have become the ends in themselves.

Let me be more concrete. Study of a rat's learning behavior in a maze or the vicissitudes of a dog's flexions does not in itself assure us of greater knowledge of man's learning processes until we have somehow bridged the gap, both conceptually and empirically, between the level at which we are observing and the level for which we wish to account. For example, we need to establish either that the response repertoires of rats and dogs are in all significant respects similar to those of human beings or that the differences are not important. It appears to me that the human capacity for language and self-reflection is either absent or only vestigially present in the other two animals. Can propositions dealing with human learning leave out these two factors?

All of this leads us back to a familiar problem: how the psychologist can become the master rather than the slave of the scientific method. I submit that the first rule of simplification (three rules will be offered) is that *we start from and keep in central focus the natural phenomena which aroused our curiosity and about which we wish to know more or to verify present ideas.* When colleagues in the first Conference on Research in Psychotherapy (Rubinstein & Parloff, 1959) discussed this question, they bogged down on what is "natural" and "naturalistic observation." "The relationship between the therapist and the patient in psychotherapy," some pointed out, "is usually far removed from natural social intercourse. Then what is so naturalistic about observing actual psychotherapy?" Here frequency of occurrence in human experience has been substituted for the habitat of the phenomena. If we are interested in understanding psychotherapy and in translating our understanding into scientific propositions, it is irrelevant (with regard to naturalistic observation) that psychotherapy represents a very atypical interpersonal relationship.[3] "Naturalistic observation" means to observe psychotherapy in its habitual setting, a situation initiated by a person in considerable psychological discomfort, in which the helper assumes that the personality of the patient makes him vulnerable to this discomfort over a wide range of environmental circumstances, and in which both parties set out to achieve a change in the personality of the patient. Is the situation of a college sophomore student in the introductory course in psychology, whose curiosity may even be subordinate to his desire to fill a course requirement, an acceptable equivalent of that of the patient in psychotherapy? Is the task we give him, are the mutual understandings about the length of the relationship, and are the other mutual commitments equivalent to those in psychotherapy? Where equivalence cannot be assumed, is it safe to assume that any features which are not present in our experiment are irrelevant to the propositions being tested?

It is hoped that this array of questions has established adequate ground for the second rule of simplification: *the degree to which we can safely depart from the naturalistic setting is proportional to the amount we already know about the phenomena in question.* It takes a great deal of knowledge to move from the natural setting into the laboratory, to be able to give the answers that establish the equivalence of simplified events to those of everyday life. What is interesting about this rule is that it conveys a different from the usual feeling about laboratory experimentation. Many of us have fallen prey to the seductive belief that, if one wants to make progress toward knowledge, the laboratory is the answer. This rule reverses the usual relationships. The useful application of laboratory methods or, for that matter, any of the other, less extreme

---

[3] The atypicality may not, however, be irrelevant to the question (Goldstein, Heller, & Sechrest, 1966, Chap. 5) of the transferability of the effects of psychotherapy.

modes of simplification must rest on progress in our knowledge rather than serving as a means to early progress. Experimentation and the laboratory are not the vehicles for upward mobility for the have-nots of the scientific world. The psychologist who chooses to simplify without knowledge becomes method-bound rather than curiosity-motivated and falls into a form of pedantry.

"Hold on," someone says, "might not an investigator through an intuitive leap into the laboratory, have achieved a correct set of simplifications and thereby be off to a running start in the accumulation of knowledge?" Obviously, this is possible and we might be able to cite examples, but such successful ones are rare. It is also clear that in a climate which encourages this leap—in some departments of psychology it is even required for the doctoral study—we must have some way of knowing whether we are following a path that will lead to vast open vistas or one that ends in a blank wall. This leads to a third rule of simplification: *if it is not based on prior knowledge, simplification should be accompanied by the early establishing of empirical bridges between the simplification and the naturalistic phenomena to which it is intended to refer.* This is probably Northrup's (1947) intent in introducing the term epistemic correlation, which he defines as " a relation joining an unobserved component of anything designated by a concept by postulation to its directly inspected component denoted by a concept by intuition. Thus an epistemic correlation joins a thing known in one way to what is in some sense that same thing known in a different way" (p. 119).

The urgency of the need for such correlations varies with the nature of the concepts being used. In learning theory, for example, the concepts are defined closely enough to the intuitive level of observation as to make less pressing such epistemic correlations, except where we try to go across species or to deal with the learning of actions surrounded by complex personal meanings and associated with deep motivations and emotions. On the other hand, when personality theory addresses itself not to general formulas for response acquisitions and decay, which I consider the province of learning theory, but to the natural laws of development and their relations to the varieties of persistent organizations of responses which differentiate persons, it gravitates toward postulational concepts far removed from concepts by intuition. After all, it was personality testing which made it necessary to add "construct validity" to our classifications of the varieties of validities. As the APA Committee on Test Standards (1954) pointed out and Cronbach and Meehl (1955) elaborated, a construct cannot be fully represented by any single observation. Working at such levels of complexity, it is easy to imagine constructs which are so incoherently related to observations as to achieve scientific unreality, or observations which tap the construct at only the most superficial and peripheral level, yet become reified as fully adequate representations. Ego strength, resistance, and defense are examples of constructs susceptible to either of these two mistreatments.

When operating from constructs far removed from the intuitive, the absence of an adequate base of epistemic correlations multiplies the danger of being led up a magnificently engrossing blind alley of the sort that has been so characteristic of some stages of our past history.[4] Many of us with an eye to the spectacular progress of physics harken to the argument that progress in science is marked by the increasing departure not only of its language but even of its experience from those of the common culture and of commonsense (Oppenheimer, 1958). The physicist builds his laws around chains of observations all of which are based in the laboratory. Why not follow his lead? Why *must* the psychologist return to the commonsense level of observation? After all, science is marked by *un*common sense. Let us not be misled. The physicist has a rich accumulation of translations from abstract mathematical propositions and laboratory experience to experience in the general domain. With increasing knowledge these translations can occur at more widely spaced intervals reflecting accumulating confidence in their connection to reality, created by such highly dramatic demonstrations as the explosion of nuclear weapons. There can be no doubt that the concepts and observations of the physicist have applications to the physical phenomena of everyday experience. Unhappily, too many systematic laboratory efforts by psychologists have been marked by long-delayed application or even the absence of application to the area of daily living and, where applied, have not been characterized by significantly large effects. Perhaps the disdain for "applied research" displayed by some experimental psychologists conceals a fear of discovering such weakness.

In any case, the preceding argument invalidates the assumption that basic research can proceed without applied research. Sooner or later the scientist must take his products out of the rarefied atmosphere of the laboratory to discriminate illusion from reality. Heller (1971) states the aspiration that bridging research will move it in opposite directions. Instead of analogue research seeking to simulate established psychotherapeutic practice, he suggests that it can be a source of innovation of new methods of achieving change. Bridging research is still necessary, he points

---

[4] MacKinnon (1953) expresses the same fear when he advocates keeping the level of theory close to data and to phenomenal concepts. He wants psychologists interested in personality to accumulate a large number of empirical relationships before moving to the level of hypothetical constructs.

out, to insure that simplified personal states and the conditions of change are transferable to clinical settings.

EVALUATION OF SIMPLIFICATIONS

Having formulated some rules for avoiding oversimplification in research strategies in psychotherapy, I turn with some trepidation to the payoff question of whether these rules enable us to evaluate the various forms of simplification which have been attempted. Are the rules sufficiently specific to permit discrimination, or are they so ambiguous that each of us, using his own frame of reference, will be able to rationalize on purely personal grounds both acceptance of his favorite strategies and rejection of those he finds alien? The first rule, to keep in focus the natural setting of the phenomena which gave rise to one's curiosity, seems straightforward. It prescribes that the means not be converted without explicit acknowledgment into an end. But the second rule, to depart from the conditions surrounding the original phenomena only so far as already established knowledge permits, does not yield to a uniform application. This can only be a process of judgment, with room for differences of opinion. Similarly, the third rule, that a laboratory simplification made without the knowledge which bridges the gap between original setting and laboratory should be validated early by studies designed to bridge this gap, is open to wide differences in application. How early is early?

The most important application of the rules will be to serve as stimuli toward accumulating the kinds of observations that make for good simplifications and that validate their relevance. The way the rules will work can be illustrated by applying them to the simplifications we have reviewed. Taking them in the order described, let us examine the use of interviews as a way of studying psychotherapy. As was specified earlier, most of these are conducted as assessment interviews with applicants for a job or patients entering a psychiatric service. In some instances, the subjects have been not actual applicants, but only potential ones. Clearly, except perhaps for the patients, one characteristic of the original situation which is absent in the experimental one is the motivation to change oneself. Furthermore, there are subtle but important differences in the aura surrounding the interviewer. In psychotherapy, he enters in the role of healer, which connotes professional commitments of confidentiality and the high priority of the subject's welfare. In most cases, the patient has made a prior effort to learn something about the therapist, if only whether he is recommended by another professional. Certainly, from the beginning of their series of interviews the person of the therapist is an important object of scrutiny. None of the above figures prominently, if at all, in experimental interviews. Even in diagnostic interviews, there is more attention to the task that is or will be assigned and to getting it over with. Are these missing features significant for the phenomena under study? If the purpose is to establish a baseline for an individual's interpersonal behavior, we must ask about the representativeness of this particular situation. Can we assume that a person's behavior while applying for a job will be similar in respects significant to his personality to the way he would act in a learning situation or a recreational situation shared with a member of his family?

There seems to be no established answer. Personality implies certain continuities across situations, but much of this is to be demonstrated. Matarazzo et al. (1968) did carry out a bridging study, conducted within ongoing psychotherapy, which demonstrated that the kinds of dependencies between interviewer and interviewee, duration of utterances and silences, and numbers of interruptions obtained in experimental interviews were also to be found in psychotherapy. This is an important contribution, but does not complete the task required before generalization can be made for all kinds of behavior and for all situations. Intuitively, one feels that certain situations tap different regions of the personality and are, therefore, not interchangeable. Thus the application of our rules identifies the need for further bridging studies involving subjects and clients or patients differentiated with regard to relevant personality variables.

Turning to another example of an interview as a simplification, I have always felt some discomfort about Dibner's confirmatory test of my ideas about the relation between ambiguity and anxiety. His patients might have been puzzled and confused by the interviewer's failure to make clear to them what he wanted to learn from them, and this puzzlement and confusion would naturally be translated into speech interruptions. This seems a one-dimensional version of a multidimensional conception of a sensory-deprived interpersonal encounter. In the succeeding period many investigators have delved into these complex questions only to amplify the complexity and to obtain only partial clarification. A fuller discussion of this subject will appear in the next chapter.

When we turn to artificial therapist response situations, the very label "artificial" stimulates doubts about authenticity. In this instance, we must consider not only the characteristics left out but a new one added. Most prominently omitted from the artificial situation, in which the therapist responds to a motion picture of a therapeutic interview, is the experience of being a participant in an on-going interpersonal relationship. The subject-therapist is basically an observer. He is not experiencing being the direct object in a highly charged relationship which can hardly avoid being provocative to the recipient. Added to the situation are the rivalries and frustrations experienced when the actual therapist's responses depart from those that the subject-therapist considers appropriate. Under such circumstances, the latter's response may aim to show what is wrong with the real therapist's reactions or may simply express his protest against such "wrongheadedness." The above possibilities demand an early empirical demonstration of a continuity of therapist style from actual clinical situation to artificial one. Unhappily, we are getting an accumulation of studies without this necessary step.

Perhaps the other kind of artificial response situation, that of using an actor-patient, is less vulnerable to such doubts. Good actors in good dramas have a capacity to convince us of the genuineness of the emotions portrayed.

It is verbal operant conditioning studies that strain our credulity the most when they are offered as simplifications of psychotherapy. Here the "patient" is a subject in an experiment whose motivations for being there are other than achieving some change in himself or his circumstances. He is there to cooperate with the experimenter. What seems so remarkable is how little change is obtained in such behaviors as the use of plural nouns or self-references. The changes reported are slight indeed compared with what could have been effected by directly asking the subject to do what was wanted! Yet these studies have established one fact which seems applicable to psychotherapy, namely, that minimal cues of the sort less likely to be under advertent control of the independent person in an interpersonal situation have the capacity to influence the dependent person when he is receiving few direct messages about his task. There is no reason why the additional characteristics of psychotherapy, bearing principally on personal involvement, can have other than an enhancing effect on the power of these minimal, unconsciously emitted cues. Please note that some investigators view these operant conditioning techniques as part of a broader class of behavior control of which psychotherapy is also a part. Under such circumstances interest shifts to the comparability of the effects to those in psychotherapy (Krasner, 1962). For the most part, we must say that the kinds of behavior modification principally demonstrated in experimental studies (e.g., the increase in the number of plural nouns or in the number of references to self) seem, speaking charitably, to be only peripherally related to those that the psychotherapist seeks. The studies of Baer (1968), Cohen (1968), and Lovass (1968) involve more meaningful behavioral targets, but these are still limited as compared to those of typical psychotherapy. The choice by Lang (1968) and Paul (1966) of phobias as targets for desensitization studies would appear to be closer to the areas of concern in psychotherapy, but one would have to question whether the phobic conditions are in fact comparable to those encountered in actual patients.

To apply these rules to my own simplification of psychoanalytic free association seems unfair and the conclusion foregone because its justification may have played a part in the formulation of the rules. Nevertheless, especially since other investigators have been and are using it, I think the exercise worthwhile, if only to place the author's biases on the record. In psychoanalytic theory there are two elements in the process of free association. One is the situational element, which explains why a person is willing to accept such an unusual task and to trust the therapist by expressing his unselected thoughts and experiences. The patient accepts the task because he is interested in—even wants desperately—the promised freedom from the psychic pain that brought him to psychotherapy and because the social role definitions of the professional healer carry guarantees about his commitments to his patient's welfare. Eventually, the accumulated experience of the therapist as a person will play its part in creating trust in him. The other element in the process is the intrapsychic one, which has been defined in terms of such factors as the amount of threat that the patient's impulses pose to him and the patterns of relating impulse to external environment that he has developed. It is these intrapersonal arrangements that psychoanalysis seeks to modify and that makes free association the method of choice because the technical specification of the psychoanalytic situation places a heavy emphasis on these intrapsychic determinants of response. In a sense, then, any self-experience in a situation of free-floating attention corresponds to free association. It remains only to create the conditions in which the person is willing to communicate that experience.

The big question raised by our experimental situation is whether the conditions of trust and motivations to confide are comparable to those found in psychotherapy. This is surely a strong challenge to the authenticity of our situation, and no rationale is likely to be fully acceptable without further empirical support from studies designed to bridge the laboratory and the clinic. Our recruitment interviews, in which we brought up the issue of trust and willingness to confide, provide opportunities to define ourselves as psychologists associated with healing activities and aware of our responsibilities for the welfare of others. The subject was encouraged to express his reservations and to participate in a process of working them through to the point of deciding to volunteer, and frequently (we cannot say always) he did so. At the same time, we tried to arouse his desire to contribute to science and to make explicit his obligation to us. Added to these motivations is the tendency for persons with latent interests in changing themselves to volunteer for experiments dealing with personality. Obviously, these arrangements are not likely to have induced very deep degrees of trust or very strong motivations to comply faithfully with the instructions to free associate. It remains debatable whether sufficient trust and motivation were achieved so that the phenomena associated with intrapsychic determinants of response became available. Therefore a further step is called for in which results obtained under experimental conditions are tested under clinical conditions of free association. With such bridging studies one could then feel more certain that these kinds of experimental studies and those of Colby are providing information on the nature of free association.

CONTROL WITHOUT SIMPLIFICATION

One of the major points of my argument has been that the leap into the laboratory is no guarantee of accelerating our rate of accumulating knowledge and that the step is best taken when founded on knowledge accumulated from observations taken in the natural setting. We should not close, however, before examining naturalistic studies and their peculiar difficulties. The most primitive forms of observation are those taken from either of the two participants, patient or therapist, usually the latter. Many of the data of psychoanalysis were and still are derived from the reports by Freud and his followers of the course of therapy, sometimes based partly on notes made during the process, but based mostly on retrospective reports collected at the end of hours or of longer periods. Although participant observations are data relevant to the events of psychotherapy, they must of necessity represent only one facet of it: how these events were experienced. They do not insure an "outside" view, which can be secured only through some kind of intrusion into the clinical situation. It is only a little over 30 years ago that Rogers and his collaborators launched a series of studies of psychotherapy which broke away from a dependence on observations by either of the two participants (Rogers, 1942). Electrically recorded, motion-pictured psychotherapeutic interviews and their verbatim transcripts make the phenomena of psychotherapy directly accessible to a third party.

Clinicians are not always easy in their minds about such invasions. Not only are recordings made, but also therapists are asked to respond in ways incompatible with their own theoretical orientations or pragmatically to adopt other modes of therapeutic behavior (Snyder, 1959), and patient and therapist are some times hooked up for physiological observations (Greenblatt, 1959). Where observations of the effects have been collected, for the most part on an informal basis, the general impression is that the therapist is a greater source of difficulty than the patient. Not all of the difference can be attributed to the argument that he may feel more able to protest than his patient. It has been argued by many that, when skillful therapists are involved, these invasions become only one more incident around which transference, resistance, and above all, countertransference cluster and, as such, are dealt with in the usual manner (Greenblatt, 1959).

In any case, as the client-centered group has shown, there are many meaningful studies via "experiments of nature" to be made with only minimal intrusion into clinical events. Particular theoretical frameworks predict specific sequences of events within psychotherapy. Again, the client-centered group has led the way in compiling an impressive array of tests of its theories about the role of self-perception. It is unfortunate that a great many of these are not being replicated within psychotherapy conducted under other theoretical orientations. Studies by Speisman (1959) and Auld and White (1959) are examples of investigations testing other assumptions about in-therapy sequences. In fact, the former of these two, done within our own research program, represented an effort to pit against each other client-centered, orthodox psychoanalytic, and John Rosen-centered conceptions of the sequential relationship between client resistance and interpretation. This study, which was a clinical forerunner of Colby's experimental demonstration mentioned earlier, obtained results more closely fitting the orthodox psychoanalytic version. Auld (1968) reviewed a series of studies testing psychoanalytic conceptions of process.

I conclude this chapter with the observation that there is need for research to be carried on over the whole range from the virtually unmodified clinical setting to the most abstracted and simplified laboratory setting. The great need is for such a disparate set of observations to be planned within a common frame of reference of the original issues as a basis for building adequate empirical bridges between levels of observation. Only then can we obtain the increase in convergence that is so necessary to the accumulation of knowledge.

CHAPTER 5

Setting Factors in Psychotherapy

Chapter 1 included a survey of differences in stances of various theories toward the basic treatment situation. The striking position would seem to be that of psychoanalysis, which assigns a central role to free association and other accompanying technical specifications designed to reduce situational determinants of the direction and content of the patient's verbal and affective responses. This means that, after the preliminaries between patient and psychoanalyst have resulted in a mutual agreement to attempt treatment, the patient experiences a working relationship with another person that is far removed from his usual experience. The "basic rule" removes the usual assumed aim to be relevant, to maintain continuity and coherence. This unmonitored condition of expression, which risks great self-revelation, is accompanied by a relatively brief acquaintance with the other person on which to base so much trust. The couch as a technical accompaniment of free association, the analyst's limited verbal interpolations, his position in the periphery of the patient's vision, and the priority he gives to the patient's as compared to his own response all combine to throw the patient back on his own resources to a degree not frequently encountered in other relationships. It is clear that the readiness of a patient to collaborate in such a process will be influenced by prior information, by prior experience in situations somewhat similar, and by faith-inducing experiences.

In this chapter I will examine different versions of the basic treatment situation and the kinds of questions that have been answered about them and the ones that remain to be answered in order to understand how setting factors influence the effects of psychotherapy. We need to concern ourselves with the avenues and the reasons whereby persons come to seek psychotherapy, their expectations, attitudes, and preconceptions, the setting where the therapy takes place, and the range of tasks and role requirements imposed. Though we will try to separate the effects on psychotherapy of prior social influences and of the basic working situation from the effects of technical parameters in the therapeutic process, therapist and patient personality factors, and the interactions among them, their organic relationship will force, at times, arbitrary decisions either to postpone consideration of a particular overlapping factor (e.g., therapists' expectations) or to consider that factor from two points of view.

THE PSYCHOTHERAPEUTIC SITUATION

The resurgence of psychotherapies based on extrapolations of academic theories of learning and associated laboratory studies raises the question of how we define psychotherapy. The term has been used to refer to a situation in which a healer works through psychological as distinguished from physical or physiological means to bring about change in a person's behavior and experience. Hence we do not intend to include in psychotherapy such treatments as brain surgery, drugs, or electroshock. Psychotherapy has traditionally referred to the influence of the therapist through his relationship to the patient and the tasks he sets him. The alternative of influencing the persons who are part of the patient's daily life has usually been differentiated from psychotherapy by the term environmental manipulation. Implicit in this distinction is the assumption that psychotherapy is indicated when the patient's inter- and intrapersonal conflicts and discomforts arise from what he brings to situations, whereas environmental manipulation is indicated when the primary source of the difficulties lies in the situation itself.

This older distinction between psychotherapy and environmental manipulation requires renewed examination in light of the appearance of new kinds of environmental manipulations. One is the management of reinforcement contingencies in various institutional settings (Ayllon & Haughton, 1962; Baer, 1968; Cohen, 1968), and the other is the developing specialty of community mental health (e.g., Iscoe & Spielberger, 1970) and its effort, in part, to influence personality development and functioning by changing the social system. These new concepts of environmental manipulation differ from the older ones in that they seek more general changes than are implied in situational treatment. Whether or not the goals are couched in terms of personality, the aim is to change the individual's response system in a way which applies to a broad range of situations. Most of the efforts of community psychologists which come under the rubric "primary prevention" fall into the class of teaching, socializing, or upbringing rather than psychotherapy. The latter process is directed toward deficits which are such that the usual attempts to rectify them in the individual's daily life prove unavailing. There still remains the possibility that this assumption of unavailingness is unwarranted.

The work of Baer (1968) and his associates illustrates the possibility that psychotherapy may best be carried out through modifying the behavior of those in the target person's life space. Baer dealt with problem children in nursery school. One was a 3-year-old girl who exhibited a high rate of crawling on all fours. The teacher had taken this to be a form of regression, precipitated by the birth of a new baby, and responded by attending to the child very sympathetically, especially when she crawled. When the teacher, on instruction, began to ignore her crawling behavior and to attend to her constantly whenever she was upright for any reason, a normal pattern of upright behavior rapidly emerged. From my point of view, the teacher's modified behavior matched typical parental responses designed to encourage a baby to give up crawling for walking. It is possible that the teacher's original assumption was correct (after all, one does have to account for the return to crawling behavior that signaled the problem), but she had bypassed the simplest remedy, which was to reinstate the previous learning process. The crucial question is whether all self-defeating behavior can be modified simply by reinstating the usual learning conditions and, if so, whether this applies to all age groups. The burden of proof would seem to lie with those, including this writer, who assume that there are conditions of persons where cognitive and motor sets organized around complex motives block the effectiveness of the usual teaching operations.

Even in advance of formal proof, psychotherapists have seemingly concluded that the more meaningful way to work with their clients or patients is within a special setting rather than *in vivo*. With the average adult, of course, working *in vivo* would prove inconvenient and time consuming, if not impossible. Even in the traditional approach there are variations to be considered—inpatient or outpatient, group or individual. There are only a few systematic studies of such questions. Information regarding the relative usefulness of working on an inpatient or an outpatient basis is hopelessly confounded with the influence of patient characteristics that lead to hospitalization, namely, degree of disturbance. Perhaps one way to bring the influence of hospitalization within the reach of empirical investigation would be to select special features of it. An important one would appear to be its function as a way of imposing limits on the patient. There have been several attempts to point to the potential usefulness of studying the role of limits in psychotherapy (Bixler, 1949; Ginott, 1959), but little actual research has followed. We would want to know what responses are to be expected from different kinds of persons to various forms of limit setting. Later in this chapter I will discuss the therapist's commitments as a feature of the working alliance. The setting of limits could be viewed as a feature of the working alliance between patient and therapist.

When we consider questions about the relative effects of individual versus group versus family therapy, the data available can only scratch the surface of the complexities. For example, the relative effectiveness of individual and group therapy (e.g., Baehr, 1954) must be examined for what effects, by which individual or group methods, for what kinds of patients.

Two kinds of developments may have produced a convergence of recent research on the issue of leaderless groups. One factor may be the increased emphasis on coping behavior, which led Rothaus and his associates (Rothaus et al., 1963) to experiment with human relations training, a part of which includes concern with leaderless groups (Rothaus et al., 1967). Using the context of human relations training, Rothaus and his collaborators have argued that the presence of a therapist may produce some undesirable consequences, for example, the suppression of leadership, competition for the attention of the therapist, restricted development of member autonomy, and inhibition of frankness and trust. In studies of leaderless groups, Rothaus, Johnson, and Lyle (1964) found that such patients became less illness-centered, less dependent, and less self-preoccupied; furthermore, they interacted more (Rothaus et al., 1966). But others have reported contradictory results, especially in studies where the same groups met with and without leaders. Both Seligman and Sterne (1969) and Salzberg (1967), working with hospitalized neurotics, found that leaderless conditions were more likely to be accompanied by discussion of more conventional topics, less personal and dealing with the general hospital environment, than under therapist-led conditions. This was true despite the fact that under leaderless conditions patients were more likely to comment spontaneously and speak longer. Truax (Truax & Carkhuff, 1965b; Truax, Wargo, & Volksdorf, 1970) has produced evidence not only that hospitalized patients and institutionalized juvenile delinquents act differentlp in leaderless sessions but also that this difference is associated with less gain from therapy, using external criteria.

Ambiguity as a Critical Aspect of the Traditional Situation

Most versions even of behavior therapy have involved a patient in a relationship to a therapist. Thus one natural approach for trying to understand the process of psychotherapy and thereby improve its effectiveness is to analyze and test questions about the basic working conditions. In defining ambiguity as a feature of the working relationship (Bordin, 1955), I was trying to capture a unique feature of the psychoanalytic approach, namely, the effort to create conditions that fix attention on internal stimuli toward action and highlight them. Thus an external stimulus deprivation interpretation was given to the concept of ambiguity. Osburn (1951), while showing that raters responded to this attribute in unidimensional terms, demonstrated also that ratings were negatively correlated with the responsivity of the therapist (number of responses per unit of time) and the number and specificity of other activities defining self or situation (e.g., initiating topics). Unfortunately, ambiguity has other meanings and connotations.

A major alternative interpretation of ambiguity refers to the emission of contradictory cues. These cues can be in the form of suggestions, commands, or expressions of approval and disapproval. Heller's studies of ambiguity included conditions in which it was defined as the emission of evaluative statements equally divided between negative and positive (Heller, 1968a; Davis, 1971). Such a condition is well designed to bring about the opposite result from stimulus deprivation, in that it tends to focus attention on the person emitting gratifying or hurting statements and distracts attention from the flow of thoughts and feelings being experienced.

Another distinction with regard to ambiguity as characteristic of the therapeutic situation is between defining a task ambiguously and unambiguously defining an ambiguous task. The task of free association is open ended and therefore ambiguous, but it can be clearly defined. As Greenson (1967) has pointed out in his discussions of the working alliance in psychoanalysis, the analyst must concern himself with the patient's need for self-esteem, self-respect, and dignity. Thus, instead of imposing rules and conditions without explanation, Greenson specifies, "All new or strange procedures are explained to the patient. I always explain to the patient why we ask him to associate freely and why we prefer the couch" (p. 214). Furthermore, in psychoanalysis or other treatment situations which make use of the dynamics of ambiguity, the setting factors include a patient's clear request for help and the establishment of the basis for a working relationship. In many of the analogue studies, the subject-patient-client is usually not very clear about what is expected. Yes, he is a subject in an experiment. He may have received further definitions, such as the fact that the experiment has to do with the study of personality or with methods of psychotherapy. He may be motivated by curiosity about psychology, about himself, or about both; he may be simply fulfilling a course requirement that he put in a certain amount of time as a subject in an experiment. A situation created by such combinations of conditions is surely going to focus attention on the experimenter-therapist. In a therapy which follows Greenson's precepts the therapist has clarified the relation of the conditions of ambiguity (stimulus deprivation) to the mutual assumption of patient and therapist that resolution of the former's difficulties is to be found in what is happening in him rather than in situational pressures. Such understandings and states of mutual agreement are not, of course, to be achieved simply and easily, nor are they maintained at a uniform level.

We shall return to this topic when discussing the influence of expectations and socializing for patient roles.

In considering the effects of ambiguity in a therapeutic relationship, then, we must assume that the patient's motivations in seeking therapy, the personalities of both patient and therapist, and the nature of their working alliance will all need to be considered. When the patient understands that the ambiguous elements of the therapeutic work situation are designed to help him come to terms with inner forces which lead to maladaptive behavior and unsatisfying experience, he will be able to engage in effective therapeutic work, that is, to talk and relate to the therapist around the significant issues in his past and present life. This does not mean that he will be free of discomfort or completely and uniformly fluent. On the contrary, ambiguity refers to a setting factor which is only one part of the process. All approaches to psychotherapy tend to consider additional process issues, revolving around various kinds of therapist interventions and their timing in terms of patient and therapist interactions. In addition to how motivated for therapy the patient is and how well he understands that he is one of the important sources of his own difficulties, the patient's personality can be expected to play a part in the influence of ambiguity. By focusing attention on himself as the source of his problems, ambiguity becomes a source of anxiety. Most clinicians assume that there is a curvilinear relation between level of anxiety and productivity in psychotherapy. Depending on the patient's vulnerability, which may be a function of the range and effectiveness of his capacity to cope with anxiety or defend against it, the patient may at high levels of ambiguity reach such a high level of anxiety as to become so immersed in anxiety-reducing operations that he has little attention or energy to devote to therapeutic work. The therapist's personality plays its part despite the seeming contradictions in the psychoanalytic notions of neutrality and the blank screen. Building on the work of Stone (1961), Greenson has pointed out that these are not absolute and that an effective working alliance can only be built upon evidence that the therapist is interested in the patient and respects him with all of his difficulties and faults.

These lines of thought pose a whole series of empirical challenges, some of which have been partially met. The complexities involved have prompted an early turn toward the use of analogues (Dibner, 1958). Siegman and Pope (1968) performed a series of studies, using female nursing students as subjects in standardized interviews divided into two topic areas, one neutral and the other anxiety arousing, with questions in these areas divided at two levels of ambiguity-specificity. They were following up previous naturalistic studies by Lennard and Bernstein (1960), who found suggestions of a reciprocal relationship between therapist and patient informational input. These prior studies found that ambiguous therapist remarks were followed by relatively long patient responses and specific therapist communications by relatively brief patient responses. Additionally, relatively unproductive patient responses were found to follow specific therapist communications, and relatively productive patient responses to follow ambiguous therapist communications. When the informational relevance of the patient's response was evaluated, the results suggested that, although ambiguous interviewer remarks tend to elicit longer patient responses, they may not elicit more relevant[1] information.

Siegman and Pope (1968) turned to analogue studies because they wished to unconfound the interviewer's ambiguity-specificity level from the anxiety level inherent in the particular topical focus. They found that, though interviewee responses were longer following ambiguous interviewer remarks, these responses were characterized by somewhat greater superficiality. They concluded, however, that the greater increase in productivity resulted in an absolute increase in information, even though accompanied by greater occurrence of superficial responses. These results are somewhat at variance with those reported by Heller (1968a), also from analogue studies, that the least feedback to subjects was most facilitative of self-disclosure. Since Heller's findings applied to those who had been found from independent indices to be primed to discuss themselves openly in personal terms, the differences in the two studies are reconcilable. This state of being primed for personal disclosure is, of course, the condition that characterizes psychotherapy. Kaplan (1966) contributes a further nuance of evidence by including Bordin's (1966c) Free Association Scale as one of her dependent variables. This scale, going beyond the personal content, relates to the expressive qualities of the interviewee's response. All of her subjects were placed in a room by themselves. Ambiguity was varied by giving half of them the usual instruction to free associate and the other half the instruction to "talk about the things you would talk about if you were a patient who comes to a therapist." Kaplan's finding that high-anxiety subjects responded differently according to level of ambiguity may be taken as a reflection of the same factors as existed for Heller's primed-for-self-disclosure groups, except that Kaplan's high-anxious subjects responded with greater affect and spontaneity in the problem-focused and therefore less ambiguous conditions. These two results are reconcilable if interpretable as evidence of a curvilinear relationship between anxiety and ambiguity. The free association condition

---

[1] This kind of research can be plagued by theory-based differences in interpretations of what is relevant and what is superficial information.

actually represented more ambiguity in this experiment than in the clinical situation in that the experimenter-therapist was not even present in the room.

The last point introduces the consideration that there are many features of the therapeutic situation which may be subject to varying degrees of clarity. In my original statement (Bordin, 1955), I identified three general aspects: the patient's task, the goal of the therapy, and the thoughts and personality of the therapist. One perplexing problem is how safe it is to vary the ambiguity of these three aspects in quantitative terms without concern for their Gestalt qualities. For example, Davis (1971) used ratio of interviewer negative and positive evaluative responses as an index of ambiguity, and an equal proportion representing the greatest ambiguity. In trying to account for the failure of ambiguity to predict subjects' rate of requesting further interviewer communication, he felt forced to question whether this unpredictability of direction of interviewer evaluation was in fact perceived as ambiguity. This points up an additional pitfall with regard to the use of ambiguity as a variable in research in psychotherapy: it is important to distinguish objective ambiguity, defined by the general pulling power of a stimulus complex, from subjective ambiguity, which is defined in terms of an individual. A particular stimulus complex which is defined as objectively ambiguous in the sense that no one percept is favored over others, as demonstrated by the variability in response obtained from a large number of persons, may be responded to with a clearly and strongly experienced percept by a particular person. This is illustrated by the probably apocryphal story about the patient who protested during projective testing about being shown "dirty pictures." Some (e.g., Clemes & D'Andrea, 1965), have even equated ambiguity with the discrepancy between the actual characteristics of the interview relationship and the patient's prior expectations. In my view such factors are dealt with most usefully in terms of social setting influences (to be discussed later in this chapter) and in terms of client personality differences.

Thus far, most studies have been directed at variations in ambiguity of either the task or the personality and reactions of the therapist. Concern with ambiguity of the task is intimately related to studies of anxiety as related to ambiguity. Siegman and Pope (1968) demonstrated that verbal indices of anxiety, which Dibner (1958) used to test whether greater anxiety was associated with greater ambiguity, can be subdivided into those that reflect uncertainty taking the form of brief filled or unfilled pauses during the search for a basis for response, and those that represent speech disruption itself, including longer silent pauses which reflect a defensive slowing down of speech and are accompanied by other defensive maneuvers. Studies by Heller and his students (Heller, 1968a, 1968b;

Davis, 1971) have varied the clarity with which the interviewer's messages could be heard, but have not been concerned either with the question of whether or not these messages involved the task or with the interviewee's responses of anxiety or uncertainty.

These studies and those of Siegman and Pope did bear on the effects of ambiguity about the therapist's reactions and personality. In some instances, interviewer and interviewee were separated by an opaque screen; in others, control of lighting made the interviewer visible when he spoke. In general, results of these manipulations are consistent with Siegman's and Pope's conclusion that ambiguity of the interviewer's verbal messages is associated with increased productivity, but that reduction of relationship-relevant cues inhibits productivity. To determine whether these latter results can be taken as partial confirmation of Greenson's contentions regarding the importance of the working alliance and of Rogers' contentions concerning the central importance of empathy, regard, and genuineness, or should be interpreted as evidence that the "blank screen" features of the psychoanalytic situation are counterproductive, would require further and more definitive research in which variations in feedback occurred against the backdrop of a well established working alliance.

My emphasis on the stimulus deprivation element in ambiguity suggests that the data from experimental studies of sensory deprivation are relevant. Very well documented is the fact that many subjects in studies of prolonged sensory deprivation report considerable anxiety, often at a panic level, accompanied by hallucinatory experiences (Heron, Doane, & Scott, 1956; Solomon et al., 1961; Zuckerman, 1969). The need for studying individual differences—and some preliminary work in this area has been done (Goldberger & Holt, 1961; Azima, Vispo, & Azima, 1961; Stewart, 1965)—is emphasized by reports that sensory deprivation experiences had a salutary effect on the condition of hospitalized schizophrenic patients (Gibby, Adams, & Carrera, 1960).

Psychic Processes During Free Association

Psychoanalytic emphasis on the intrapersonal determinants of behavior and experience leads to many implicit propositions regarding the psychic processes that ambiguous conditions facilitate. The reported hallucinatory responses occurring under conditions of extended sensory deprivation can be taken as evidence supporting Freud's ideas that the conditions of free association facilitate the expression of primary process thinking. On the other hand, verification of the suggestion that schizophrenic patients would profit from treatment by sensory deprivation would appear to challenge this idea. Presumably, the problem with schizophrenics is not so much to facilitate access to primary process aspects of experience as to enable them to utilize these experiences more constructively than before. Most therapists have reported that modifications *away from* the stimulus-depriving elements in classical psychoanalysis were required for effective work with such patients. Something of the same problem for psychoanalytic explanations is created by my finding (Bordin, 1966b) that hospitalized psychiatric patients responded as effectively to the associative task in an analogue situation as did college students free of overt signs of psychiatric difficulties. On the other hand, the same investigation offered evidence that, within the college student sample, differences in rate of perception of reversals in reversible figures and the style of perception on the Rorschach were related to associative performance. Of particular interest with regard to Rorschach performance was the fact that an index reflecting balance of access to drive and of drive control (Schneider, 1953) showed the same positive relation to adequacy of response as its developer had found in actual therapeutic interviews. In further analyses of my data, Mann (1965) found differences in style of free association among subsets of the college student subjects classified by the Minnesota Multiphasic or the Rorschach. Using criteria based on previous research, she identified "hysteric," "obsessive," and "borderline" personality types, all these being persons without psychiatric history. Some of the observed differences were in accord with expectation; for example, obsessive personality types displayed more self-observation than did hysterics and were less overtly inhibited, and borderlines showed more primary process responses than either of the others. But other results were surprising; for example, obsessives also displayed greater involvement and as much spontaneity as did the hysterics, and borderlines were generally more similar to the obsessives than to the hysterics.

Client-centered constructions give only a slightly different emphasis to the nature of the associative process.[2] Although not placing as much emphasis on stimulus deprivation, the client-centered work style is typically nonintrusive with an emphasis on client response coming on its own initiative. Rogers' description of the therapeutic process in terms of client experiencing (1959b), a culmination of earlier starts by Gendlin, and later elaborations (1968) by the latter bear many similarities to psychoanalytic conceptions of patient experience in complying with the free associative task. Gendlin found that the degree to which the individual displays an initial ability to attend to himself forecasts the effectiveness of

[2] Interestingly, Weitzman (1967) argues that the reliance on patient imagery in the desensitization process leads to a free associative process which may be a hidden ingredient in that form of behavior therapy.

client-centered therapy and agrees with my earlier conclusion (1964) that response to the free associative task can be taken as an index of soundness of personal functioning. Using a highly simplified laboratory analogue, Gendlin et al. (1968) has reported an initial series of studies directed to uncovering the sources of individual differences in this capacity to attend to one's experience, which he calls "focusing ability," and the ways whereby it can be modified. Client-centered thinking leads to an emphasis on self-ideal discrepancies as a source of individual differences and to the analysis of self-reference in free association. Stollak et al. (1967) reported that the subjects expressing most satisfaction with themselves spoke more about themselves in the present tense and used more feeling words during a 15-minute period of solitary free association than those expressing self-dissatisfaction.

As has already been mentioned, there are many aspects of the classical free association situation, each of which may facilitate or retard the desired process. Only a start has been made at a systematic identification of the independent effects of the ingredients that make up the situation. Colby (1960), using a 30-minute analogue, presented evidence that subjects incorporated more references to significant figures in their lives into their free associations during periods when the experimenter was present in the room than when he was absent. This suggests that the interviewer-therapist not only influences general productivity but also may help to bring about a greater focus on interpersonal issues and thereby facilitate transference phenomena. But, of course, more needs to be done about investigating the interactions among therapist ambiguity, working alliance, patient, and therapist personality factors. Martin, Lundy, and Lewin (1960) compared the effects of talking into a tape recorder with those of talking to a therapist, either under regular conditions or in a situation where the therapist was restricted to nonverbal means of communication. The subjects were college students who volunteered for a brief psychotherapy experience and were seen for five 30-minute sessions. The regular group showed a tendency to increase its approach to emotionally important material during the course of the interview in succeeding sessions, whereas the tape recorder group displayed an opposite tendency, with the nonverbal group falling in between. It is surprising that there has been so little examination of the effect of the physical position of lying on the couch. Morgan and Bakan (1965) in a sensory deprivation situation found that subjects who were lying down produced more visual hallucinatory reports than those sitting up. Berdach and Bakan (1967) reported that subjects produced more early memories and distributed toward the earlier age while lying down than when sitting up.

This absence of studies regarding the influence of various aspects of the situation prevails whether or not one is concerned with the classical psychoanalytic situation. Mintz (1971), citing the lack of examination of the influence of how therapists handle fees, suggested that therapists' prudery regarding money might be one reason for the neglect of this factor. Haase (1970) tried to study the effect of spatial distance between therapist and client by analyzing the reactions of subjects to photographs showing therapists at distances ranging from 30 to 88 inches from their clients. He found that preferences concentrated on distances of less than 60 inches. Finally, one set of investigators (Kasmar, Griffin, & Mauritzen, 1968) compared the effects of two contrasting environments, a "beautiful" and an "ugly" room, on patients' self-rating of mood and their ratings of the psychiatrist-interviewer after an undefined 20-minute interview. Their failure to find effects of room atmosphere on either mood or response to interviewer may reflect on the crudity of the experiment more than anything else. Both the "ugly" and the "beautiful" rooms were windowless! Furthermore, 20 minutes in what may have been a relatively meaningless interaction may have little generalizability.

Time Framework of Relationship

Though there is a range of difference in viewpoints, most theories of psychotherapy place considerable emphasis on the strength of the personal relationship between therapist and patient. Surely, then, the time boundaries within which that relationship functions are also important. Two persons have much greater opportunity and experience greater stimulus to become emotionally involved with each other if they meet every day than if they meet once every 2 weeks or if they meet with no definite commitments to meet again. Though the "50-minute hour" is traditional, therapists in public agencies under the pressure of heavy case loads have been known to cut down to briefer meetings. A few agencies have policies that rotate therapists rather than maintaining a consistent relationship. At the other extreme, the technique of the marathon group involves meeting continuously for as long as 10 or 15 hours or within the period of a single weekend. When beginning a psychoanalysis, therapist and patient are committing themselves to a process expected to extend beyond a single year and probably for several years. The many questions surrounding the length and frequency of interviews and the duration of the relationship have scarcely been touched.

As might be expected, the greatest skepticism about the special significance of the relationship comes from among those approaching psychotherapy from a behavior therapy standpoint. Although Wolpe[3] has explicitly stated the importance of relationship variables, Lang, Melamed, and

[3] See comment by Lazarus in Klein et al. (1969, p. 262).

Hart (1970) offer evidence that an automated, depersonalized process of desensitization achieves essentially the same results as a personalized one. Kahn and Baker (1968), whose study relied on telephone followup for the dependent variable, offer additional data. Krapfl and Nawas (1969) provide similar evidence, but their study is tainted because the subjects were qualified by their capacity to produce imagery in response to a questionnaire. Thus their sample population was already selected as those who would function in an impersonal situation and therefore lacks generality. In fact, Nawas later (Nawas & Pucel, 1971) reports evidence that pseudo-desensitization has an effect and concludes that relationship factors cannot be ruled out. Others have emphasized the importance of faith and hope in the desensitization process and the degree to which the behavior therapist augments these through his own feelings of confidence and through the use of prestige (Klein et al., 1969; Wilson, Hannon, & Evans, 1968). On the other hand, Geer and Katkin (1966) seek to underline the superficiality of the relationship as a factor by illustrating the transferability of the therapist in a report on the treatment of an insomniac.

Most of the naturalistic studies of duration and frequency have used global rather than specific dependent variables. One of the most extended investigations lends little encouragement to those who wish to promote one frequency over another (Imber et al., 1957, 1968; Frank, 1961). It does suggest, however, that there is a lower limit of frequency below which psychotherapy becomes markedly less effective. With outpatient neurotics, individual therapy for 1 hour a week was pitted against group therapy for 1½ hours a week and what was intended to be a minimal amount of therapy, individual sessions lasting not more than ½ hour every 2 weeks. None of the patients was seen for longer than 6 months. Patients under all three conditions experienced some immediate relief from distress. Although at 6 months those in the minimal therapy group had improved least in the area of social effectiveness (overdependence and disruptive aggressiveness), the difference was not pronounced after 5 years. This led Frank (1961, p. 213) to speculate that frequency, perhaps even psychotherapy itself, is eventually of little consequence. But this conclusion may need to be modified in light of data obtained when patients were followed up 10 years later. Among those reached, the patients seen in the minimal treatment condition were judged to be significantly lower in social effectiveness than the others, although not in personal discomfort. Naturally, the attrition of the sample at the last followup weakens confidence in the results.

Two other naturalistic experiments offer weak evidence in support of the assumption that frequency makes a difference. In one of them (Lorr et al., 1962) Veterans Administration outpatients were randomly assigned to be seen twice a week, once a week, or every other week, with controls to make the durations of the relationship comparable. No differences assignable to treatment frequency were observed after 4 and 8 months. At the end of a year, a 23% loss on followup plus the fact that only about half remained in therapy forced a cruder analysis in terms of treatment frequency for the two samples, those still in and those out of treatment. Within each group, those seen with greater frequency reported improvement in characteristics seemingly similar to Imber et al.'s variable of social effectiveness. At 3 years (McNair et al., 1964) these gains were maintained and even augmented by some improvement, especially in regard to anxiety. In a further analysis at that time, the total number of interviews the patient received, as distinguished from the number of months over which the treatment stretched, was positively correlated with improvement. The other investigation (Heinicke, 1969), an unusual one in that it compared psychoanalytic treatment of young boys four times a week with treatment once a week, unfortunately included only four in each group. These small numbers undermine confidence in statistically significant evidence of differential improvement favoring the more intensively treated group in three of four rated factors (ego integration, flexibility, and peer relationships) and in tested improvement in reading and spelling. Although the rated factors were based on diagnostic testing, they represent possibly contaminated evidence because the ratings were made by the therapist rather than the diagnostician.

Two treatment situations, at opposite extremes of intensity of relationships, have hardly been exploited in either naturalistic or analogue research. As mentioned, the weekend encounter or marathon group represents one extreme of an intensive relationship, albeit brief in calendar terms. Using indices of group cohesiveness derived from research on small groups in social psychology (e.g., feelings of belonging and attraction), Dies and Hess (1971) found evidence favoring a marathon group over a conventional one for comparable hours of meeting. Meador (1971), reporting descriptively, found that the eight members of a weekend encounter group reached various stages of freedom of self-disclosure more rapidly than has been reported for groups not using the weekend format. The other treatment setting is a brief-contact clinic (Moos & Clemes, 1967), so arranged that each patient sees a different therapist each week. What effect does such fragmentation have? Are therapists interchangeable? The studies that could bear on these questions (Moos & Clemes, 1967; Moos & MacIntosh, 1970; Van Der Veen, 1965; Houts, MacIntosh, & Moos, 1969) have confined themselves to the question of therapist and patient consistency. The summing up of results suggests that patients are consistent, reflecting their personalities, and that therapists are less consistent, reflecting their responsiveness to patient and situational variations. In a Veterans

Administration outpatient clinic where turnover in therapists is forced by rotation of trainees, Meyer and Tolman (1963) found that most patients manifested a reaction to forced change of therapist and that the majority (49 of 68) were unfavorable.

Most investigations of the influence of duration of treatment have confounded this factor with frequency of interviews and have been concerned mostly with the more global question of how patient personality contributed to early or premature termination, or whether duration of the relationship was correlated with outcome. In most field situations, duration represents so complex a set of factors as to defy definitive analysis. In addition to situational conditions that make it impossible for a patient to continue in treatment, such as physical illness, unemployment, or transfer to another city, the patient may exercise his option to terminate, either because he is satisfied with the changes achieved, has given up hope of achieving his goal, or is expressing an impulsive or defensive reaction to the emotional vicissitudes of treatment. The therapist may exert specific, even arbitrary, influences on duration as a reflection of his conception of the usual period required to achieve adequate change or as a function of his personal reactions to the particular patient (Stieper & Wiener, 1959).

Rank (1945), concerned with will, stressed treatment as an opportunity for the individual to come to know and accept his own capacity to express feeling and initiate action against a backdrop of clear therapist self-definition. This position led him to attach importance to the facing of endings and to suggest the tactic of fixing particular ending dates. The only systematic studies of this way of using the time factor of which I am aware (Henry & Shlien, 1958; Shlien, Mosak, & Dreikurs, 1962; Muench, 1965) inevitably confounded the tactic of setting a terminal date with variation in duration of treatment. Shlien and his collaborators found that clients for whom a limit of 20 interviews had been set reached the same levels as clients for whom no limits had been set (seen for an average of 37 interviews) and seemed to reach these levels earlier in their abbreviated treatment. Moreover, this effect of time-limited therapy applied when either client-centered or Adlerian therapists were involved. Within an eclectically oriented counseling center, Muench (1965) compared a group of 35 clients for whom an arbitrary time limit, from 8 to 19 interviews had been set with two groups for whom duration was allowed to vary. One group, called "short term," was seen for from 3 to 7 interviews; the other, "long-term" group, for 20 or more interviews. Time-limited therapy was found to be as effective as short-term treatment and more effective than long-term, independently of therapist skill and severity of client disturbance. More information is needed about the specific effects on how the patient works and feels when a definite ending date has been set.

THE SOCIAL FRAMEWORK

Sociologists and social psychologists give us good reason to believe (if commonsense were not enough!) that the ease with which a person adopts a prescribed pattern of behavior is influenced by prior social conditioning toward that role. Through direct and indirect experience we learn to expect to behave and, in fact, do behave in certain ways with healers, teachers, priests, and prophets. Depending on the role, we anticipate demands for certain kinds of disclosures and complementary kinds of responses. In any psychotherapeutic relationship, no matter of what variety, patients and therapists will have initial expectations not only about the degree to which the patient is likely to improve as a result of the therapy offered, but also about the specific roles that each will play in the therapeutic relationship. Role expectations pertain to the working arrangements of the therapy, its technical requirements, such as frequency and length of sessions, the duration of treatment, and, especially, the types and levels of activity required of the participants. Patients and also therapists, even though training and personal therapy seek to neutralize such effects in the latter, meet with preset attitudes toward each other. These attitudes run the gamut from derogatory prejudices about color, religion, class, sex, or nationality to faith and overestimation, sometimes involving these same characteristics or specifically attached to occupational role.

At this point we will review questions and evidence regarding the influence of expectations on the processes of therapy and on perceptions of its outcome, the sources of expectations in the individual's social history, the influence of different varieties of manipulations of attitudes toward the therapist, and the use of different methods of inducting or socializing the patient to his role.

Sources and Influence of Expectations

A client or patient enters therapy with a complex of wishes, hopes, and anticipations that have been forged out of the combination of his personal needs, impressions obtained from television, motion pictures, and other media and from friends and acquaintances, and the effects of the specific referring person. Apfelbaum (1958) found three independently varying therapist role expectations among a sample of 100 individuals seen in a university outpatient psychiatric clinic. Using patient responses to Q-sort items, he identified three clusters: (1) nurturant—patient expects guiding, giving, protective therapist; (2) model—expects a well adjusted therapist who is neither protective nor critical; and (3) critic—expects a therapist to be critical and analytical, and willing to accept considerable responsibility.

Undoubtedly, social class and ethnic group participate in the formation of preconceptions regarding the role requirements of being a patient, the roles of psychological helpers, and the features of the working relationship between the two. One personal influence on expectations is the severity of the stress which motivates the quest for therapy. Goldstein and Shipman (1961) report a correlation of .53 between a preinterview report of symptom intensity and expectations of symptom reduction, which corresponds with other, less controlled reports, for example, that of Lipkin (1954). As Goldstein (1962) has pointed out, research and theory on level of aspiration, as well as clinical theory, suggest a curvilinear relationship between expectation and motivation. According to level of aspiration theory, fear of failure leads to setting either very low aspirations to increase the likelihood of reaching them or extremely high aspirations which reduce the onus of the failure because virtually no one could be expected to reach such heights. Psychodynamic theories utilize the ideas of patterns of defense against anxiety to account for the same behavioral phenomena. Unfortunately, Goldstein's and Shipman's data give only partial support to the expectation of a curvilinear relationship. They found evidence for curvilinearity in the relationship between expected and reported reduction in severity of symptoms, but are silent on the question of linearity between severity and expectation, leaving the suspicion that there was no evidence.

The view of the patient's expectations as, in part, a function of his personality has been little investigated, with thus far indeterminate results. Goldstein and Heller (in Goldstein, 1962) included in their studies of client and therapist expectations analyses of Minnesota Multiphasic Inventories (MMPI) completed by both patient and therapist. Although there were some results for therapists, to be discussed below, there was no relation between personality measures and expectations of symptom reduction. On the other hand, Berzins, Friedman, and Seidman (1969) found that outpatients classified by the A-B scale, developed to differentiate therapists successful with schizophrenic patients from those successful with neurotic patients (Betz, 1962, 1967), exhibited differing expectations. Patients classified as similar to A therapists (those more successful with schizophrenic patients) were more likely to anticipate that the therapist would assume a passive role and that they themselves would do much of the initiating, and to be rated high by their therapists on characteristics descriptive of neurotic patients. Thus, the A personality may be associated with neurotic-type characteristics and be prone to expect the kinds of therapeutic style exhibited by B therapists. Apfelbaum (1958) found suggestions in mean MMPI profiles that the patients who enter psychotherapy expecting the therapist to take either the nurturant or the critic role are maladjusted and distressed than those who anticipate a model psychotherapist.

There has been much concern about the influence of social class and ethnic factors on the willingness of patients to seek psychotherapy and the kind of psychotherapy they will be offered (Hollingshead & Redlich, 1958; Schaffer & Myers, 1954), and some direct investigation of the relations between these factors and expectations regarding psychotherapy has been made. There have, for example, been several suggestions that lower- and working-class patients are more likely to be unsophisticated, unpracticed, and even grossly misinformed about psychological kinds of treatment, and to bring to therapy an array of values, life styles, and expectations of treatment which are widely discrepant from those of their primarily middle- or higher-class therapists (Riessman & Scribner, 1965; Gould, 1967). Hollingshead and Redlich (1958) found distinct class differences in favorableness of attitudes toward psychiatrists and toward psychotherapy as a means of dealing with emotional problems, and in accuracy of information regarding practitioners and treatment processes. Others (Overall & Aronson, 1963; Goin, Yamamoto, & Silverman, 1965) have further documented the inaccuracies of lower-class knowledge regarding psychotherapy.

One specific influence on the patient's anticipations regarding psychotherapy is the person who refers him, another area which is sparsely investigated. Goldstein and Shipman (1961) reasoned that psychiatrists, psychologists, and social workers were likely to communicate confidence and expectations of improvement when referring for psychotherapy. They combined persons who received this kind of referral with those who referred themselves into an expected favorable group and compared them with those who were referred by friends or others. Although those referred by mental health specialists displayed greater confidence in psychotherapy, as indicated by their willingness to refer a friend, there was no difference between the two referral groups in terms of expectations of improvement. Uncertainty about the nature of self-referrals and referrals by friends, which in this survey were treated differently, adds to the inconclusiveness of our knowledge.

Turning to therapists, we might expect that a major source of their expectations regarding process and outcome is their training and experience in psychotherapy. Strupp (1960) has been a major source of data regarding the effects of theoretical orientation (which usually reflects form of training) and experience. He found that, when matched for experience and the presence-absence of personal analysis, psychiatrists, more than psychologists, were modest in their goals and alert to the possibility of acting out responses. Although the results are less certain because of possible confounding with other factors, Strupp found that client-centered therapists were more optimistic in their expectations for improvement than psychoanalytically oriented therapists. Theoretical orientation as well as accumulated experience, no doubt, leads to expectations regarding patients presenting particular personality characteristics and patterns of pathology. Strupp (1960; Wallach & Strupp, 1964; Strupp & Williams, 1960) has shown that the therapist's expectations of improvement and, to a lesser extent, his liking of the patient are associated with his judgments of ego strength, insight, capacity for self-observation, defensiveness, emotional maturity, and social adjustment. The earlier cited studies of differences in treatment received according to social class suggest the need for examination of the effects of their own social class and other cultural conditioning factors on expectations and other biases of psychotherapists. Beyond the literature on countertransference, I have found little specific research on personality as a source of therapist's expectations. Goldstein and Heller (in Goldstein, 1962), using an inventory designed to tap expectations regarding Apfelbaum's (1958) three therapist roles and relating these to therapists' MMPI scores, found differences in personality according to the role the therapist anticipated. Therapists who anticipated adopting the nurturant role gave evidence of depression and perceived others as more dominant and forceful than themselves. Those who expected to assume the critical role were low in depression and in role playing and empathy. And, finally, those with model role expectancies showed greater role-playing and empathic abilities.

When we turn from the source of expectations to their influence, we must take into account the separate as well as the combined influences of the patient's and the therapist's expectations. Moreover, we must distinguish between pseudo and real effects. If the estimate of the effects depends on observations biased by the observer's expectations, then the bias, as Rosenthal (1966) has so amply demonstrated, may result in pseudo effects. On the other hand, favorable expectations, which Frank (1961) has discussed under the heading of faith, may make a person more susceptible to actual change.

As Frank (1961) pointed out, the placebo control group as a necessity of research designs evaluating the effects of treatments in medicine or in psychotherapy testifies to the reality of the effects that anticipation of change exerts on the changes obtained. Indeed, this frame of mind is an integral part of an effective partnership with the therapist. This working relationship consists of the patient's acute sense of his own complicity in his discomforts, as well as his optimism about his own and the therapist's capacity to bring about change, complemented by comparable feelings on the therapist's part. There is a reasonable mutuality of positive feeling for each other, and the patient finds it both reasonable and possible to engage in the therapeutic work that the therapist requires.

Direct evidence that patient and therapist expectations, individually and in interaction, influence outcome is remarkably spotty, considering the almost self-evident importance of these factors and the large number of indirect data testifying to their reality. Heine and Trosman (1960), sampling new referrals to an outpatient clinic, found that those who continued in treatment beyond 6 weeks were more likely to anticipate an active collaborating role than those who discontinued and were more likely to see their problems as involving behavior change rather than medical or diagnostic information. On the other hand, degree of conviction that treatment would help was unrelated to duration. These results elaborated on the finding of Gliedman et al. (1957) that patients whose reasons for seeking therapy were congruent with the expectations of their therapists were more likely to remain in treatment. Goldstein (1960) found that only therapists' expectations of change were significantly related to duration, and that both sets of expectations were unrelated to the patient's report of improvement. Goldstein and Shipman (1961), as mentioned previously, did find a positive but curvilinear correlation between patient expectancy and report of improvement. In addition, they found that the favorableness (optimism?) of the therapist's attitude toward psychology and psychiatry correlated positively with patient-perceived improvement. Taking the interaction of patient and therapist attitude into account did not add any further information. Krause's (1967, 1968) investigations in a social work setting of motivations for treatment offer evidence that clarification of the presenting problem, the benefits sought, and the costs of treatment influences continuance. Thus there is a dearth of systematic evidence of independent observation of patient improvement as a function of patient or therapist expectations. There is, however, experimental evidence, reviewed below, that procedures designed to socialize the patient for his therapeutic role and to manipulate his expectations do influence the process and the outcome, independently evaluated.

Several investigations (Chance, 1959; Appel, 1960; Lennard & Bernstein, 1960) provide evidence that expectations influence the process. They point up the fact that discomforts are created and corrective processes are stimulated when there are discrepancies in the role expectancies of the partners in the therapeutic enterprise. Lennard and Bernstein (1960), who conducted by far the most searching study, found that such discrepancies were accompanied by increased focus on the working relationship and by evidence of strain in communication.

Socialization and Manipulation

By far the greatest impact of the examination of expectancies has been its stimulation of a sociological and social-psychological view of the therapeutic relationship. The client or patient enters a therapist-dominated culture. The therapist, supported by his fellow therapists and by his previous experience with patients, has a clearly developed mode of response predicated on particular norms of patient response. Because his own sense of certainty as to what he is about requires that the patient play a certain role in their partnership, the therapist must be concerned with socializing the patient to the reciprocal demands of his role (Lennard, 1962; Orne & Wender, 1968). Furthermore, convinced of the importance of patient faith for outcome, the therapist turns his attention toward influencing that faith by manipulating his own attractiveness and authority.

An early practical response was to offer group therapy, with revolving membership consisting of those on the waiting list, as a means of inducting patients into therapy (Dibner et al., 1963). Dibner and his associates found that patients who received this kind of preparation remained in individual therapy longer. In the intervening period questions regarding modes of socializing and their effects have been expanded and refined. The different modes of socialization tried have included an anticipatory interview (Orne & Wender, 1968), a client model, presented through either a video-audio tape of an interview (Truax & Carkhuff, 1967) or a programmed learning text (Parrino, 1971), and explanatory statements offered during the course of treatment (Blanchard, 1970).

The most thorough naturalistic studies of the effect of socialization processes have been made by Frank and his associates of the Phipps Clinic of Johns Hopkins (Hoehn-Saric et al., 1964; Nash et al., 1965) and by Truax and his collaborators (Truax & Carkhuff, 1965b; Truax & Wargo, 1969; Truax, Wargo, & Volksdorf, 1970). Using a preliminary "role induction interview" inspired by Orne and Wender (1968), the Hopkins group demonstrated that neurotic outpatients who received this interview attended treatment more faithfully, were judged more improved by their therapists, and were independently rated higher in social effectiveness than controls lacking this special treatment. In addition, these patients rated themselves more improved than the controls with regard to the symptoms selected as the targets of therapy. In addition to this evidence of greater improvement, ratings by independent observers and by the therapist indicated that the experimental patients offered fewer relationship difficulties and conformed more closely to role expectations than the control patients. The more experienced the therapist, the greater were the effects of socialization. Whereas the Hopkins group was concerned with individual therapy, the Truax group tested the usefulness of a socialization process for group therapy as applied to hospitalized, largely psychotic patients, to outpatients, largely neurotic, and to institutionalized juvenile delinquents. Their socialization procedure consisted of presenting a 30-minute tape recording of "good" patient therapy behavior. Using changes on the MMPI as a criterion, these investigators found that hospitalized and neurotic patients given such prior orientation profited by it, but that the institutionalized delinquents did not. Emphasizing the need for socialization for lower-class patients, Heitler (1971) demonstrated the usefulness of a role induction interview in furthering the working relationship. For a Veterans Administration hospitalized population consisting largely of patients classified as social classes IV and V, observations of group therapy demonstrated that patients prepared by the socialization interview, as compared to controls, exhibited lower time latencies for voluntary participation, communicated more frequently and at greater length, and generally tended to engage in more self-initiated self-exploratory efforts.

Although a number of analogue studies have been stimulated by the foregoing naturalistic research, they have tended to lack convergence. There has, for example, been no systematic effort to compare the relative effectiveness of different methods of socialization. Especially glaring is the absence of a thoroughgoing study of carefully developed socialization as a feature of the ongoing relationship. This would need to be further subdivided into socialzation by therapist example, socialization by delineating and clarifying expected patient roles and explaining their significance for reaching the mutually shared goal, and socialization by differential reinforcement. Jourard and Jaffee (1970) illustrate one aspect of such research by showing that greater interviewer self-disclosure was accompanied by greater subject self-disclosure. Powell's (1968) analogue study points up the fact that interviewer self-disclosure can function as a reinforcement rather than as a model, but evidence that classes of response other than those reinforced also increased suggests the possibility that something other than either modeling or reinforcement was taking place. Since self-disclosure is seen as a psychological process intimately associated with freedom from psychopathology (Jourard, 1964), Heller (1969) makes a germane comment that needed research on modeling must "specify why those in need of psychological help have not been able to profit from observing the behavior of others before entering psychotherapy. If observational learning is so widespread in our society, why are patients unable to resolve their difficulties on their own by observing the adequate solutions of others?" (p. 524). This comment gives further significance to Heller's emphasis on the need for clinical trials to test the clinical relevance of analogue research on modeling.

Within the framework of the use of models to prepare clients or patients for therapy, a number of investigators have employed analogues to examine the effects of several conditions and to compare modeling with other preparatory procedures. Myrick (1969) sought to compare an audio versus a video presentation with a control of no presentation of a model. Although he reports an order of effects which finds audio greater than video, and this in turn greater than no model, on amount of self-reference, little confidence can be placed in his finding, considering his willingness to reject the null hypothesis with a p value of .25. Spiritas and Holmes (1971) found that sex of the model operated independently of preparation as an effect on the duration of female subjects' responses, but only preparation influenced revealingness. Studies by Heller and his students (Heller, 1968b) suggest that modeling procedures are more effective than verbal reinforcement in eliciting and sustaining self-disclosure. Whalen's (1969) demonstration that a filmed model had to be accompanied by detailed verbal instructions to elicit interpersonal openness in a small group situation raises the question of the participation of cognitive elements in preparation for therapy. The question of the role that cognitive factors play is further underlined by the showing of Marcia, Rubin, & Efran (1969) that phobias about snakes and spiders can be modified as well by expectancy manipulation (explanation, authority, faked evidence of change) as by desensitization.

There is a discernible, though sometimes fine, line between preparing the patient for psychotherapy and engaging in manipulations designed to influence his progress. Taking off from emphases on the social influence view of the psychotherapeutic dyad (Goldstein, Heller, & Sechrest, 1966; Goldstein, 1966), Strong (1968) seems to be suggesting that such perceived characteristics of the therapist as his status, attractiveness, and reputation for expertness or trustworthiness be brought under the therapist's control, that is, manipulated. In fact, a number of investigators have sought to demonstrate that these factors will influence counseling or psychotherapy, albeit, thus far, in an analogue situation. Undergraduates listening to recordings formed more positive impressions of therapists to whom higher status was ascribed (Price & Iverson, 1969). Greenberg (1969) found that undergraduates reacting to a tape of simulated therapy were influenced in their feelings of attraction and receptivity to influence by prior sets regarding the therapist's warmth and expertness. Set regarding warmth appeared more potent than that regarding expertness. Two experiments (Hartley, 1969; Strong & Schmidt, 1970) have demonstrated that credibility can be manipulated, but Strong and Schmidt did not get much of an effect and used this weak effect to account for their failure to find that trustworthiness influenced self-evaluation. In a similar analogue, this time manipulating interviewer attractiveness, Schmidt and Strong (1971) demonstrated an effective manipulation, but found that attractiveness also showed little effect on self-evaluation.

A recently published report of a research program under Goldstein's leadership (Goldstein, 1971) underlines the gap here between the effects of manipulations when studied in analogues versus naturalistic conditions. The Syracuse group tried to test the degree to which the attractiveness of the therapist and the patient's willingness to engage in therapeutic self-disclosing behavior could be influenced by manipulating the patient's set regarding the therapist's warmth, expertise, and effectiveness. In addition, they examined the influence of models, role playing, and therapist-patient status distances. Their main interest was in comparing college student and adult patient populations, the latter mostly lower class, less well educated, and less intelligent. They found striking differences in the effectiveness of their manipulations, the college population being more responsive. It happened, however, that in the one instance where the college subjects were in fact clients seeking psychotherapy for neurotic problems the results of the manipulation for attractiveness were less clear cut. On the other hand, as already noted, the patient population was marked by negative results. This suggests the possibility that patient populations, especially when in actual psychotherapy, may not be influenced by the same means as nonpatient subjects.

THE WORKING ALLIANCE

Perhaps the best way to synthesize the foregoing concerns with social influences and the previously described questions about the basic therapeutic situation is to focus on the working alliance between the patient and the therapist. Through conceptual explication and empirical investigation, we should direct attention to the ways in which the working relationship evolves and the consequences of different patterns. Most of the ideas and research discussed in this chapter become organized, then, under the set of headings outlined below.

Clarification of the Contract

The necessity of explaining the difficulties that brought him into psychotherapy, plus the impact of the therapist's views, modifies and inevitably enlarges the patient's ideas of the goals toward which he will work. In a sense, this mutual agreement regarding goals is never static, but always undergoing change. A patient's quest for therapy is precipitated, for example, by his increasing sense of his inability to attain satisfying intimate relationships or by a feeling of having reached the end of his rope in his anxieties and fears regarding relationships with supervisors and other authoritative persons. His initial concentration is on these target symptoms. The therapist's experience and theoretical commitments lead him to expect connections between these targets and other problematic aspects of the patient's behavior and experience. Accordingly, the two of them engage in an exploratory period of testing each other to establish a mutual understanding of aims, methods of work, and time, effort, and money to be expended. Therapists, whether governed by personal predilection or theoretical orientation, may be expected to differ in the amount of time and attention they give to the establishment of such an initial understanding and the explicitness with which it is treated (Menninger, 1958; Greenson, 1967). When therapeutic work occurs over an extended time, conditions are likely to arise calling for modifications in this mutual understanding that I call the *therapeutic contract*. Observation of this aspect of the working alliance is not confined to the initiating phases of therapy.

The Working Situation

Within the terms of the working alliance and as a feature of the therapeutic contract, the therapist specifies certain modes of work, which were discussed earlier in this chapter under the general heading "The Psychotherapeutic Situation." Here we are concerned with the impact of the different kinds of tasks that the therapist sets and the ways in which he sets them. To what extent must patients be taught the skills that the performance of these tasks requires? Are there certain traits that are prerequisites to being able to learn these skills? To what extent does a particular task require the adoption of particular sets, or the attainment of certain understandings? How different or similar are the tasks that accompany the applications of alternative theories of psychotherapy?

Development and Variations in the Integrity of the Relationship

If we do assume that therapeutic work entails a personal relationship, then the heart of the working alliance resides in the bonds that mark this relationship. To what extent are they marked on the patient's side by sets created by his past experience, culturally or socially defined, or artificially created either by referral or entrance procedures? Here I would include studies that have dealt with efforts to influence the patient's feelings of trust and confidence and attraction to the therapist. Research must be directed toward the question of how robust are the effects of such setting factors against the impact of considerable direct and intimate experience in the actual relationship. In other words, what is the relative strength of earned as compared to manipulated feelings of trust, faith, and attraction?

Examination of the earned or developed bonds in the working relationship takes us into areas that will be covered in two later chapters, when I consider the personality of the therapist and that of the patient as determining factors in psychotherapy. Primitive observation suggests the truism that persons differ in the kind and strength of the relationships they establish and in the types of persons to whom they can relate. For the person experiencing emotional difficulties, of whatever type or origin, there arise feelings of vulnerability, self-distrust, self-criticism, and concern for self-esteem, all of which may be expected to require certain complementary reactions on the part of the helper if he is to be able to enter into an effective working relationship. This would be one way to view the accumulating evidence (Rogers et al., 1967; Truax & Carkhuff, 1967) that therapist empathy, respect, and genuineness influence the effectiveness of psychotherapy. Raush and I (1957) have suggested that the degree to which the therapist is willing to commit his time and, especially, resources for those the patient lacks or is temporarily unable to use represents an important ingredient in the formation and maintenance of the working relationship. At least one inquiry (Williams, 1959) found that client-centered therapists typically offered less commitment than psychoanalytically oriented ones. Since very few patients and therapists were represented in this study, however, this difference may be a sampling artifact. Elsewhere (Bordin, 1965b), I have proposed that the amount of commitment by the therapist necessary to facilitate a working relationship will differ according to the amount and configuration of conflicts over dependency experienced by the patient.

One approach for clarifying the significant features for personality change in psychotherapy is to focus attention on the influence of the basic setting in which psychotherapy takes place. Most psychotherapists have assumed that their influence must be mediated through a personal relationship, but empirical demonstration of this has thus far been scarce and results have been mixed. The question of personality-impersonality must be further broken down to determine whether its influence is to be understood in terms of ambiguity-stimulus deprivation, ambiguity-uncertainty, or impersonality as mechanized processing.

There is accumulated evidence that uncertainty, probably interacting with lack of trust or outright distrust, retards the expression of openness and spontaneous self-examination. But the influence of sensory deprivations on the psychic processes of self-experience and self-examination is only just beginning to be examined. Much more research is needed on the interaction of degree of self-disclosure by the therapist and the characteristics of the task he sets on the patient's behavior and experience in therapy.

Apart from the personality characteristics of the patient, which will be considered later, research must be concerned with estimating the effects of prior conditioning and setting factors on the patient's response to psychotherapy. Although the direct evidence is less than clear cut, there is strong indirect evidence that a patient's expectations influence the ease with which he enters into the patient role and his rate of improvement. The strongest evidence for this comes from demonstrations that the process and the outcome of individual and group therapy can be facilitated by preparatory socializing measures. Relatively little is known about the comparative effectiveness of alternative preparatory measures and, especially, about the value of socialization within the process through the building of a working alliance, as compared to preparation before entering the relationship.

Beyond obvious indications that patients are initially influenced by cues reflecting on their therapist's expertness, authority, attractiveness, and credibility, it is not yet apparent how research on the manipulatability of such features can be applied in psychotherapy.

CHAPTER 6

Therapeutic Intervention and the Change Process

Chapter 2 directed attention to the kinds and levels of change in behavior and experience that psychotherapy seeks and that therefore are most appropriately used as evidence of effectiveness. The inherent continuity of observations within psychotherapy with those outside and after psychotherapy was emphasized. Chapter 2 also examined the problems of translating this inherent continuity into a demonstration and understanding of what changes as a result of psychotherapy. Having in Chapter 5 reviewed the influence of setting factors on how changes come about, I intend at this point to analyze our present state of knowledge of the effects of therapeutic interventions and to highlight the important questions that challenge our insight and ingenuity.

TAXONOMY OF THE CHANGE PROCESS

As many have argued, to be fully validated a theory and its associated pattern of psychotherapy must be able to articulate the kinds of actions of the therapist, whether verbal or nonverbal, intended as communications or as spontaneous expressions, which interact wtih patient actions or expressions to mediate the succession of changes culminating in the enduring patient behavior and experience sought as an end product. In other words, we cannot escape the necessity of dealing in detail with the events occurring during the patient's and therapist's time with each other.

The terms of that detailed observation will be derived from the particular orientation adopted by the investigator. Dollard and Auld (1959), for example, developed a scoring system for interviews based on a psychoanalytic view of behavior. Since this view emphasizes the motivational sources, especially the unconscious ones, of behavior and experience, their observations concentrate on inferences regarding such motives as sex, love, dependency, anxiety, and hostility, as drawn from the verbal communications of patients. Their psychoanalytic view of the change process leads them to choose further categories of patient behavior geared to the task of free association. These include associations and other communications that represent confirmations of interpretations and interferences (i.e., resistances) with the work of therapy, which, more than anything else, consists of seeking to comply with the rule of free association. Similarly, their categories for therapist behavior include responses judged to raise patient motivation, reduce tension, thereby rewarding, label, connect, or discriminate (i.e., interpret), and, symmetrically with resistance, responses which interfere with therapeutic progress and are, therefore, errors.

The greatest contrast to the terms employed in the psychoanalytic view of the change process is to be found in the portion of behavior therapy research that stems from the operant conditioning view (Sherman & Baer, 1969). More than any other group, the operant conditioners are concerned with what people do, not what they think, feel, or wish. Hence analysis of the change process becomes a recording of selected target behaviors, for example, the emission of self-references, frequencies of communication with children or adults, occurrences of stuttering, stammering, or other nonfluencies in speech. The behavior of the change agent is classified in terms of negative or positive reinforcement. The other prominent behavior therapy method, desensitization, is marked by a greater willingness to employ experiential classifications. To begin with, anxiety is held to be the central source of the difficulties that bring patients to psychotherapy, and the therapeutic process is designed to reduce the experience of this feeling in the troubling situations. The typical process involves visualization of versions of the troubling situation, arranged in a hierarchy of ascending anxiety. Thus a central feature of the change process becomes the patient's reports of anxiety as the therapist assigns situations to be visualized after the induction of a relaxed state. Studies of desensitization under actual field or comparable controlled conditions have not usually subjected the process to detailed examination. Instead the main emphasis has been on the end product. Lang (1969) has been the main source of studies examining the mechanics of the desensitization process. For the most part he has pursued the strategy of experimental controls of such factors as the therapist and the therapeutic relationship, and the roles of hypnosis and relaxation. He has reviewed the work of others bearing on experimental extinction and cognitive sets as explanations of the desensitization process.

As client-centered theory has evolved, observations of client behavior have concentrated on the quality of experiencing, which would seem to overlap considerably with ideas about the psychic process of free association. In deep levels both of experiencing and of free association the patient is open to the flow of thoughts and feelings being generated by either inner or outer stimulation, and is able to experience them without distortion and to use them in his behavior and report (cf. Rogers, 1969b; Bordin, 1966c). The client-centered emphasis on the atmospheric effects of therapists' attitudes has led to the development of scales for rating therapist genuineness and his regard for the patient. The work of the therapist is captured in the accuracy and sensitivity of his understanding. For the most part accurate empathy is relegated, together with genuineness and regard, into a view of the change process as being governed solely by atmosphere, rather than assigning effects to specific interventions (Rogers et al., 1967).

As I pointed out in Chapter 3, there are infinite sets of observations of process that can be defined by shifting from linguistic to paralinguistic to kinetic levels and from shifts within these levels, by selecting out particular contents (e.g., Strupp, 1957; Freedman et al., 1951; Leary & Gill, 1959; Ekman & Friesen, 1968). There have been relatively few efforts to examine how interwoven are various systems of process observation. The most thorough empirical study thus far reported (Mintz, Luborsky, & Auerback, 1971) included virtually none of the kinds of observations used by behavior therapists, but did sample a number of client-centered and humanistically oriented attributes. The largest number were drawn from the psychoanalytic framework. Fifteen experienced therapists, predominantly psychoanalytically or eclectically oriented, contributed 2 successive early interviews recorded with each of 2 patients. Starting with 110 patient and therapist variables, this research group used a rough method of examining correlations to reduce the number to 19 clusters and 8 single items, divided into 19 therapist and 8 patient variables. A factor analysis of these 27 measures for the 60 interviews resulted in four principal factors, three of them representing therapeutic modes and the fourth representing a broad evaluative dimension applied to the patient.

The factor accounting for the largest variance was labeled "optimal empathic relationship and included such standard client-centered variables as acceptance and empathy. "Therapist fast speech tempo," which was also included, may correspond to the attribute of genuineness stressed in client-centered views. But this factor also includes therapist reassurance and warmth and the rater's liking of the therapist's calm nonjudgmentalness, as well as ratings of expertness embodied in such characteristics as perceptiveness, security, and skill.

The second factor in the triumvirate reflecting therapeutic mode was identified as "directive mode." In addition to including that variable, it encompassed ratings of activity, experiential approach, intrusiveness, therapist interpretations and impact, hostile defensiveness, and creativity. Of interest is the fact that this study, unlike that of Sundland and Barker

(1962), found therapist activity, intrusiveness, and interpretation at the same pole as experiential approach. When Sundland and Barker asked psychotherapists to select statements descriptive of their practices or attitudes, they found a general bipolar factor with the experiential and analytic items at opposite poles. Whether the differences between the results of Sundland and Barker and those of Mintz et al. reflect the difference between what therapists report and what they do or involve different interpretations of "experiential" is difficult to determine.[1] There are no clearly evident differences in definition to support the latter explanation, but the similarity of the formal definition does not preclude differences among raters and therapists.

The third treatment mode seemed to identify the core of the change process as captured in this sample of interviews. This factor was labeled "interpretive mode with receptive patient" and was the only treatment factor in which there was appreciable participation of patient variables. The two variables most heavily loaded on this factor were patient receptiveness, defined as an opposite to resistiveness, and a six-item composite including therapist interpretive activity and its impact on the patient. Other heavily loaded variables were therapist perceptiveness and focus on transference and patient hostility to others. Since the methods of analysis cannot disentangle sequence issues (i.e., whether it is the patient's behavior that is influencing therapist response or vice versa), these data cannot be taken as clear evidence supporting this view of the change process. Some weak undermining evidence, moreover, is offered by the fact that the therapists' ratings of success and patient satisfaction, although correlated with the sex of the patient (females were more successful and satisfied), with ratings of patient health versus distress, and with patient hostility to others, were unrelated to therapeutic mode. Although the outcome measure has many limitations, it cannot be completely discounted.

It is of interest that McNair and Lorr (1964a), working with extensions of the Sundland-Barker approach, also found three therapeutic technique factors: psychoanalytically oriented techniques, emphasizing interpretive activity directed toward resistance, unconscious motives, and understanding the influence of the past; impersonal versus personal affective approaches to the patient, in which items ranging from detachment to spontaneity predominate in bipolar loadings; and directive, active therapeutic methods, also bipolar, featuring the therapist versus the patient setting

---

[1] There is, of course, the alternative explanation that different therapists and/or patient samples were involved. This may be so, but Mintz and Luborsky (1970) found essentially the same results in a P-technique factor analysis of a single case of client-centered therapy.

treatment goals. On the other hand, Wallach and Strupp (1964) somewhat precariously, because only 17 items were involved, extracted six factors, of which they identified four. "Maintaining personal distance" and "keeping verbal interventions at a minimum" seem related but not identical to the technique issues highlighted by the other studies. The other two factors, "preference for intensive therapy" and "psychotherapy seen as art," have more to do with attitudes than technique.

A project headed by Howard and Orlinsky concentrated on the subjective experiences of therapist and patient. At the end of each of at least eight consecutive sessions, 60 patients, all women, and 19 therapists, 8 of them women, were asked to respond to a therapy report form designed to elicit information on the content of the dialogue, feeling process, therapeutic relationship, exchange, and session development. One analysis of these data (Howard, Orlinsky, & Hill, 1969) related the therapist's feelings to the patient's experience in 28 cases with highly suggestive results. Striking differences are observed in the feeling responses of male and female therapists to this set of female patients. Whereas male therapists were largely unaffected at points where the patient is reporting "intrusive dependence with embarrassed tense therapist," the female therapists showed a marked tendency *not* to feel "nurturant warmth," *not* to be "feeling good," and *not* to feel "uneasy intimacy." Both male and female therapists gave marked affective responses to erotic transference resistance but in different and sometimes opposite ways. The males tended to feel "disturbing sexual arousal" and *not* to be "feeling good." The females tended very strongly to feel "uneasy intimacy" and, in lesser degree, to be "feeling good" and to feel "resigned," "nurturant warmth," and *not* "suffering." When the patient is reporting "courting the rejecting therapist," the female therapist tended *not* to be "feeling good," *not* to feel "nurturant warmth," and to feel a "sense of failure." The male therapists reported little more than a feeling of "disturbing sexual arousal."

Another study of subjective experience (Lorr, 1965) relied solely on the patient's report at single points during the process of treatment, varying from 3 months to no more than 10 years, thereby providing only inferential evidence bearing on the change process. Since the 523 patient respondents were drawn from 43 Veterans Administration outpatient clinics, we can assume that this study reflects primarily a male patient's view. Lorr identified six factors in analyzing the intercorrelation matrix of 65 items descriptive of therapist behaviors. Three of the factors, "understanding," "accepting," and "independence-encouraging," were positively related to the patient's ratings of improvement and satisfaction and the therapist's rating of improvement, but the effect of the last of these was negligible. Two other factors, "authoritarian" and "critical-hostile," were, not unexpectedly, negatively associated with the criterion ratings, but at low levels, close to zero in the case of the therapist's improvement rating. The sixth factor, "acceptance," corresponded very closely to the by now familiar "accurate empathy" attribute. "Accepting" seemed to be a broad factor with interest, nurturance, and egalitarianism appearing to play equal roles.

It would be illuminating to apply the terms of the change process to examples of the work of highly experienced proponents of specific forms of psychotherapy. So far, there have been three efforts to compare well known practitioners, but all of these have been confined to comparisons of therapeutic style rather than more encompassing comparisons of the change process. The oldest of these studies, by Strupp (1957), was more limited in that many aspects of Gestalt and behavior therapies were unrepresented. Analyzing a published case each by Wolberg and Rogers, Strupp used seven categories of therapeutic activity and five of dynamic focus, the latter referring to whether the therapist "goes along" with the patient or introduces a different focus. In addition he rated therapist responses for degrees of inference, initiative, and warmth. The two therapists, as might be expected because they had published the cases for illustrative purposes, differed in ways that mirrored the differences in their recommendations with regard to technique. Wolberg varied his intervention over the course of therapy, using the full range and more of an external focus, more initiative, and greater inference. Rogers steadily confined himself to clarifications from an internal frame of reference, with limited inference and initiative.[2]

Films of interviews by Rogers, Perls, and Ellis with the same patient provide the basis for data in the other two studies, in which the results are less fully determined by prior selection on the therapists's part. Both Shostrom and Riley (1968) and Zimmer and Pepyne (1971) sought sets of ratings designed to reflect the full range of therapeutic styles. On an armchair basis, Shostrom and Riley arrived at 10 attributes on which therapists were to be rated: caring, ego strengthening, encountering, fostering feeling, interpersonal analyzing, pattern analysis, reinforcing, self-disclosing, value reorienting, and fostering re-experiencing of past learnings. Rogers and Perls presented a somewhat similar profile to the extent that ego strengthening, encountering, and fostering feeling were prominent in both styles. They were most clearly different (no statistical tests of significance are offered) in regard to caring, where Rogers was rated as manifesting more, and interpersonal analyzing and reinforcing, where Perls was rated higher. Raters found it more difficult to rate Ellis distinctly in terms of these attributes. Most characteristic of him was pattern analysis

---

[2] Not enough nonneutral ratings of warmth could be obtained to warrant analysis.

and value reorienting. None of the three was rated as markedly self disclosing or as different from the others in this respect. The same was true of fostering re-experiencing, but this may have been an artifact of the limited situation.

Zimmer and Pepyne (1971), seeking for a set of variables that would cut across theoretical orientations, defined 31 classes of counselor response, which on factor analysis reduced to six items, providing a basis for differentiating the three therapists. One of the six, interrogating, represented by probes and rhetorical questions, showed no differences. Rogers differed from Ellis in being more passive in structuring and less given to rational analysis; Rogers and Perls differed on all counts. Perls was even less prone to rational analyzing than Rogers, less prone to passive structuring, and less inclined toward summarizing and reconstructing, but considerably more likely to press or even command specific patient responses and to confront. Interestingly, Ellis and Perls differed only in the former's greater use of rational analysis.

ATMOSPHERIC INFLUENCES ON CHANGE

As was suggested above in discussing client-centered views of the change process, change need not be attributed to specific interventions but can be connected to broad, enduring conditions of the therapeutic relationship. Perhaps the experience of energetic optimism in a helper is sufficient to release and facilitate self-corrective forces. This idea certainly makes contact with some of our experiences. Similarly, at other times, we have had experiences of the calming and facilitating effects of the gentle, steady, low-keyed helper. Is the psychotherapist's contribution to the change process a function of such general attributes as friendliness, liking and interest in patient, tempo, and general active or passive stance?

There has been a tendency to group such factors under the heading of "warmth." The facilitating conditions of accurate empathy, acceptance, and genuineness stressed by client-centered theory have customarily been subsumed under this heading. But not everyone has treated warmth as an atmospheric variable. Although identifying a set of attributes similar to the client-centered triad, Raush and Bordin (1957) spoke in terms of modulations of these influences, depending on the nature of the patient. For example, they suggested that with certain kinds of patients (e.g., paranoid or otherwise distrustful ones), the therapist's efforts to understand run the risk of being experienced as threatening and even intolerable intrusiveness. Similarly, although they would concede that the therapist's spontaneity surely serves a general function, perhaps comparable to genuineness, of facilitating growth in therapy, they suggested that the sensitive therapist will naturally dampen his spontaneity in response to the impulsive patient or one who is momentarily fighting a desperate battle with poorly integrated impulses, where stampeding him into impulse expression will not be therapeutic. One of the Raush-Bordin attributes of "warmth," commitment, is distinctly different from the client-centered set. These authors define commitment as a therapist's willingness to offer his resources as substitutes for those that the patient lacks or is momentarily unable to use. These resources can range from time to the imposition of controls as temporary substitutes for self-control. The range and sequence of the appropriate level of commitment will differ between overtly dependent and counterdependent persons and with the level of anxiety about dependence (Bordin, 1965b).

Empirical Evaluations of Warmth

However defined, warmth seems to be well established as a significant feature of the therapeutic relationship. Strupp, Wallach, & Wogan (1964) found that a patient's sense of the amount he had changed during psychotherapy was closely linked to his estimate of the therapist's warmth and the latter's respect and interest. By far the majority of direct studies of therapist warmth have relied on ratings of accurate empathy, respect, and genuineness, as defined by client-centered therapists. Research at Wisconsin (Rogers et al., 1967; Truax & Carkhuff, 1967; Van Der Veen, 1967; Truax, 1970a; Kiesler, 1971), at Johns Hopkins (Truax, Wargo, et al., 1966a, 1966b), and at Kentucky (Truax, Wargo, & Silber, 1966; Truax, Wargo, & Volksdorf, 1970) has produced consistent evidence that these three attributes are related, albeit weakly, to rated, self-report, and test measures of improvement and to the level of self-exploration exhibited during the process. Thus we seem to have for the first time a more definitive basis for establishing a clear effect of psychotherapy than can be provided by gross tabulations of studies, varying drastically in severity and type of presenting problems, methods of treatment, training and commitments of therapists, and criteria of change (Eysenck, 1952, 1965; Levitt, 1957; Meltzoff & Kornreich, 1970). The latter kinds of investigations, no matter how well intentioned, become parades of our ignorance clothed in scientism. In such shotgun surveys the special understandings attained by various groups of therapists are pretty much canceled out in a process which maximizes the error variance and overloads the dice in favor of the acceptance of a null hypothesis that is in fact false (i.e., the conclusion of no effect).

At the same itme, I find much ground for uneasiness about the evidence for the effects of client-centered-defined warmth. The small amount of variance accounted for opens the door to the possibility of hidden factors which would change our perspective on the meaning of the results. How are we to understand these three attributes: accurate empathy, respect, and genuineness? In most studies, they are found to intercorrelate to the extent permitted by their respective reliabilities, giving rise to the suspicion that perhaps in fact only one attribute is being captured in the rating process, a conclusion reached by Muehberg, Pierce, and Drasgow (1969). After a factor analysis revealed one factor with loadings roughly equivalent to the reliabilities of the ratings, this set of investigators suggested a "good guy" label for the trait. Yet in two investigations, genuineness was negatively correlated with empathy and respect. With regard to one of these (Truax, Carkhuff, & Kodman, 1965), Truax and Carkhuff (1967) suggest that "when two conditions of the therapeutic triad are highly related but the third is negatively related, the prediction of outcome should be based on the two that are most highly related" (p. 92). But Garfield and Bergin (1971), who also obtained a negative correlation between genuineness and the other two, found that neither of the two positively correlated ratings nor the negatively correlated one showed other than a chance relationship to a range of outcome measures.

Any careful reader of Rogers must conclude that he sees these three therapeutic stances as deeply laid attitudes, perhaps functionally interrelated, and certainly not as skin-level masks to be worn or dropped at the therapist's whim. How can this view be compatible with studies in which the conditions are manipulated experimentally (Truax & Carkhuff, 1965a; Pierce, Carkhuff, & Berenson, 1967; Holder, Carkhuff, & Berenson, 1967)? In these investigations, the effects of successive periods of offering high and low levels of the facilitating conditions on the depth of self-exploration by patients, in one instance, and by experimental subjects, in the other two, were demonstrated. Surely, if such results are taken seriously, we must find a contradiction between the view of these therapeutic ingredients inherent in the theory and the empirical view provided by the particular methods of assessment. Truax (1966c) has, in fact, suggested and even demonstrated that Rogers and other client-centered therapists respond differently to their clients, depending on the level of self-exploration being exhibited, and that the therapeutic ingredients represent interpersonal rewards offered as reinforcements of this kind of patient or client behavior. This is, of course, no more than behavior therapists have been claiming and demonstrating in laboratory studies (cf. Krasner, 1962). With remarkable resiliency, Truax has taken such demonstrations as evidence of the compatibility of client-centered and behavior theory. I think it is self-deluding to overlook the fact that a differential offering of warmth is the definition of an evaluative relationship, one that offers rewards or punishments (at the very least, withholding of rewards) on a basis decided by someone other than the client. Be that as it may, the contention has attracted both independent confirmation and disconfirmation, the differences being attributable, perhaps, to differences in procedures. Vitalo (1970), using a Taffel-type sentence construction task, demonstrated conditioning and extinction effects for experimenters, preselected on the basis of their work as therapists as being high on the three warmth variables, and no conditioning and extinction effects for low experimenters. Namenek and Schuldt (1971) found an effect for high and low experimenters for rate of emission of words belonging to the response class "human," in a Greenspoon type of interview situation, but the growth curve departed from the normal curve of learning in showing a marked decrement during the middle phase of the learning period. Waskow (1962), using a situation simulating therapy more closely than in the preceding two studies, found that selective reinforcement influenced expression of content but did not affect expression of feeling.

Traux's (1966b) failure to demonstrate that removal of access to the client's communications influences ratings has led to strong critiques of his interpretations of the construct validity of accurate empathy ratings (Chinsky & Rappaport, 1970). Although his counterargument that raters were making use of the sequential order of the therapist's responses to infer features of the excised client communications may have some validity (Truax, 1972), this remains to be demonstrated. Moreover, I must agree with the retort of Rappaport and Shinsky (1972) that ratings based on such slender and inferential observations must be very susceptible to the influence of purely verbal stylistic communication patterns, citing evidence from Truax (1970b) and Caracena and Vicory (1969) that accurate empathy ratings were positively related to the number of words spoken by the therapist and the proportion of the therapist-client conversation spoken by the therapist.

One group of investigators has taken a somewhat different approach to assessing a factor closely associated with genuineness: the vividness of the therapist's expressive style in client-centered interviews. Looking at three characteristics: (a) freshness of words and word combinations, (b) voice quality, and (c) functional level—whether focused on inner or outer view, Rice (1965) demonstrated a tendency for therapists manifesting generally high levels of all three characteristics to show more favorable therapeutic outcomes. A later study (Duncan, Rice, & Butler, 1968), using purer paralinguistic indices, compared "peak" and "poor" treatment hours, selected as such by nine therapists. Each therapist was asked to submit one of each type of interview, representing different clients. Each therapist was left free to use his or her own criteria, but informal comments suggested that "peak" and "poor" corresponded to the identification of interviews where therapy generally was proceeding successfully and unsuccessfully. Three patterns of paralinguistic behavior were identified through factor analysis, one being descriptive of peak interviews, the other two of poor interviews. Rice and Wagstaff (1967) turned attention to the voice quality and expressive stance of clients as features of the process, expressive stance being much more linked to content; for example, one category was defined as "objective analysis and description (of self)." They found that by the second interview clients who agreed with their therapists in reporting considerable change could be differentiated in voice quality and expressive stance from those for whom the agreement was to a conclusion of minimal or no change. Moreover, attrition could be predicted even from the first interview. The results were not completely clear cut in that, when one includes groups for which the judgments of therapists and clients did not agree, the group in which clients rated themselves high while therapists rated their changes low was even lower in expressive indices than the purely low-rated groups. Nowhere in this series of investigations is there the kind of evidence that permits a decision as to whether we are dealing with factors solely reflecting the change process or atmospheric variables dictated by the personality of the therapist or client. Furthermore, I regret that Duncan et. al. did not add an analysis of client expressive style à la Rice and Wagstaff to their analysis of peak and poor hours.

EFFECTS OF RELATIONSHIP-ORIENTED INTERVENTIONS

As an alternative to the view that it is atmospheric factors that mediate change, we turn to the effects of specific interventions. First we should note that there is no automatic contradiction between these two views. It is certainly possible that both the general features of the therapeutic relationship and specific kinds of interventions play a part in the process of change. Rogers had, however, seemingly committed himself to the position that certain kinds of interventions, interpretive ones, impeded therapeutic progress. Interpretive activity, according to Rogers (1951), leads only to intellectual knowledge; "for behavior to change, a change in perception must be *experienced*" (p. 222, italics his). Moreover, diagnosis which is intimately linked to a readiness to offer interpretations inevitably engages an antitherapeutic evaluative attitude. Later, Rogers seems to have decided that therapists with theoretical orientations which embrace diagnosis and interpretation may still advocate and adopt these basic attitudes of acceptance and orientation to the client's inner experience (Rogers et al., 1967,

p. 98). Cochrane (1972) sought an empirical test of the compatibility of the diagnostic and experiential approaches, asking psychotherapists-in-training to respond in a simulated psychotherapeutic situation. Whether the subject received prior diagnostic information, couched in either psychoanalytic or experiential terms, or no information, no differences in empathic communication and inference were observed. Thus this study failed to demonstrate incompatibility, but the artificiality of the situation and the use of inexperienced therapists make for inconclusiveness.

Apart from empirical demonstration, it appears that theories of psychotherapy which emphasize relationship factors in change are not in disagreement about the importance of atmospheric factors. Even Wolpe and Lazarus (1968), writing from one viewpoint of behavior therapy, can speak of the essential role of empathy and a trustful relationship. They warn their fellow behavior therapists that they cannot do without accepting the patient or without using other similar personal influencing processes (pp. 23–29). The question, then, remains as to the kinds of interventions within a therapeutic relationship that advance the patient toward his goal.

To avoid oversimplification, we must pause for a larger look at these relationship approaches. What marks all of them is that they see the individual as caught in a fixed way of viewing and responding in relationships. Whether taking a psychoanalytic position (transference), a client-centered one (external evaluation), or a Gestalt or transactional one (interpersonal games), the therapist sees the patient as frozen into a single set of postures as a result of earlier relationships founded in his family and unresponsive to the realities of current relationships. In these approaches the conception of the goal of therapy is that the grip of these perceptual and action sets will be loosened, freeing the individual to respond realistically and in an ultmately more satisfying and meaningful fashion. He acquires this modified response to his current relationships through the experiences he has in his relationship to the therapist.

The psychoanalytic version of how the therapist intervenes to bring about change is by far the most complex of all. As was suggested in Chapter 5, it presupposes the setting conditions of the task of free association and of the working alliance. It stipulates that interpretations be centered initially around the specific effects of transference on the patient's compliance or noncompliance with his therapeutic task. The time at which interpretations are offered and the amount encompassed in any one interpretative communication are geared to the vividness of what the patient is presumed to be experiencing and to that pace of the progression of experiences which will ensure that it does not become an intellectual exercise.

Other views incline to the position that the psychoanalytic version is unnecessarily complex. As has been suggested, Rogers believes that the basic therapeutic relationship is in itself not only necessary but even sufficient for change to take place. The Gestalt and transactional therapists believe that their perspectives on the patient's present relationships allow them to concentrate on particular features of the patient's perception and experience in such a way as to truncate what in psychoanalysis is a long-drawn-out process. On the other hand, someone like Ellis (1962) simplifies to the point that only the central processes of cognition and reasoning are important, and, therefore, this view will be discussed later.

Empirical Evaluations of Effects of Interpretations

At the outset, we encounter some definitional problems. There is little doubt that the ultimate aim of psychoanalytic interpretative activity is, as Colby (1963) states, to disclose to the patient previously unnoticed or unacknowledged aspects of his behavior and experience and their causal correlation to other aspects of which he is already aware. Yet, as Loewenstein (1963) makes clear and Colby (1963) acknowledges, psychoanalysts use the term interpretation to designate any communication in which the therapist offers the patient a view of the latter's present or past behavior and experience. For example, Loewenstein labels as an interpretation his suggestion to a patient that he must have been a bad eater as a child and must have had many fights with his mother when she tried to persuade him to eat, this response being triggered by 2 months of the young man's being unable to remember anything in his life or to tell what occurred to him and finally inviting the therapist to declare that he was no longer interested in having the patient talk to him. Thus much of the psycho-analyst's interpretive activity will be indistinguishable from the client-centered therapist's reflections and, especially, his clarifications. Indeed, Levy (1963) has argued persuasively that, once their strictures against the misuse of interpretation are taken into account, psychoanalytic and client-centered therapists are alike in seeking to stimulate understandings in their patients slightly beyond those they currently possess but still within their grasp.

A moderate amount of evidence of the effects of various features of interpretive activity has accumulated. Working from a psychoanalytic framework, Colby (1961), Dittmann (1952), and Speisman (1959) have examined the influence of interpretation on therapeutic work. Using an analogue to therapeutic free association, Colby demonstrated that interventions calling attention to causal correlatives were followed by longer responses than those following interrogative inputs. Similarly, Speisman, searching actual therapeutic interviews, found that interpretations rated as slightly beyond the patient's current level of awareness were more likely to be followed by a decrease in resistence than interpretations which either fell more within or further beyond the patient's level of awareness. In an intensive analysis of interview protocols for a single case, Dittmann found that patient progress was greater in units where the therapist was responding at a level deeper than pure reflection, meaning that he was going beyond the patient's current level of awareness. An unusual feature of Dittmann's pioneering study, one which is yet to be pursued, was the beginning of a comparison of the effects of focusng on particular aspects of the patient's behavior or experience. Dittmann, distinguishing between response focuses on feeling and behavior, found greater patient progress in units where the therapist responded to both, as compared to responding to either feeling or to behavior alone.

In other studies, the outcome was not so clear cut. In an investigation exemplary for its multifactorial design, Ashley et al. (1957) compared reflective therapy, essentially client centered, with leading therapy which seemed to be a hodgepodge of interpretation, interrogation, advising, suggesting, encouraging, and didactic informing. The major evidence was for no differences for methods, except for greater tendencies of clients to respond to leading methods with more guardedness but to have been rated by the therapist as more improved. Six therapists, graduate students with some prior experience, each carried out both kinds of therapy, so that the therapist's ratings cannot be seen as simply reflecting attachment to a particular mode. An early client-centered study by Bergman (1951) compared the frequency with which client self-exploration and insight followed reflections or clarifications, as compared to structuring or interpretation. From his description it is clear that in these 10 cases from the University of Chicago Counseling Center what was classified as interpretation came most often in response to a client's request for confirmation or for suggestions as to how to continue self-exploration. Under these circumstances, interpretation becomes some positive response to that request in the form of either a suggestion or an interpretation. Bergman found that more client self-exploration and insight followed two reflection of feeling categories than either clarification or interpretation.

It is difficult to know what to make of Grossman's (1952) research, which was flawed by the experimenter being also the therapist. Grossman, admittedly biased toward a client-centered view, matched two sets of volunteers for an experiment in psychotherapy in which each received three interviews, one set marked by the therapist offering "surface" responses and the other by his offering "deep" responses. The members of the group receiving surface responses were less satisfied with the therapy and felt that the therapist placed greater responsibility on them, but followup revealed no differences between the groups in a test of self-insight.

Against his own bias, the therapist rated the deep-response group as gaining greater insight. Equally unclear as to the conclusions one may draw was Gordon's (1957) comparison of leading and following psychotherapeutic techniques in an analogue situation. Male college student volunteers were instructed under hypnosis to imagine a mildly traumatic incident and then to forget it. Following techniques were defined in terms of the client-centered categories of restating, reflecting, and clarifying; leading techniques, in terms of asking questions, making suggestions, and the like. The dependent variables were the time taken to recall the forgotten experience and the expression of hostility. Leading techniques were superior in speed of recall, but no differences in hostility were elicited. There are obvious questions about the correspondence between experimentally induced and clinical repression and the relation between experimentally defined "leading" and the central issues in clinical interpretation. Frank and Sweetland (1962) followed a tradition of categorization established by Snyder (1945), except that two categories referring to forcing insight and seeming to consist of partial interpretations were added. Contrary to Snyder, Frank and Sweetland found that clarification and interpretation were therapeutically productive. In addition, forcing insight was most productive of all.[3]

To sum up this part of the research, there appears to be a weight of evidence to support the contention that therapist interventions which seek to add something, but not too much, to the patient's awareness do facilitate patient work. Much more documentation than now exists, however, is needed to establish the connection between patient work and outcome. The best data so far have come from the client-centered group. Rogers et al. (1967) have demonstrated relationships between the client-centered process scale and more enduring external measures of outcome, such as the MMPI. Moreover, Gendlin et al. (1968) have begun the process of establishing a network of relationships between focusing ability (a form of self-exploration) and such other relevant variables as physiological indices of arousal, productivity on the TAT, personality measures taken from Cattell's inventory, and responsiveness to hidden figures.

Notice how simplified the issues have become. With few exceptions, observations are centered solely on the general character of the therapist's communications and on a specific feature of the patient's response, namely, how effectively he is working. What of the feeling aspects of the patient's

[3] Rottschafer and Renzaglia (1962) take a somewhat different tack when, after some reanalysis of their data, they offer weak evidence that counselors whose style is marked by a higher proportion of leading interventions are more likely to elicit dependent responses from their clients.

reaction? Haggard, Isaacs, and their collaborators have probably done the most so far to include a concern with affect in their studies of process (Isaacs & Haggard, 1966; Alexander & Isaacs, 1964; Garduk & Haggard, 1972). Isaacs and Haggard (1966) outline a notion of the developmental aspects of relatability, incorporating six levels of affect, which would seem to have the potential for transforming the concept of transference into process observations. In earlier studies, Dittes (1957) and McCarron and Appel (1971) had investigated the psychophysiological aspects of affect. Dittes demonstrated in the continuous record of a single patient a progressive decline in GSR accompanying embarrassing sex statements over the course of 30 interviews. McCarron and Appel also employed GSR as an index of autonomic activity in an analysis of 1 patient-therapist pair for 12 interviews and of 12 patient-therapist pairs for first interviews. They found increasing patient (and therapist) autonomic response accompanying therapist reflection, interrogation, interpretation, and confrontation, in that order. Garduk and Haggard (1972) identified psychoanalytic interpretations, further classified them as comprehensive, moderate, or limited, and distinguished them from noninterpretations. They tested 17 hypotheses about how patient responses to interpretations would differ from their responses to noninterpretations. About half of their expectations were confirmed at statistically significant levels. In response to interpretations, patients were likely to show longer reaction times, say less words and produce more periods of silence, manifest more affect, communicate less relatively factual material, offer more oppositional and defensive associations but also more understanding and insight, and deal with more transference-related material. When Garduk and Haggard compared comprehensive with moderate and limited interpretations, they found, contrary to their expectations, that moderate and limited, treated as a combined category, were followed by more expressions of anger, hostility, and aggression and by dealing with transference-related material.

Since so much of the work of psychotherapy proceeds via the patient communicating verbally to the therapist and in free association or its equivalent (the patient is specifically instructed to "say whatever comes to mind"), there is a tendency to treat silence as nonproductive therapeutic activity or as resistance. Contrary to this view, Gendlin (1958) proposed that the vivid experience of immediate feelings so necessary to therapeutic movement was likely to occur during periods of silence. Toman (1953) had earlier offered some rich speculations regarding the usefulness of a closer examination of what was occurring during pauses in interviews. Cook (1964) sought to follow up Gendlin's ideas by selecting five successful and five unsuccessful cases from a University of Chicago sample. He extended Gendlin's thinking to suggest that too little or too much silence probably indicated defensiveness. When the client's 2-minute segments of communication were rated on Rogers' process scale, Cook found that segments incorporating the middle ranges of percentage of silence were rated highest. Unfortunately no such curvilinear relationship was established between success and silence. Instead, the more successful cases were more likely to display silences in excess of 4%; the less successful ranged over lower percentages of silence.

Murray (1954) offers another example of the kinds of research that can lead to more definitive demonstrations of the effects of therapist interventions. He analyzed expressions of hostility and defense over a series of interviews in a single case and showed that interpretation of the use of physical complaints as a defense was followed by its disappearing and being replaced by intellectual defenses.

Evaluations of Confrontation and Approach-Avoidance

When one looks at therapist interventions from outside the psychoanalytic framework, other possible conceptions of significant actions by the therapist appear. In examining the therapist's behavior in offering interpretations, some have seen it more in terms of the therapist's paying attention or "approaching" some patient expression, as compared to ignoring or "avoiding" such expressions. One group has become involved in a distinction between interpretations and confrontations, which seems rather arbitrary to me. Though Perls, Hefferline & Goodman (1951) have described a series of tasks (they call them experiments) which are designed to uncover the individual's lack of contact with himself and his environment, especially the interpersonal aspects of it, there has been little or no systematic empirical examinations of these assumptions. A study by Denner (1968), in which he sought to understand the behavior of witnesses, made use of Gestalt therapy-like exercises as a way of demonstrating that individuals who need relatively more information for decision making and are more concerned with the distinction between the real and unreal are relatively more reluctant to verbalize current and possible experiences.

The distinction between interpretation and confrontation has come from two sources (Pallone & Grande, 1965; Anderson, 1969). The former distinction, used by McCarron and Appel (1971) in the study cited earlier, emphasizes the client's unawareness and the forcefulness of the therapist's presentation as characteristics of confrontation as compared to interpretation. Anderson appears to emphasize not forcefulness, but simply the therapist's introducing a new view of the client and counterposing it to the one presented by the client himself. She goes further to distinguish between constructive confrontations (directed toward bringing the client to greater awareness of his resources and strengths) and destructive confrontations (focusing on weaknesses and limitations). Later investigators (Berenson, Mitchell, & Moravec, 1968) expanded the classifications to include experiential confrontation (where the discrepancy refers to therapist's direct experience of patient as compared to patient's experience of himself), didactic confrontation (where the discrepancy revolves around factual information) and, finally, confrontations that represent encouragements to action. Most of the research thus far has been directed toward demonstrating that confrontation is a factor over and above the three client-centered atmospheric conditions in facilitating depth of self-exploration (Anderson, 1965, 1969; Berenson et al., 1968; Mitchell & Namenek, 1972). Other sets of investigations (Berenson, Mitchell, & Laney, 1968; Mitchell & Berenson, 1970; Mitchell & Hall, 1971) have sought to compare frequency and type of confrontation according to level of functioning of the therapist whether in inpatient or outpatient treatment, and according to time period in the first interview. Apart from questions about whether the distinction is another way of treating depth of interpretation, this research seems highly superficial since it is confined to single interviews and, often, to very contrived situations.

The examination of therapist interventions as approaches or avoidances has greater substance to it. It was inspired by the application of learning theory to interview processes, particularly the role assigned to reinforcement in the acquisition of response patterns. It seems reasonably clear both on commonsense and on theoretical grounds that by focusing attention and by similar devices the therapist can invite and elicit specific kinds of communications. Conversely, through ignoring and actively disapproving, the therapist can discourage and even block the appearance of specific kinds of communications. How far does this influence go? How much importance can be attached to the principle of reinforcement as a source of the acquisition and decay of habit systems, as compared to the more transitory effect of eliciting or suppressing the expression of a particular response? Murray (1968) has suggested that an overemphasis on the role of reinforcement may constitute an oversimplification of learning theory and the learning process. Murray (1956) was also the author of an early study demonstrating that categories of client response associated with clear therapist approval increased in frequency over therapy, whereas those associated with therapist disapproval decreased.

Two sets of clients' responses, dependency and hostility, were the subjects of a series of studies, some of which have tended to support Murray's charge of oversimplification. Bandura, Lipshur, and Miller (1960), concentrating on hostility, found that clients were more likely to continue with expressions of hostility after approach responses, and, in addition to being less likely to follow an avoidance response with further expression of hostility, were, if they did continue to express hostility, more likely to change the object toward which the hostility was directed. Concentrating on dependency, Winder et al. (1962) found parallel approach-avoidance effects. Since they were confining their interview samples to the first 2 sessions, it is of further interest that, in 6 of the 7 instances where the proportion of avoidance responses exceeded the proportion of approach responses, the patients left after no more than 10 sessions without the concurrent agreement of psychotherapist and supervisor. By contrast, in all 16 of the cases where the proportion of approach responses equaled or exceeded the proportion of avoidance, therapy continued beyond 20 sessions with no premature terminations.

Caracena (1965), Schuldt (1966), and Varble (1968), students of Winder, have contributed important extensions of the evidence and raised provocative questions. Caracena, speaking of dependency, addressed the question of whether the habit was indeed strengthened by approach or merely elicited. Again working with first and second interviews, he found that client-initiated (as opposed to continuing) dependency actions did not increase for the second half of interviews, regardless of whether the client was the recipient of higher or lower than average approach responses from the therapist, leading Caracena to conclude that the dependency responses were merely being elicited. Moreover, those who initially showed a high rate of continuance of dependency statements in response to approach continued to do so less as the interview progressed, a form of behavior which suggested that, instead of having reinforcing qualities, something in the therapist's approach was operating to reduce the likelihood of the response—which is, of course, more in line with psychodynamic views. Caracena did not, however, achieve a replication of the evidence of Winder et al. (1962) that those whose dependency was not approached were likely to terminate permaturely. At the same time, unlike the finding of Winder et al., only 2 of 30 therapists, as compared to 6 of 23, approached dependency less than half the time. By the time of Schuldt's (1966) study at the same agency, therapists were averaging between 73 and 83% approach to client dependency statements, perhaps reflecting a feedback effect of the research. Schuldt extended attention beyond the first two interviews to the entire range of the therapy and, in addition to once more producing evidence in support of the elicitation hypothesis, added evidence that, far from reinforcement increasing the habit of offering dependency statements, the likelihood of the client initiating such statements decreased over the course of the therapy, despite the therapists maintaining their high rate of approach whenever such statements were made. Thus the question raised with regard to Varble's (1968) study of hostile statements, namely, whether the inconsistency of therapist approach-avoidance precluded the strengthening of this habit, does not apply to Schuldt. Incidentally, both studies were done with the same sets of interviews.

This series of investigations, then, offers reasonably solid evidence that therapists at this agency, the Michigan State University Counseling Center, give a consistently high rate of approach responses to clients' dependency statements, that these approach responses are likely to be followed by continuing exploration of these dependency issues, but that the rate of initiating such responses decreases over therapy. Alexander and Abeles (1968) explored these dependency responses in greater depth, once again over the course of therapy, but this time with a new sample. Relying on Lennard's and Bernstein's categorizations, they further classified dependency statements as to which relationship system they reflected: the primary system, the formal, structural aspects of therapy roles, goals, expectations, and frequency of meetings; the secondary system, reflecting the interpersonal relationship between therapist and client; the family system, that is, the client as a member of a family unit; or the social system, including peer, business, and teacher relationships. Over therapy, primary system statements showed a steady downward trend, whereas secondary system statements increased from the beginning to the middle and stayed at that level. Alexander and Abeles wonder whether this reflects necessarily unresolved transferences in this essentially short-term psychotherapy or the influence of a particular ideology (Kell & Mueller, 1966) which views therapy as an encounter marked by increasingly intense and reciprocal impact. Dependency statements referring to the family system decreased markedly between the beginning and the middle and then stabilized, whereas dependency statements regarding the social system did not fall until the period between the middle and the close of therapy. What remains to be done is a similar thorough examination of client communications and actions in the spheres of hostility and aggression to provide coverage of the other major areas of action and feeling around which human problems organize.

Transference and Countertransference

As suggested above, the assumed effects of earlier relationships are central to the psychodynamic approaches to psychotherapy and are embodied in the psychoanalytic concepts of transference and countertransference. The patient is expected to perceive the therapist in the same distorted ways as he does other significant persons in his life, particularly his parents, and to act inappropriately toward him as he does toward others. These distortions in perception and action are extensions of relations founded in family experience. Moreover, to his relationship with his patient, the therapist brings the effects of his own conflicts, hopefully minimal either because of highly favorable conditions of development or through personal therapy, but the transference behavior of the patient is in itself provocative and often designed to elicit the very responses from others that he is accustomed to receiving, usually in spite of dissatisfactions with this very condition. At the same time, the social roles of patient and healer impose certain similarities to behaviors experienced in other relationships. Thus the examination of transference phenomena in psychotherapy is surrounded by many subtleties and complexities requiring large process units for adequate delineation. It is these difficulties that have undoubtedly forced psychotherapists to rely heavily on clinical reports, which offer rich and vivid examples of the phenomena but, of course, lack the kinds of controlled observation needed for verification.

Although some starts have been made, definitive studies of transference in the change process are lacking. One approach has been to obtain subjective reports from therapist and patients at various points in the therapeutic process. Snyder (1961), Howard, Krause, and Orlinsky (1969), and Howard, Orlinsky, and Hill (1969), using this strategy, have produced evidence supporting the obviously mutually interactional character of the relationship; that is, there is a close correlation between the feelings of the two participants. Presumably, the therapist should exert the independent influence. Most of the time data are neither collected nor analyzed to test this question. Howard, Orlinsky, and Hill did find that therapists were more likely than their patients to view the patients and their own feelings as situationally determined. In a more searching analysis of the same data, Howard, Krause, and Orlinsky found evidence suggesting that the therapist will not necessarily feel bad when the patient feels bad, but that, when the therapist feels bad, the patient is likely to have similar feelings. There has been little followup of Fiedler's and Senior's (1952) earlier exploratory study of the use of Q sorts as a method of identifying transference and countertransference. The cumbersomeness of this method as applied to intensive process examination probably accounts for the lack of use. Its applicability as a way of examining expectations and transference readiness has already been demonstrated by Apfelbaum (1958) in his finding that the patient's expectations about the therapist cluster around three roles: therapist as nurturer, therapist as critic, and therapist as objective helper, neither nurturant nor critical.

Mueller and his associates have turned to the circumplex developed by Freedman et al. (1951) as a means of investigating transference and countertransference phenomena at the process level. This scheme for coding interactions is based on two bipolar, assumedly orthogonal variables, loving-hating and dominating-submitting, with provisions for further subdivision into octants or finer; for example, the dominate-love quadrant, subdivided and moving from dominate to love, includes teach, give, and support. Mueller and Dilling (1968) and Mueller (1968) coded therapist and client behavior toward each other, as well as clients reports of their behavior toward their parents and significant others. They found that, as therapy progresses, the client's behavior moves closer to that he has reported exhibiting toward both parents and significant others, and that over the same period the therapist's behavior toward the client becomes increasingly similar to that reportedly exhibited by parents and others. In the most complete analysis, Mueller finds evidence for mutual impacts of therapist and patient on each other, in that, when they depart from their respective role-defined patterns (i.e., support seeking for the client and support-interpretation giving for the therapist), competitive hostile behavior on the client's part is likely to be associated with similar behavior by the therapist. By relating each party's later patterns to the other's patterns in the initial interviews, Mueller found evidence of random relationships for the client but concluded that the therapist exhibits a relationship sometimes positive and sometimes negative to the patterns of behavior exhibited by the client in their initial interviews. The more competitive-hostile the client in the initial interview, the more competitive-hostile and passive-resistant and the less supportive-interpretive the therapist was likely to be in later interviews. The therapist was also more likely to be more passive-resistant in response to earlier passive resistance. Earlier support-seeking client behavior was accompanied by less passive-resistant later therapist behavior.

Twenty-five cases with more than nine interviews were classified as successful or unsuccessful by Crowder (1972) on the basis of pre- and post-MMPI's. In comparing these two sets of cases, he expected to find that therapists in successful cases would be characterized by more behavior in the supportive-interpretive quadrant and less behavior in the other three quadrants. Correspondingly, he expected successful clients to show more behavior in the support-seeking quadrant and less in the others. He found support for his assumption about therapist behavior during the late phases of therapy, but none in the middle and early phases. In the latter phases, successful therapists are *more* frequently hostile-dominating, though less hostile-submitting, than unsuccessful ones. Successful clients fit expectations in the first phase of therapy except for being more, rather than less, competitive-hostile; in the middle phases they fit by being more support seeking and less passive-resistant; no differences at all appear in the final phase of therapy.

Clearly, the results of the studies reflect the mixture of role requirements, the generalization of requirements among different roles, and the specific impact of each role on the others, in addition to the continuing influence of conflicted and distorting motivations. Much more detailed studies of the interactive process will be required to disentangle these many complex factors.

THERAPIST AS MODEL

The question of whether the therapist mediates change through providing his patient with a model for patterning his behavior is appropriately addressed at this point because it bridges relationship and nonrelationship conceptions of the change process. Commonsense observation tells us that the developing and changing person continually looks about him for others who exemplify the person he seeks to become. Publicly visible persons certainly provide influential embodiments of ideals. But it is among the persons with whom he has extended experience that the patient finds the more tangible models and the accompanying emotional attachments that transform ideals into behavioral approximations. Thus parents, older siblings, teachers, and peers provide earlier prototypes of the modeling phenomena which the psychotherapeutic relationship makes possible. Psychoanalytic thinking has subsumed the modeling process in the concept of identification, which is seen as more than imitation. It assumes a somewhat more sophisticated version of becoming the other person. Thus Schrier (1953) distinguishes between syntonic identfication, in which the patient adopts the therapist's attitudes toward him, and classical identification, in which the patient adopts the attitudes that the therapist has toward himself. The latter identification is, I think, intended to exemplify the adoption of the other's world view rather than simply his view of oneself. At the other extreme, behaviorally oriented therapists (Bandura, 1971) tend to play down the relationship issues, emphasizing instead the role of the model in calling attention to novel responses not now within the patient's repertoire or to the consequences of responses, thereby changing anticipations of the reinforcement contingencies.

Within the psychodynamic group, there are differences in the importance attached to the modeling aspects of the therapeutic relationship. Neither the classical psychoanalytic version nor the early client-centered version attaches much importance to identification. Freud and his followers conceived of psychoanalysis as a pure, objectvely scientific process, uncontaminated by exhortation and suggestion. The therapist as a person enters only through the kindly concern of the healer, but certainly not as a model. This view becomes modified as the concepts of the working alliance are developed and the therapist is seen as a model of realistic perception, as opposed to the distortions arising out of the patient's conflicts and his mechanisms for protecting himself from anxiety. Similarly, the pure client-centered view would couple modeling with all other efforts to perpetuate an external frame of reference, the source of the individual's difficulties. Psychotherapy aids the individual to free himself from his dependence on others and to attain an organismic basis for self-evaluation. Yet there has been a gradual and subtle movement in which such conditions as genuineness are transformed from conditions for achieving this desired self-evaluation to ends in themselves. With the placing of greater emphasis on therapist activity and particularly on his self-disclosure (Jourard, 1964), the role-modeling function of the psychotherapist is given not only legitimacy but also prominence.

Empirical demonstrations of the therapist functioning as a model are reasonably well established. Parloff (1960) offers two cases, with detailed observation of the process of psychotherapy accompanied by extratherapeutic ranking of topics for importance by therapist and patient independently. When Parloff categorized the therapist's responses as approving or disapproving, he found that the therapist's emission of approval and disapproval responses to topics in the patient's communications followed the therapist's ranking of these topics. More specifically, the therapist geared his approval or disapproval to the rate at which the patient introduced the topic, sometimes in opposition to the patient's own valuation of its importance. Moreover, of these two hospitalized schizophrenic patients, who initally were both relatively distant from the therapist in their valuations, the one who moved closer to the therapist was discharged as improved. Although illustrating a process of both modeling and shaping, Parloff's report underlines a situational artifact for which research in this area must allow, namely, that the therapist may be an arbitrary definer of the outcome. Just as the therapist's judgment of the patient's progress will influence discharge decisions and, perhaps, be influenced in turn by the patient's moving closer to him, the therapist's judgment of the success of therapy will be influenced in the same way. Thus the significance of Schrier's (1953) finding that the degree of syntonic and classical identfication correlated with the therapist's success rating is more limited than the result of a somewhat similar study by Rosenthal (1955), in which ratings by independent clinical judges, based on a report of an evaluative interview conducted immediately after treatment by a clinician other than the therapist, provided the outcome criterion. Rosenthal's investigation confined itself to an index of classical identification, finding that successful patients moved closer to their therapists' Q-sort of statements of moral values than did unsuccessful patients, but the amount of final correspondence was not very great. Even in the successful group values ranged from .2 to .65, suggesting that the modeling influence may not be a very powerful one. Welkowitz, Cohen, and Ortmeyer (1967), Landfield and Nawas (1964), and Ourth and Landfield (1965) are others who have offered evidence that psychotherapy is accompanied by movement toward the therapist's frame of reference. The latter two studies cast the issues into Kelly's (1955) conceptual system, which emphasizes the convergence of personal construct systems.

Farson (1961), proceeding from a client-centered framework at that time clearly opposed to the modeling hypothesis, found that in client-centered therapy clients did not resemble their own therapists at the end of therapy any more than they resembled other therapists. Moreover, he found that peer judgments of therapeutic competence and of adjustment were negatively correlated with the likelihood that a client would show increased resemblance to his therapist. Clearly, Farson's results raise important issues regarding the modeling hypothesis.

Undoubtedly the more specific the behavior targeted for change, the greater is the likelihood that modeling will have an important effect. Blanchard (1970), in an example of very specific targeted behavior, offered evidence that modeling accounted for approximately 60% of the increased approach behavior in treatment of a snake phobia.

Jourard (1964) has highlighted the modeling of self-disclosure, leading a number of investigators to give it special attention. Jourard's and Jaffee's (1970) demonstration in experimental interviews that an interviewer can influence through modeling the number of words spoken in self-disclosures can be seen as an extension of the work of Matarazzo et al. (1968), in which the duration of both speech and silence was shown to be responsive to modeling effects. Powell (1968) treated self-disclosure within the framework of reinforcement, comparing it with approval-disapproval and with reflective restatement. In experimental 20-minute interviews, self-disclosure was found to be effective in conditioning either positive or negative self-references, whereas approval-supportive statements were completely ineffective and reflective statements were effective only with negative self-references. Although these results would appear to support the power of self-disclosure, questions must be raised about the transferability of the experimental situation to psychotherapy and about the contradiction between the failure of approval in this situation and its manifest success in a large number of similar experimental studies. Powell argues, unconvincingly in my opinion, that in his situation the approving-supporting behavior represented more active involvement than in the other experiments cited and was susceptible of being experienced as nondiscriminating support, reflecting lack of understanding and disinterest.

Research in group situations has yielded a range of evidence regarding the effect of self-disclosure. Culbert (1966) found mixed results of trainer self-disclosure in T-groups. When the trainer was low in self-disclosure, group members established relationships with him or his partner; when he was high, they turned to other group members. Weigel and Warnath (1968) reported no differences in the self-disclosure rates of graduate students in group psychotherapy as a function of being exposed to therapists demonstrating role models of self-disclosure. Finally, Weigel et al. (1972) found that participants in sensitivity groups, as well as paitents in psychotherapy, were likely to view therapist self-disclosures as negative indicators of mental health.

The rising interest in group, family, and couples or marital therapy gives special interest to modeling phenomena in these situations. The research reviewed above bears on the therapist as a model. In addition, Beutler (1971) reports that in marital therapy a general tendency was evident for the spouses' attitudes to become more similar to those of the therapist, and that, though the two spouses' attitudes naturally converged, there was no relation to judged success of therapy. Weigel et al. (1972) found that therapists liked patients who self-disclosed, but did not necessarily see these disclosures as indices of mental health. The data on the reactions of group members are more fixed. Members of sensitivity groups, similar to those in the study by Kahn and Rudestam (1971), liked their self-disclosing members but had less clear-cut attitudes regarding their mental health. On the other hand, members of psychotherapy groups clearly responded to their fellows' disclosures as negative indicators of mental health, but reacted less clearly in terms of liking.

Goldstein (1967) has presented a psychodramatic technique for eliciting verbal behavior in group psychotherapy from severely withdrawn patients; he calls this "doubling," but it represents a form of modeling. The double acts as a model by giving voice to what he senses are the unspoken reactions of the mute patient. The Goldsteins' research (S. G. Goldstein, 1967; Jeanne A. Goldstein, 1971) has demonstrated the efficacy of this technique in sparking participation by these previously silent members and has shown that the participation maintained itself. This research, incidentally, might be seen as feeding data relevant to the Gestalt therapist's concern for bringing into the open the person's indirect statements of himself.

BEHAVIOR-ORIENTED INSTIGATION AND MODIFICATION

The disagreements between psychodynamic and behavior-oriented approaches to psychotherapy have been surrounded by so much polemic as to obscure the fundamental bases of controversy. It is not—I repeat, not—

that one group sees psychopathology as conditions incorporating learned response and the other does not. Rather, what is at stake is the paradigm of learning that is to be applied. Most of the behavior therapists have relied on the learning paradigms coming from research laboratories in which learning has been studied under stripped-down, simplified conditions, depersonalized and often with infrahuman subjects. In Chapter 4 I argued for the necessity for simplification as a part of research strategy, but also underlined some of the formal requirements and the needed safeguards that should accompany this process. Psychodynamic clinicians have clearly assumed that they were dealing with an acquired set of responses, as illustrated by their effort to account for them through conceptions of how past history brought them about, and have assumed also that their clients and patients were acquiring a new set of responses through their psychotherapeutic experiences.

At first glance the difference between the two approaches would appear to be that the psychodynamic group assumes that changes occur solely through changing the organism and that the behavior-oriented group concentrates its attention on situational variables. But this is, I believe, a superficial interpretation of certain evident differences in the way the two groups behave as psychotherapists. It is true that, if we take a position at some distance from both groups so as to diminish differences among subgroups within each, we see that the psychodynamic group seeks a person-centered view of the patient. Its members search for the organizing forces within the individual, which they assume to be major determinants of his responses. They set tasks that facilitate coming to understand what self-concepts or what self-representations he has acquired and how they are associated historically and currently with certain persons or certain kinds of persons. They observe differential readiness to experience particular kinds of feelings and emotions, and the ways in which these feelings and emotions are organized and interwoven with whole interpersonal response systems. One way or another, depending on the particular form of psychodynamic therapy, the psychotherapist defines his influence in terms of how it modifies these mediating cognitive and emotional systems. The behavior-oriented therapist is much more likely to concentrate on very specific problematic situations, seeking to identify the aspects of such a situation that seem to control the problematic behavior and to manipulate these externally controlling variables so as to bring about changed behavior in that situation or class of situations.

But a more careful reading of both groups leads to more complex views of the differences. Clearly both groups assume that the organism's response to present situations is mediated by past experience in the form of remembering, with or without self-reflection and awareness. Generalization from the therapeutic experience is a feature of both kinds of therapy, even when the therapy takes place *in vivo*. Even in the latter, presumably limiting case, the therapist assumes that the successful shift in response will survive either his physical absence from the situation or his secondary removal as an advisor to a person in the situation. The differences would seem to come into sharpest focus in regard to the relative importance attached to the organized character of past experience. Psychodynamic therapists stress the organized character of experience in various ways, according to their particular paradigms. The Gestalt therapist finds his organizing factors in the nature of perception; the client-centered therapist finds them in the epigenetic factors (the ground plan) for the development of self-evaluation; the psychoanalytic therapist turns to a complicated biosocial epigenetic approach which aspires to a highly differentiated, yet potentially deductive view of human behavior and psychopathology. Concern with organization is muted but not absent in the learning paradigms adopted by behavior therapists. As might be expected because desensitization makes use of imagery and related thought processes, we find Lazarus (1964) speaking of and identifying "more basic dimensions" of anxiety hierarchies. The controversy over symptom substitution revolves around assumptions about the amount of organization present in response systems. Much of the intensity of the dispute has diminished as psychodynamically oriented therapists have begun to concede that certain behavior methods may be a means of achieving fairly general changes for certain kinds of cases (e.g., Kamil, 1970), and behavior-oriented therapists have reported instances where removal of a target symptom was accompanied by many ohter changes that did not appear to be targets of treatment (e.g., Kraft, 1969).

Desensitization

Wolpe (1958), more than anyone else, has been responsible for the application of desensitization procedures to the treatment of anxiety responses, particularly the relatively focalized fears involved in phobias. When work is done with older adolescents and adults in noninstitutional settings, this behavior therapy method or a variant of it is the one by far the most frequently used. Typically, the patient is taught deep muscular relaxation. Then he is asked to imagine a graded series of scenes relevant to the phobia. Progress along this hierarchy is halted whenever the patient experiences anxiety. Wolpe attributes the elimination of the anxiety to the principle of counterconditioning. The fearful stimulus is presented while the patient is relaxed. Since muscular relaxation is incompatible with the autonomic responses involved in fear, the relaxation is conditioned to the imagined stimulus. The progressive hierarchy is important to insure that the imagined stimulus does not elicit the anxiety response in spite of the relaxation.

Stampfl, appealing to the principle of experimental extinction, offers a method featuring a flooding of anxiety, in stark contrast to Wolpe's method (Stampfl & Levis, 1967). Using the imaginal procedure, Stampfl stresses the need to go directly to all of the anxiety-provoking ramifications of the fear-producing object in a catharsis-like process. Thus in one study (Hogan & Kirchner, 1967) coeds with fears of rats were induced to imagine the most horrifying things they could about rats. They were told to think of rats running over them, entering their bodies, and devouring their organs. In a later test the treated subjects were able to pick up and pet rats, whereas untreated controls were not. Graff, MacLean, and Loving (1971) pitted desensitization against a less dramatic version of the Stampfl method in treating test anxiety and obtained no difference in effectiveness. Another investigation which found no differences between desensitization and im-plosive methods of treatment involved probably significant departures from the standard conditions. Boudewyns and Wilson (1972) selected inpatients only on the basis of MMPI indices of high anxiety, not necessarily phobias, and the willingness to volunteer. Their desensitization treatment consisted of a modification developed by Wilson and Smith (1968) in which the patient is instructed to free associate and encouraged to embellish associa-tions and situations that are particularly disturbing. All of this is preceded by relaxation training as in the usual desensitization treatment. Patients receiving either treatment were significantly improved in terms of the MMPI and behavioral indices as compared to a milieu therapy control group, but though differences favored the desensitization group, they were not significant.

This contrast in methods of achieving the same result, relief from a specific phobia, underlines the need for identifying more specifically the effective treatment factors. Little has been done in the direction of con-fronting the contradictions between desensitization and implosive therapy procedures. One natural way of resolving the contradiction is to assume that both methods stimulate cognitive or other central mediating processes which are the effective ingredients of the treatment process. For example, in comparing these two kinds of therapy, London (1964) points out that both depend on imagery and may involve discriminations between fan-tasy and reality. Instead of reacting with intense emotional states such as panic, the person learns to respond cognitively.

Since most of the research on cognitive factors has dealt with systematic desensitization, reformulations in cognitive terms are directed mainly to-ward that method of treatment. Some studies (e.g., Marcia, Rubin, &

Efran, 1969; Leitenberg et al., 1969) show that sets such as those induced by explanations, authority, and prestige are sufficient to account for the effects achieved. Folkins et al. (1968) showed that cognitive rehearsal paired with relaxation achieved the same results as the full desensitization procedure and defended this conclusion (Folkins et al., 1969) against Davidson's (1969) claim that their procedure allowed for the completion of the desensitization process during relaxation in the test trial. Davidson (1968) had found that experiences of imagery in the graded series without relaxation did not produce results comparable to those obtained with the full procedure. Yet a number of investigators have presented evidence that simple observation of a model approaching a phobic object results in marked reduction of avoidance in subsequent behavioral tasks (Bandura, 1968; Bandura, Blanchard, & Ritter, 1969; Geer & Turtletaub, 1967; Ritter, 1968; Mann, 1972). Another kind of evidence of the influence of mediating processes is adduced by Hekmat's and Varian's (1971) demonstration that by pairing the word snake with imagined experiences associated with pleasant words they could bring about changes in reported fears of snakes and in actual approach behavior. In a comparison of desensitization, counseling on study methods, and attention focusing, an amalgam of positive suggestion and rehearsal intended as one control, Allen (1971) found a surprisingly large effect on both grades and self-reports of the control procedure. Finally, Rehm and Marston (1968) showed the effectiveness of an amalgam of desensitization and self-reinforcement as a method of treating anxiety in social relations with females. In this treatment, the individual takes himself through a hierarchy of behaviors, keeping records and awarding points to himself according to the part of the hierarchy represented.

Two major efforts at incorporating this impressive evidence of the importance of mediating factors have been made. Goldfried (1971) suggests that "what the client learns is a means of actively coping with the anxiety rather than an immediate replacement for it" (p. 229). He proceeds to suggest modifications in procedures designed to highlight this concept for the client and to emphasize the relaxation part of the process. Murray and Jacobson (1971) propose a broader notion that the process involves a direct change in beliefs about the self and one's ability to deal with fears. This idea is echoed by Lazarus (1971): "When discussing behavioral procedures, it is important to specify whether or not one adheres to strict behavioristic stimulus-response mechanisms in assessment and therapy, or whether one's system also takes cognizance of central mediational processes (such as a person's self-concept and other cognitions)" (p. 349).

Relaxation and a gradual increment in the anxiety-provoking potentials of the imagined or real stimuli, which together are aimed at insuring that the patient experiences the stimuli without anxiety or with minimal amounts, are procedures that differentiate desensitization from implosive therapy. Although Folkins et al. (1968) demonstrated an effect for relaxation independent of cognitive rehearsal, they did not control for other kinds of cognitive factors, for example, expectancy or the goal of establishing self-control. On the other hand, Zeisset (1968) did seek to control for such factors as therapist interest, suggestion, attention, warmth, and confidence in the efficacy of treatment and found that the control group did not differ from a no-treatment control, yet relaxation plus application training produced results comparable to those obtained with desensitization. It is unlikely, however, that Zeisset removed all cognitive factors since his relaxation treatment included discussions and illustrations of the use of relaxation in everyday activities, especially those involving interpersonal stress. On the other hand, Davidson and Hiebert (1971) found little effect attributable to more than simply instructing the patient to relax (giving no actual training), and Sherman (1972) added a new dimension by providing evidence that, at least in the case of fear of water immersion, *in vivo* experience is a vital source of variance. Cooke (1968) found that desensitization procedures with or without relaxation were equally effective and were superior to relaxation alone or to a period of hierarchy construction without the rest of the procedure.

The confusion created by the simplifications which are so prominent in research on behavior treatments is illustrated by Lomont and Edwards' (1967) investigation of the relative efficacy of systematic desensitization and extinction in snake-phobic college students. They achieved the contrast by equating two experimental groups so that they differed only in that the desensitization group was required to engage in muscle relaxation in the presence of the imagined anxiety hierarchy items, while the extinction group tensed their muscles during this time. This is a far cry from the extinction process in implosive therapy. Hence their results, although relevant to the role of relaxation in desensitization, shed little light on a deeper resolution of the seeming contradictions between the two therapies. Germane to this point is the fact that this investigation, contrary to other ones, found no decrease in fear of snakes in the extinction group.

As the above review suggests, most of the work done has reflected the point of view of the earlier developed desensitization treatment. Fazio (1970), in evaluating the reality testing and supportive aspects of implosive therapy, using college students with fear of insects, found greater reductions in phobic behaviors associated with reality-supportive discussions than with implosive therapy. Since a no-treatment control was absent, there was no index of the net effect of treatment. There were some indications that implosive treatment may have increased the phobic behavior.

Although behavior therapists in general and those who practice systematic desensitization in particular believe that relationship factors such as trust and confidence in the therapist are vital to obtain the patient's cooperation and collaboration, they do not consider the relationship sufficient to account for the effects of treatment. Moreover, unlike psychodynamic therapists, who assign to specific relationship experiences the important determining influences, the desensitizers are convinced that the vital ingredients of the change process are to be found somewhere in the specific conditions and procedures of stimulus presentation. Thus there have been a number of studies designed to demonstrate that specific relationship factors are not required in order to obtain the effects of therapy. The most carefully designed of these experiments (Lang, Melamed, & Hart, 1970) set up an almost fully automated process and found evidence, including physiological measures of anxiety, that the automated, depersonalized treatment achieved the same results as the usual, more personal methods. Although in its original form systematic desensitization called for drawing up an anxiety hierarchy tailored to the individual patient, research (e.g., Emery & Krumboltz, 1967) has shown that standardized hierarchies can be used with no visible decrement in efficacy. Some of the other demonstrations of the viability of mechanization of the treatment process have been flawed by gross sampling defects. For example, Krapfl and Nawas (1969) ruled out subjects who did not give appropriate imagery responses in a prelminary questionnaire. Since this procedure could be seen as a preliminary test of a person's capacity to function in an impersonal situation, they can be said to have demonstrated only that it is possible to preselect subjects who can be helped as much by mechanical as by personal means.

Since all of the demonstrations, including that of Lang et al., involved volunteers presenting phobias not necessarily severe enough to interfere seriously with their daily functioning or to force them to present themselves as patients, questions of sampling leave moot the question of the general applicability of mechanical methods. Along this line, Rhoads and Feather (1972) offer clinical evidence that some failures in desensitization turn out to be attributable to the familiar psychodynamic phenomena of transference and resistance. Similar possibilities were suggested to Ryan and Gizynski (1971) from their survey of a sample of ex-patients of behavior therapists.

Operant and Aversive Therapies

As I have stressed several times before, a major feature of laboratory-based learning theories is their emphasis on the directive power of negative and positive reinforcements. Although allowances are made for reinforcements the power of which is derived from the social and personal history of the individual and which are interpersonal in character, the main thrust is toward a more mechanical definition of the change process. Indeed, much effort is devoted to demonstrating that the supposedly highly personal, individualized psychodynamic processes are reducible to the essentially impersonal forces of reward and punishment (Krasner, 1962). A great deal of research effort continues to be expended in this direction (e.g., Cole, 1965; Dicken & Fordham, 1967; Hekmat, 1971a, 1971b) seemingly more for polemic than for heuristic gains. For the most part, operant methods are mixed in with other behavior-oriented interventions, as the behavior therapist works, like other clinicians, in a practical, sometimes intuitive, sometimes purely experimental (sometimes frustrated and desperate!) way. For the most part, purely operant methods have been applied to institutional processes of control of psychiatric patients (Ayllon & Azrin, 1968), juvenile delinquents (Cohen, 1968), and autistic children (Lovaas, 1968).

A major question is how far changes brought about by purely operant methods will generalize. This question is raised particularly with regard to verbal reinforcement. Ullmann, Krasner, and Collins (1961) showed that patients' behavior in group therapy sessions could be influenced through verbal reinforcement of emotional words before these meetings. But Suinn et al. (1971) found that they could influence approach behavior toward a boa constrictor by snake-phobic subjects but could not modify their fear reports in a more generalized fear-of-snakes questionnaire schedule. This failure is particularly troublesome because the verbal reinforcements were applied to the expression of generalized attitudes toward snakes rather than toward boa constrictors in particular. In a very carefully designed study, Lapuc and Harmatz (1970) established clear increases in positive self-references through verbal reinforcements. Generalization was tested by responses to five self-concepts on the Semantic Differential Scale, by responses on the Manifest Anxiety Scale, and through nurses' observations of ward behavior. The only generalization effects obtained were in the patient's responses to the Semantic Differential Scale, and these were dissipated within 48 hours. Probably most disappointing was the the failure to demonstrate generalization to the behavioral level in the wards. Thus far, it would seem that purely verbal reinforcement has relatively brief and weak generalized effects.

The aversion therapies involve the use of painful and unpleasant stimuli as consequences of undesirable responses in order to create an avoidance of such responses under the conditions that have been evoking them. Typically, these stimuli are used to eliminate various kinds of socially disapproved behaviors, either addictive (e.g., alcoholism) or socially or sexually deviate, which may or may not be deemed undesirable by the individual himself. The instances in which the behavior is not deemed undesirable by the individual are associated with the social treatments inherent in public discussion and with the legal codes governing penal practices. There is clearly a distinct difference between experiencing impersonally painful stimuli and being subjected to the deliberate application of pain by another person. The experience of all of us documents the fact that the nature of the individual's relationship to the person controlling the painful stimuli will determine whether a desired generalized avoidance of the response is achieved or whether only very limited control is reached, accompanied by anger and rebellion that gives rise to other kinds of socially undesirable behavior. The experience of parents in socializing their children and of the state in reforming criminals is replete with both kinds of outcomes.

This as yet incompletely explicated effect of the interpersonal relationship in determining the success or failure of aversive controls probably accounts for the variability in outcomes of aversive therapy (Feldman, 1966; Kalish, 1965; Rachman, 1965). The context of psychotherapy more nearly fits the situation in which the individual himself is dissatisfied with the addiction, deviate behavior, or compulsive response and seeks to bring it within his control. But research on this class of conditions has not yet clarified the necessary and sufficient determining factors. Some of the thetheoretical problems can be illustrated by Cautella's (1966, 1967) covert sensitization technique. As in systematic desensitization, Cautella trains a patient to relax and then asks him to visualize a relevant scene, such as bringing a glass of alcohol to his lips. Then the patient is instructed to imagine himself becoming sick to his stomach and vomiting. This, Cautella reports, results in avoidance of the drinking behavior, suggesting that the presumably pleasant relaxation does not inhibit the unpleasant feeling associated with imagining the aversive stimuli. Yet in systematic desensitization the same conditions of relaxation are used to inhibit fear, making approach behavior possible. Murray and Jacobson (1971) suggest that aversion therapy operates primarily by changing the individual's beliefs about himself. In fact, Cautella (1967) suggests that an important reason why aversion therapy is successful is that the individual develops feelings of self-mastery and a sense of being able to control his own life and behavior.

RATIONAL INTERVENTIONS

We have seen that many of the contradictions in the alternative methods of behavior treatment and in the results of investigations suggest that such mediating processes as self-constructions or other modes of thinking may be the central determiners of response and that the processes of change, where successful, require change in these systems of thought. In discussing psychodynamically oriented approaches to therapy, I pointed out that interventions directed toward cognitive processes were seen as necessarily embedded in the therapeutic relationship, meaning that the required changes in cognition can be achieved only if the content of the cognition is an extension of the experience in therapy. For example, the patient's awareness of his unrealistically resentful attitude in certain kinds of competitive situations can affect his further experience and change his actions when this understanding is reached through experiencing such reactions in the context of transference and resistance. But there are those who, though certain of the primacy of mediating processes, take a much more didactic view of the change process. Ellis (1962) is, perhaps, the most influential articulator of this view of a "rational therapy." Since he came to his present views via a prior espousal of psychodynamic views, he is fully aware of the importance attached to feeling and emotion as components of the central organizing structures. But he assigns a secondary significance to the affective components, asserting that "human emotions are largely a form of thinking or result from thinking [and proceeding from that assumption] it would appear that one can appreciably control one's emotions by controlling one's thoughts." Following this line of argument, Ellis proposes that therapy proceed by an almost syllogistic process of uncovering illogical thinking and showing the patient how it is causing and maintaining his disturbance and unhappiness. Teaching is an all-pervasive feature of human relationships, and even some of those whose orientation is basically psychodynamic aver that the importance of general informational learning in therapeutic relationships has been underrated (e.g., Murray & Jacobson, 1971).

The research base in psychotherapy for these assertions is as yet relatively limited. Ellis (1957) tried to document his conclusions by summarizing his success rates during the periods when he practiced psychoanalysis and psychoanalytically oriented psychotherapy, as compared to his more recent practice of rational-emotive therapy. Obviously, in view of the conclusions he had reached, his report of his cases could show nothing other than superiority for the latter method. Other contrasts with rational-emotive therapy have included desensitization (Nolan, Mattis, & Holliday, 1970) and fixed-role therapy (Karst & Trexler, 1970). In comparing rational-emotive therapy with systematic desensitization for the treatment of fear of rats, Nolan et al. (1970) found slight evidence favoring the latter. Suggestive of some of the questions that become evident on closer examination of so-called rational treatment processes is the fact that this process included the therapist picking up a rat to demonstrate that it was an easy task, an action which suggests a hidden modeling factor in the treatment.

Kelly's (1955) notions about the central importance of personal constructs lead to treatments designed to aid the individual in gaining greater flexibility by exposing him to as wide a range as possible of alternative constructions. Karst and Trexler (1970) compared this "rational" method with rational-emotive therapy as applied to public-speaking anxiety and found little difference in results. A later investigation (Trexler & Karst, 1972) dealt only with rational-emotive and demonstrated effects, as compared to an attention-placebo control which had been absent in their earlier study.

Much closer to didactic processes not tied to therapeutic relationships was an effort to influence procrastination and distraction in the study behavior of students by means of didactic material sent through the mail (Sieveking et al., 1971). Self-reports showed a significant change, but grades, the only direct behavioral evidence, revealed no effect.

The fostering of self-monitoring processes, usually from a behavior modification point of view, might be seen as closely allied to other rational interventions. McFall and Hammen (1971), comparing different forms of self-monitoring, varying the amount and type or schedule of self-reinforcement, found no differences among them in their immediate effects on smoking behavior. Since reviews of the smoking reduction literature show that no treatment technique has to date achieved lasting successful effects (Kreutzer, Lichtenstein, & Mees, 1968; Bernstein, 1969), not much can be made of these results. Going somewhat beyond self-monitoring, Meichenbaum and Goodman (1971) taught impulsive children to increase their self-control by helping them to make up deficiencies in their mediating behavior. Through modeling the child was taught to raise questions with himself about the nature and demands of tasks and to give himself instructions.

Our review of research on therapeutic interventions reveals encouraging signs of movements toward a more direct empirical confrontation among alternative approaches. So far, few if any approaches have been ruled out. What seems more likely is that more definitive knowledge will enable us to understand which kinds of therapists will be most effective using particular methods with specific types of persons presenting specific kinds of problems. The next chapter discusses the role of the therapist as a person in his treatment, and chapter 8 considers the patient as a factor.

CHAPTER 7

The Personality of the Therapist
as an Influence on Psychotherapy

In this chapter I propose to examine questions bearing on the extent to which psychotherapy is solely a matter of technique, the degree to which education and training in themselves can make a therapist. In other words, we will examine whether the kind a person a therapist is, beyond his specific preparation, influences the effects of his therapy.

Such questions, seemingly straightforward when stated, become exceedingly complex when examined more deeply. From two points of view, the separation of personality from the technical specifications for psychotherapy would be judged as meaningless or impossible. Those who espouse a radical version of behavior theory and of behavior therapy are likely to dismiss the term personality as meaningless. Rejecting the reality and/or the utility of constructs directed at organizations of behavior and hypothesized organizing forces, they say that, when speaking of either personality or psychotherapy, we come down to specific acts which the individual learns in accordance with learning principles. Since they deny any difference between psychotherapy and other learning situations, such as those in either socializing or formal teaching, they assume that the therapist learns, whether informally or formally, the behaviors in his repertoire and that the raising of questions regarding personality adds no new dimensions. At the other extreme are those who believe that psychotherapy is simply an expression of the personality of the psychotherapist and that technical specifications and techniques are artificial designations. They lean toward an emphasis on the art of psychotherapy, even to the point of distrusting science and its methods.

Clearly, both of the groups just defined might leave us at this point because I start by assuming that it is worthwhile to adopt as a trial hypothesis that psychotherapy learning situations are not identical with all other learning situations and that technical specifications are differentiable,

[1] This chapter represents an expanded and modified version of an earlier paper (Bordin, 1968).

even though with difficulty, from personality. As I have hinted at various points in preceding chapters, I see psychotherapy as being directed at conditions against which the usual efforts at teaching and socializing have failed. My psychodynamic orientation is derived from the belief that, far from being unconnected or arranged in chance fashion, the individual's experiences are arranged and organized in a form dictated by the biosocial conditions of development, broad outlines of which are evident though not fully understood. The physical and psychological helplessness with which we start life means that experiences with caretakers are very significant in organizing strivings, perceptions, anticipations, and actions. Under ideal conditions, which of course can only be approached but never met, the individual's development prepares him to be maximally responsive to present circumstances without becoming, as it were, a piece of driftwood at the mercy of the elements. The separation of technical specifications from personality is useful in the same way here as in many other formal learning situations. The more we know about the formal requirements of psychotherapy, the more can be specified and accomplished in the formal training of psychotherapists.

THE THERAPIST AS A SOURCE OF VARIANCE

When we turn to an empirical examination of the questions associated with the personality of the therapist, one important test of the relevance of such questions is whether the therapist contributes a significant part of the variance in processes and outcomes in psychotherapy. If psychotherapy were a purely technical process which varied as a function of the patient's personality and needs, the variance attributable to the fully trained therapist would approach the vanishing point. The effectively functioning therapist would vary from patient to patient as a function of the circumstances and the therapeutic requirements associated with each one. That therapists have a set toward situational variations is suggested by the finding of Howard, Orlinsky, and Hill (1970) that therapists' reports of their feelings seemed much more responsive to the particular session, that is, were more situationally determined, than were patient's reports. A clearer statement of the situational set is contained in Hammer's (1968) discussion of how interpretive technique must be varied according to the pathology of the patient. He suggests, for example, that in working with an obsessive patient the therapist should give relatively free rein to his emotional expressiveness, but that with the depressed patient his expressions of warmth should be conveyed in acts of concrete giving. If, on the other hand, one takes a client-centered view that atmospheric variables (i.e., warmth) are the important determiners, we would expect to find that therapists are the major sources of variance, being little influenced by either patients or specific interactions.

The optimal conditions for investigating such questions call for a sample of patients to interact with all members of a sample of therapists, a highly abnormal situation in respect to the way psychotherapy is conducted. Two situations, one set up as a mode of normal operation and the other evolving out of research needs, have permitted empirical investigations. In the course of their study of the applicability of client-centered therapy to hospitalized schizophrenic patients, Rogers et al. (1967) encountered much resistance from the patients selected for therapy. Therefore they created a ward availability project in which a ward containing 24 chronic schizophrenic patients had eight therapists available for 2 hours each for a total of 16 hours spread over each week. This permitted exploratory periods of approach wherein patients had interviews ranging in length from only a few minutes to close to an hour with more than one therapist. Of the 24 patients, 11 saw four or more therapists and 8 saw four different therapists, each more than once. For reasons not made clear, actual analysis was done on data for 3 patients who had seen five therapists more than once. In the other situation (Moos & Clemes, 1967) a brief-contact outpatient clinic was designed for patients who had difficulty in establishing a good relatively prolonged relationship with one therapist and had a history of either many hospitalizations or many abortive attempts at psychotherapy, yet were susceptible of being helped through an "institutional transference."

Unfortunately, the results of studies on these two populations leave our basic questions unanswered, despite some propitious conditions. In both investigations, the samples of therapists were relatively homogeneous in terms of training, and in at least one study they were homogeneous also with regard to theoretical orientation. But the findings are not completely reconcilable, despite the valiant effort by Moos and MacIntosh (1970) to portray them as such.

The client-centered research (Van Der Veen, 1965) chose, in observing the therapist, to examine atmospheric variables. It was not surprising, therefore, that Van Der Veen found therapists contributing a major source of the variance in levels of accurate empathy and congruence, even though patients and therapists, through interview interactions, were also significant contributors. This means that a large portion of the variance in these characteristics came from consistent differences among therapists across patients and interviews. Incidentally, with regard to patient behavior, patients were the major source of variance in terms of level of experiencing and degree of recognition and concern with personal problems, as compared to therapists and interviews or interactions.

The brief-contact clinic with rotating therapists permitted more random pairing of patients and therapists and even replicated studies. Moos and Clemes (1967) set up a research design employing four patients and four therapists, all of the latter being in the middle of their second year of training. Both patients and therapists were observed in terms of the same kinds of behavior: total number of words spoken, percentage referring to feeling, percentage referring to actions, number of questions, and number of "Mm-humm's" emitted (seen as reinforcements). Though Moos and Clemes found a strong patient, compared to therapist, effect on patient behavior—that is, who the therapist was did not contribute materially to patient behavior—they also found that therapist behavior varied almost equally as a function of the therapist, the patient, and the interaction. In another investigation from the same clinic (Houts, MacIntosh, & Moos, 1969), this time directed at role-linked behavior (i.e., "be businesslike toward doctor," "suggest new ways of looking at her problems"), once again patients and interactions were important sources of variance in therapist behavior, this time overwhelmingly so. Responding to the differences between their reports and the results of Van Der Veen, Moos and MacIntosh (1970) replicated the earlier study, this time adding ratings of patient problem expression and therapist accurate empathy. The analysis of the more general verbal behavior confirmed Moos and Clems (1967), but little significant variance was found for either problem expression or accurate empathy, and whatever significant variance existed was contributed by patients to their own behavior as well as to the therapist's behavior.

Whether these differences in results are attributable to the difference between a client-centered and what I take to be a more eclectically oriented style of therapy or to special sampling differences in involving patients, therapists, or both, it is impossible to say. The therapists in the brief-contact clinic were in relatively early stages of their professional development as compared to the client-centered therapists, but were much more homogeneous in their experience. Although it may not be feasible to replicate these research designs in other centers, it should be possible to gather many more data on therapist variation from patient to patient and at different times with the same patient. Truax's (1966c) analysis of Rogers' differential behavior in response to different classes of patient behavior is an example of the further studies that are feasible.

THERAPIST TRAINING AND EXPERIENCE

The less articulated our conception of the necessary processes in psychotherapy, the more general are the processes of preparing psychotherapists and the greater room there is for the personality of the therapist to function decisively. As is clearly evident in the case of hehavior therapy, where the specifications for action become very concrete, the preparation of the therapist is relatively specific and leaves less room for his personality to play a role unless it influences his level of mastery. More importantly, whether the necessary phenomena of psychotherapeutic treatment are seen in concrete interventions and instigations or in terms of attitudes and understandings, the important question bearing on the role of personality is how amenable it is to formal training. The question becomes more complicated to the degree that formal preparation takes on some of the characteristics of psychotherapy and is designed to modify personality rather than specific function as a psychotherapist.

Strupp (1960) carried out by far the most extensive investigation of experience differences among functioning psychotherapists. Observing them in his analogue situation in which they offered their own responses at selected juncture points while observing a film of a psychotherapeutic interview, Strupp found no relationship between experience and diagnostic formulations about the patient; he reported, however, that the more experienced therapists were less likely to ask exploratory questions, but were more likely to show initiative, introduce a change of focus, or give more interpretive responses focused on dynamic interpersonal events, and were slightly warmer. Using a slight modification of Strupp's film analogue, Ornston and her colleagues (Ornston et al., 1968) found that, when compared with first-year psychiatry residents, fully functioning psychotherapists, psychiatrists, and psychologists, used more nonquestioning responses and averaged more words per statement. These differences seemed to reflect a tendency for the novice therapist, when faced with an ostensibly disturbed and agitated film patient in a first interview, to be preoccupied with obtaining information from the patient. On the other hand, it appeared that the main thrust of the experienced therapist was to impart information to the patient. Followed up 6 months and 1 year later with the same filmed interview (Ornston, Cicchetti, & Towbin, 1970), the residents at both later points performed in a manner essentially similar to the experienced therapists. Although this pair of studies suggests a specific effect of training and experience, the use of the some film situation leaves a specific habituation effect as a possible alternative explanation.

One series of studies (Bohn, 1965, 1967; Parsons & Parker, 1968) centered around the directiveness of responses to three kinds of college student clients: typical, hostile, and dependent, portrayed in a taped interview with interruptions at selected times to permit responses by observers. The three investigations involved comparisons of untrained college students with graduate students in training for counseling (Bohn, 1965) and with medical students and psychiatrists (Parsons & Parker, 1968), and a comparison of graduate students at the beginning and the end of a didactic-experientially conducted seminar in counseling and psychotherapy (Bohn, 1967). Directiveness was defined positively by four directive categories of reassurance, persuasion, direct question, and forcing the topic and negatively by four nondirective categories of simple acceptance, restatement of content, clarification of feeling, and nondirective leads. The general trend of the results showed that experience and training led in the direction of less directiveness and of differences according to the client; in all groups the dependent "client" elicited the most directiveness. Moreover, when the college students and graduate students were classified for dominance on the basis of the California Personality Inventory, no effects for this aspect of personality were visible (Bohn, 1965).

A further investigation using the same taped interviews (Lovitt, 1970) focused on therapist's approach-avoidance behavior with somewhat different results. Adult college-educated unemployed women, college students of both sexes, psychiatric attendents, and professional therapists, including those receiving psychiatric, social work, and psychological training, were the groups compared. In these comparisons, the experience factor was more complicated in that psychiatric attendents exhibited less approach behavior than either of the lay groups and professional therapists the most approach behavior. There were differences attributable to the clients, with the dependent (for some reason designated by Lovitt as "friendly") ones eliciting the most approach behavior from all groups. But all groups other than the professionally trained therapists tended to display more approach behavior to the hostile than to the typical (neutral) client.

Beery (1970) was interested in the effect of experience on a therapist's ability to respond with acceptance in the face of patient hostility. She compared professional therapists (no less than 4 years of experience) with graduate students in clinical psychology in an analogue situation involving a "friendly" and a "hostile" patient. The experienced therapists were warmer than the graduate students and all therapists responded more warmly to the "friendly" patient, but there were no interaction effects.

Truax, Carkhuff, and their associates have devoted considerable attention to developing an integrated didactic and experiential approach to training for the three client-centered stances of accurate empathy, acceptance, and congruence (Truax, Carkhuff, & Douds, 1964). This teaching process seeks to incorporate some of the aspects of psychotherapy, especially those represented by these three facilitating conditions of relationships. In one investigation Carkhuff and Truax (1965) demonstrated that lay hospital workers and graduate students could through this kind of training be brought to function at a level approximately equivalent to that of highly experienced psychotherapists. Utilizing an experimental interview around personal problems, Martin, Carkhuff, and Berenson (1966) showed that trained counselors offered higher levels of the three conditions than the subject's self-designated best friend. Moreover, another investigation (Pierce, Carkhuff, & Berenson, 1967) produced evidence that the degere to which the trainer possessed these three characteristics influended the outcome of training. Finally, Martin and Carkhuff (1968) added evidence of personality change in a constructive direction, based on the MMPI, as an accompaniment of training. Carkhuff (1966) was moved by this impressive set of findings to suggest that psychotherapy could be turned over to specially trained laymen, with the doctoral level practitioner free to function as a consultant. This would seem to represent a too hasty acceptance of the three conditions as all that is needed in psychotherapy. A more specific question can also be raised, namely, whether a purely didactic approach would accomplish the same results. Berenson, Carkhuff, and Myrus (1966) addressed this question without very clear results. When three groups of college students, one receiving the prescribed training, the second only didactic training, and the third no training, were compared, the only clear superiority was between the first and the third group.

We have to say that the evidence thus far suggests that experience and training, although influential, do not in themselves fully account for the therapist's behavior and his effect on his patient. At the same time, the work of Truax and Carkhuff raises the possibility that formal training directed at specific aspects of therapeutic responses may bring them sufficiently within control as to render negligible the residual effects of those parts of the therapist's personality that are untouched by formal training. As more features of the therapeutic relationship are validated for their effects and possible specific types of training directed toward them are tested, we will be able to arrive at more definitive answers concerning the direction and importance of the therapist's personality.

THE PERSONAL DEMANDS OF THE THERAPEUTIC SITUATION

The personality of the therapist may be important in psychotherapy to the degree that it facilitates or interferes with his ability to respond in ways that further progress and to avoid responses that impede progress. The advancement of evidence of this sort will necessarily depend on the identification and validation of the facilitators and inhibitors of therapeutic progress. The research basis for such identifications was considered in Chapter 6.

Some investigators have tried to avoid the problem of pinpointing the specific demands of therapeutic relationships by simply comparing the personal characteristics of therapists shown to have different success rates or judged to be different in competence. This is such a crude approach, so filled with uncontrolled sources of variance, as to render meaningless either positive or negative results. If success rates are the criterion and negative results are obtained, we do not know whether the reason is that the particular therapeutic methods represented are irrelevant to success or the personality characteristics sampled are irrelevant to the methods or to success or both; positive results leave us in the same dilemma of separating method from personal influences. The use of competence criteria only compounds the ambiguity to the extent that the relation between judgments of competence and actual success in psychotherapy may be unknown.

More important than the ambiguity of the results is the probable introduction of large amount of error variance, because it is likely that the true state of nature is that success and its associated competence depend on varieties of treatment activities organized according to the particular characteristics and needs of specific patients and involving complexes of personal characteristics of therapists. Failure to control for these complexities introduces so much error variance as to multiply the likelihood of negative results. This probably accounts for the largely negative findings in a number of such "shotgun" studies (Holt & Luborsky, 1958: Burdock, Cheek, & Zubin, 1960) ; Brams, 1961; Campbell, 1962).

If it turns out, as I believe it will, that there are relatively few general demands of therapeutic work and that most demands must be specified in the context of the needs of particular patients and the requirements of particular stages of the therapeutic process, we must turn to a more sharply focused research strategy of an intensive study of specific demands. Although some investigators will prefer to await firm empirical demonstrations of the relevance of particular therapist response systems to the ultimate outcomes of psychotherapy, others will be willing to back their convictions about relevance with such intensive studies in advance of validation of their belief. Such choices require no special defence, but it is pertinent to point out that examination of the way in which meeting the requirements of the therapeutic role of ambiguity, for example, makes specific personal demands on the therapist may contribute toward greater precision in the design of studies aimed at validating the therapeutic role of ambiguity.

Conditions That Facilitate a Working Alliance

In Chapters 5 and 6 I analyzed research done or needed to demonstrate how the working alliance is forged and how it influences the process and outcome of psychotherapy. Prominent among the positive influences on the working alliance is the therapist's communication of the sensitivity and accuracy of his understanding, his acceptance, and the inner freedom to be able to show his own feelings when appropriate. Some of the latter attributes are intimately related to the therapist's liking the patient and to his interest in the patient or in the particular problem. What personal factors or dynamics make it possible for a therapist to respond sensitively with acceptance and genuineness? Psychodynamic approaches suggest that a person who is not finely tuned to his experience of himself will suffer limitations in his ability to sense the inner experiences of others. This, along with the level of his anxiety and the modes or effectiveness with which he copes with anxiety, will not only influence his sensitivity but the way in which that awareness is expressed in the therapeutic relationship. Finally, the gratifications that the therapist seeks and obtain from his work will influence sensitivity, acceptance, and openness. Therapists who are excessively dependent on therapeutic relationships for interpersonal gratifications or who cannot permit themselves the gratifications normative to the work may be expected to exhibit limitations in this sphere as well as in other technical functions.

The major efforts of investigators have been directed toward examining personal factors related to empathy, with some distinctly positive results. Allen (1967) asked supervisors on the basis of case reports in a group supervision situation to rate counselor-graduate students for general competence, willingness to acknowledge own feelings, and responsiveness to client's feelings. In addition, each counselor's response to the Strupp (1960) film was rated for responsiveness to feelings. Using the rating of general competence, and the two ratings of responsiveness as criteria, Allen found that the Rorschach Index of Repressive Style (Levine & Spivack, 1964), which seems to be a measure of the degree to which subjects are comfortable enough with their own thoughts and feelings to give themselves over to imagination and whimsey, was significantly positively related to general competence but fell short of that level of relationship to either of the other two criteria. The counselor's willingness to communicate his own feelings was positively related to both general competence and responsiveness to client feelings as rated by the supervisor. Neither measures of intellectual competence nor measures of level of academic performance related to any of the three criteria.

Allen's finding of a relation between Rorschach performance and empathic sensitivity is somewhat at variance with an earlier study that concentrated on human movement responses (Mueller & Abeles, 1964). In a situation where 28 graduate students rated their own and each other's fifth interviews with one of their clients for activity-passivity and for appropriateness of responses, Mueller and Abeles used senior staff ratings of the same interviews as a standard. The M scores, derived from Holzman's modification of the Rorschach technique, were not significantly related to the accuracy with which each therapist perceived himself or others or to the appropriateness of his responses. These scores correlated only with the accuracy with which he was perceived by others. Yet the more accurate a therapist was in his perceptions, the more accurately he was likely to be perceived by others. Another study (Passons & Olson, 1969), somewhat similar to Allen's in the populations sampled and in methodology, found once more that the counselor's willingness to communicate his own feelings, this time rated by peers, was positively related to the supervisor's rating of the empathic sensitivity that the counselor offered to his clients. Unlike the preceeding investigation, this one also found a positive relationship between openness and the empathic sensitivity of the counselor's response in the Strupp film situation. Of two cognitive style variables, the Rokeach Dogmatism Scale was unrelated to either criterion, but the Color-Word Test of cognitive flexibility was positively related to empathic sensitivity as displayed in the Strupp situation. Peer ratings of ability to sense feelings were related to the display of empathic sensitivity toward one's own clients.

Further support for an intimate relationship between the therapist's style in communicating his own feelings and his empathic sensitivity is offered in Fish's (1970) comparison between beginning psychotherapist's reports on their emotions and ratings of their sensitivity provided by clients or by independent raters responding to tape recordings of eight session with these clients. Fish had expected to find that the complexity and differentiation with which the therapist communicated regarding his emotions would forecast his accurate empathy. In addition, he rated these communications for the depth of feeling attended to in them. He found no relations to the client's rating, but depth of feeling attended showed a clearly positive relation to tape-rated empathy, and complexity approached such a relation. Bergin's evidence that depression and anxiety, as reflected on the D and Pt scales of the MMPI, are negatively related to empathy as rated from recorded interviews is on firm ground because it is based on replicated studies (Bergin & Solomon, 1970; Bergin & Jasper, 1969). The importance of replication is underlined by the fact that relationships to needs as tapped by the Edwards Personal Preference Inventory did not survive.

The inconsistencies of results, depending on whether the criterion is based on case reports or direct observations of therapeutic behavior or on ratings obtained from clients, are further extended in three investigations directed at the three therapy-facilitating conditions of empathy, respect, and genuineness. Whereas Foulds (1969) found many significant relationships between the 12 scales of the Personal Orientation Inventory, dealing with attitudes toward self-actualizing behavior and experiences, and empathy, genuineness, and total score, Winborn and Rowe (1972) in a faithful replication found only random relationships. These studies relied on taped interviews for ratings of the facilitating conditions. Furthermore, it should be noted that Foulds found no relationships to respect. Yet Donnan, Harlan, and Thompson (1969) report that Factor A on the 16 PF (Warm, Sociable vs. Reserved, Detached) correlated positively with respect as rated by clients. Mature, Calm was *negatively* related to genuineness, as compared to a positive relationship for Tender-minded, Sensitive. Finally, Adventurous, Socially Bold was positively related to ratings of trust. A specially limiting feature of the populations studied was that all were prospective college freshman interviewed once in a group, once individually for 30 minutes, and then the next day for 1 hour as part of a precollege orientation program. McClain's (1968) finding that results on the 16 PF correlated differently for men and women with a criterion of counseling competence suggests that lack of control for sex may be one source of inconsistencies in studies.

The mood or frame of mind of the therapist might be expected to influence his relation to his clients or patients. Whereas Howard and Orlinsky (Orlinsky & Howard, 1967; Howard, Krause, & Orlinsky, 1969; Howard, Orlinsky, & Hill, 1969, 1970) have concentrated on the therapist's feelings during the therapy hour, Gurman (1972, 1973) investigated relationships between therapist's moods as ascertained apart from the therapy hour and the level of facilitative conditions offered to the patient. In a preliminary study (Gurman, 1972), he asked 12 experienced therapists in training to record ratings of their moods for 14 consecutive nights and obtained process ratings on recorded samples of their therapeutic work. There were positive correlations between average self-ratings of elation (as differentiated from depression), tranquility (anxiety), sociability (withdrawal), and overall mood with gross functioning. Only elation was related to empathy, whereas all mood ratings were related to warmth (acceptance-respect) and all but sociability to genuineness. Then Gurman (1973) selected three high- and three low-functioning therapists for further study of their moods just preceding the therapeutic hour. Each therapist contributed a number of consecutive taped interviews (ranging from 5 to 12) from the latter half of a treatment process with one patient. Before each interview, both therapist and patient reported on their moods. Unexpectedly, Gurman found evidence that high-functioning therapists functioned better under dysphoric moods, whereas the opposite was true for low-functioning therapists. Reasoning from previous evidence that high-facilitative therapists are happier and freer of psychological discomfort (Bergin & Jasper, 1969; Bergin & Solomon, 1970; Gurman, 1972) and that they are less dependent on therapeutic relationships for satisfying their needs, Gurman views these results as supporting the notion that high- and low-facilitative therapists differ in the feelings that accompany good therapeutic hours. Since these moods preceded the therapeutic hour, we are compelled to view the mood as influencing the effectiveness of the therapist. Moreover, there is no obvious explanation for the difference of the effect of mood according to the therapist's base functioning level. Perhaps an effort to replicate Gurman's finding is the first step toward unraveling this mystery.

Surely, one factor contributing to the formation of a good working alliance is the purely personal reactions of like and dislike felt by the patient and therapist for each other. Unfortunately, this seemingly straight-forward proposition becomes vague on closer examination. Do "like" and "dislike" refer to physical attraction and aversion, behavioral attraction and aversion, trust and distrust, interest and indifference, or respect and contempt? Mayeroff (1971) distinguishes liking from caring, which he defines as helping a person to grow and actualize himself. Yet some have treated liking as identical with warmth (caring, respect, acceptance). In fact, when Strupp, Wallach, and Wogan (1964) asked therapists to rate the degree to which they liked a patient and related this response to a great many other therapist ratings, they found a cluster of intercorrelations which they labeled "warmth of the relationship," including the therapist's emotional investment in the treatment, the amount of warmth he felt, and his estimate of prognosis before therapy. This warmth rating was shown to be related to the patient's feelings about the therapist and to both the patient's and the therapist's ratings of the success of therapy. On the other hand, McNair, Lorr, and Callahan (1963) failed to find any difference in therapist's liking for patients who eventually withdrew prematurely from therapy, as compared to those who stayed.[2] Stoler's (1963) evidence that likable patients are more successful in psychotherapy warns us that re-search designs must be arranged to provide a discrimination as to whether the therapist's liking or the patient's likability is the important factor. In view of the fact that his raters were themselves therapists Stoler warned that his results may reflect a reaction to whether the patient was conform-ing to the role of "good" patient rather than some general personality trait which influences the therapist's ability to provide effective therapy.

As yet, there have been no definitive followups of Stoler's study to demonstrate that either therapist liking or patient likability has conse-

[2] They did find, however, that therapists had expressed more interest in the pre-senting problems of stayers as compared to defectors. But Garfield and Affleck (1961) obtained negative results for this kind of interest.

quences observable in the therapist's behavior in therapy. Abeles made one attempt in this direction as part of a pair of studies of how the personality of the therapist may influence his tendency to like his patients. In one investigation for which only a brief report is available, Abeles (1964) found no relation between liking and empathic understanding, but reported that ease of liking was inversely related to the therapist's hostility and anxiety responses on the Holtzman Inkbolt Technique. In collaboration with Mills (Mills & Abeles, 1965), he demonstrated that for therapists in the beginning stages of training need for affiliation and nurturance predicted liking, but that this relation did not hold for therapists in a later stage of training or for experienced practitioners. From smaller, less reliable indications, Mills and Abeles were stimulated to speculate that prospective therapists are drawn to their vocation out of their needs for affiliation and nurturance, but that experience teaches them that satisfying such needs with clients they like will lead to adverse therapeutic results, thereby leading to a stifling of these needs (low negative correlation with liking) during the later stages of training and to only a more limited level of satisfaction (low positive correlation with liking) at mature levels of experience. They did not examine directly the relation of liking to willingness to approach client hostility or dependency expression during counseling, but did relate such behavior to need for affiliation and nurturance. No relation to approach to dependency was found, even when the therapists were grouped by experience. With regard to approach to hostility and need for nurturance, the pattern followed that with respect to liking, in that the beginning group exhibited the strongest positive relation, the mature group showed a more moderate one, and the advanced training group tended toward a negative one. This pattern, however, was not repeated with affiliation, where degree of relation varied inversely with experience in a simple linear fashion.

Wogan (1970) offers observations regarding the influence of the therapist's personality on the patient's liking him. Two weeks after therapy had begun (the patient being seen two to three times a week) each of 82 inpatients was asked to rate his therapist (1 of 12 psychiatric residents) for degree of liking, both patient and therapist having been administered the MMPI before therapy. The patients tended to manifest more liking for more anxious therapists and those higher on a somatization factor. Since anxiety was similarly related to patient ratings of ease of communication and therapist repression was negatively related both to ease of communication and to patient's rating of speed of progress, Wogan speculated that a patient both liked his therapist and showed more progress if the therapist was able to acknowledge some forms of unpleasant experience in himself and tended not to deny symptoms.

Obviously, the therapist's personality may have a direct influence on the working alliance. For the most part the research reviewed thus far has been oriented toward the positive contribution of the therapist's personality to his ability to contribute to the working alliance. But, as I stated earlier, psychodynamic ideology suggests that personal conflicts may interfere with optimal therapeutic responses. Such conflicts may distract the therapist and thereby detract from his empathic understanding, make him susceptible to hostile or avoidance reactions, or foster a vigilance toward himself and others which inhibits the genuineness and spontaneity of his responses.

Direct examinations of effects of personal conflicts specific to the working alliance are virtually nonexistent. Cutler (1958) related conflicts over style of interpersonal relations to accuracy of recall of psychotherapy, to the devotion of the therapist's response to his task, and to threshold for perception of tachistoscopically presented interpersonally relevant verbal stimuli. He reasoned that one way to identify a personal conflict was by uncovering differences between the therapist's perception of his customary patterns of behavior toward others and the perceptions of his peers. With two therapists as subjects, Cutler compared their recalls of the events of therapeutic hours with typscripts of the same hours. He found that in their recalls they systematically over- and under-emphasized those of their interpersonal actions that corresponded to the direction of the descrepancies between their self-ratings and those of their peers. While their recalls of their patient's behaviors tended to distort the same trait as they distorted in perceiving themselves, the similarity in the direction of distortion was not as consistent. As an index of the adequacy of the therapist's response, Cutler coded therapist response units as task or ego (defensively) oriented and found that ego-oriented responses were significantly more likely to occur after instances in which the patient's behavior represented a mode that was conflict laden for the therapist than after neutral behaviors. To show that the distorted recall probably reflected impaired sensitivity, he turned to the tachistoscopic laboratory technique. He had hoped to demonstrate a continuity between the therapist's patterns of defensive distortion in self-description and in perceptual threshold. Instead, he found that the two therapists tended to display a heightened threshold toward conflict-relevant stimulus words whether or not they displayed over- or under-sensitivity toward the relevant behaviors when rating themselves. These latter results bring to mind Gurman's (1973) evidence that highly facilitating therapists function in a more effective way when in a dysphoric mood.

On the other hand, Bandura (1956) failed to obtain corresponding results when supervisor's rating of psychotherapeutic competence was the dependent variable. In this instance, peer and therapist ratings of anxiety around sex, hostility, and dependency were obtained. Neither self-rating about anxiety nor discrepancy between self and peer ratings was found to correlate significantly with ratings of competence; only peer ratings of anxiety in each of the three areas correlated (negatively) with competence. No test for curvilinearity, which would have corresponded to Cutler's over- or underemphasizing, was applied to the discrepancy scatter plots.

One other investigation (Milliken & Kirchner, 1971) offers related data but is marred by ambiguities regarding its generalizability. Its subjects, master's degree candidates in counselor education, lacked any counseling experience and were asked to respond to videotaped simulated counseling in which an actor portrayed four states: anger (directed toward the counselor, who was not shown on the videotape), anxiety, positive affect, and typical (normal) affect. After viewing the tape, the subjects were asked to report on their observations of the verbal and nonverbal behavior of the "client" both in recall terms and in response to a series of true-false items. Accuracy of observation was related to score on the IPAT Anxiety Scale. In 10 or 11 comparisons, higher anxiety was associated with poorer performance, but only 3 achieved statistical significance, primarily in response to the objective items. The main source was the influence of anxiety on objective report in the anger situation. Somewhat anomalously, the other situation in which anxiety related to impaired observation was the relatively neutral one.

Maintaining Ambiguity

Once we move beyond the demands of the working alliance, specifications of the necessary demands of psychotherapy have been less well established and are, therefore, much more subject to disagreement. Discussions in preceding chapters have touched on the relevance of maintaining loose situational determinants of patient behavior through ambiguities in the definition of the task and through leaving many aspects of the therapist's thoughts and feelings undefined as necessary preliminaries to important therapeutic events. One might expect that an inactive, relatively self-effacing style will come easily to some persons but not to others. Moreover, the therapist's anxieties and conflicts can be expected to have a bearing on his tolerance for ambiguity. Hence preferences for interpersonal style, cognitive style, and personal anxieties and conflicts might all be expected to influence the therapist's maintenance of ambiguity in therapeutic work.

Research bearing on this subject has barely scratched the surface, being limited in quantity and marked by contradictions, indirection, and, in some cases, oversimplification. The reasonable notion that sensitizers, seen as more obsessive-compulsive, need more than do repressors to maintain structure in an interview was supported by the results obtained by Kaplan (1967) in an analogue study rather distant from psychotherapy. His subjects were undergraduate students who acted as interviewers or interviewees, in a situation where the interviewer's task was to get to know the interviewee, whose task was to cooperate as honestly and as completely as possible. The sensitizers were clearly more active (presumably, more structuring) than the repressors, the groups being so classified by the Byrne scale. Cannon (1964) chose somewhat related scales from the Omnibus Personality Inventory, Repression and Suppression (RS) and Schizoid Functioning (SF), but his dependent variable was the therapist's report on his own feelings toward his patient after the initial interview. Cannon found that RS and SF were high-negatively correlated with each other and showed significant but low correlations in opposite directions to a therapist's tendency to express positive attitudes toward his patient; RS was positively related. The differences in these scales from the Byrne scale may be more important than the similarities between the two. Since Parker (1967) defined his dependent variable as directive or nondirective response classes, in terms of the former representing "those which tend clearly to lead, direct or control the verbal activity" and the latter "those which would tend to give responsibility for choice of area and direction of verbal activity to the client [it also included those responses which reflect or clarify affect]," we may take this variable as roughly equivalent to ambiguity, though it leaves out the factor of frequency of therapist response. Using Gough's Adjective Checklist, Parker identified one group of counselors high on need for dominance and another group low on need for dominance and found that the high ones were more likely to respond directly in initial interviews. Since earlier studies by Hardy (1948), using a wide variety of inventories and semiprojective measures od dominance, and by Bohn (1965), using the California Personality Inventory, found no evidence of relationships to a similar classification of counselor behavior, replication of Parker's study is needed.

One pair of investigations looked into the influence of cognitive flexibility, with findings differing, perhaps, as a function of differences in counselor behavior observed. Whitely et al. (1967) obtained supervisory ratings of counselor effectiveness, defined in terms of cognitive flexibility displayed during the counseling process and in supervision. This very specific criterion was shown to be clearly predicted by measures of cognitive flexibility based on the Rorschach and on the coding of written responses to two selected case reports. Jackson and Thompson (1971) used the two case reports of Whitely et al. and Budner's measure of tolerance for ambiguity, but their criterion measure of effectiveness, also supervisor's rating, was more generally defined. Their negative results with regard to both predictive measures may reflect this difference. One other study gave attention to cognitive attitudes, this time in the context of

Kelly's (1955) model for describing cognitive processes. By means of an adaption of the Role Construct Repertory Test for clients as stimuli, Gottesman (1962) related measures of permeability and complexity to indices of mastery of client-centered therapy as rated by practicum instructors and by raters of samples of interviews. The participation of maintenance of ambiguity as a weighted factor in such a rating is, of course, indeterminate. It is likely that maintenance of a moderate level of ambiguity is embedded in the client-centered pattern, so perhaps some significance can be attached to Gottesman's results showing that permeability and complexity, especially the former, may be positively related to mastery of client-centered therapy.

There has been only one attempt to see whether the therapist's conflicts influence his behavior, controlling level of ambiguity. Rigler (1957), applying Cutler's (1958) techniques for identifying areas of conflict in interpersonal behavior, in addition to investigating the concomitant physiological level of anxiety as indicated by GSR, coded for level of ambiguity maintained. Rigler reasoned that patient expression of behavior that was conflict ridden for the therapist or his own expressions of such conflict-ridden behavior would stimulate increased anxiety, to which the therapist would respond by structuring the situation. After identifying conflict areas, Rigler asked three therapists to listen to recordings of their own interviews while obtaining continuous records of skin conductance level. The results suggested that physiological arousal in therapists occurred in response to patients' expression of behavior conflict laden for the therapist, but not in response to his own behavior. When Rigler related anxiety displayed while listening to level of ambiguity, he found significant positive relationships between anxiety and structuredness for 3 of the 5 interviews involving one of his three therapists. For another there were two such relationships in 11 interviews, and for the third, of the two significant relationships in 8 interviews, one was in the negative direction. For all interviews, there was no significant tendency for relationships to fall in the positive direction. Reflecting on these results, Rigler concluded that his expectations had not taken sufficient account of the possibility that some therapists may respond consistently or under certain circumstances with passive (i.e., ambiguous) responses, rather than structuring responses to anxiety.

Therapeutic Interventions

There is good reason to believe that the therapist's personality will participate in the forms of intervention he masters and to which he feels drawn. For example, it seems likely that cognitive style (e.g., flexibility, permeability, or complexity) will influence the subtlety and aptness of the interpretations that a therapist offers and will extend to their effects. His very willingness to engage in more active interventions (e.g., interpretation or behavior instigation vs. reflection) may be influenced by active or passive components in his personality.

Virtually all of the sparse formal research that exists on these questions has been directed at negative features of personality such as are embodied in the psychoanalytic model of countertransference. The one study which even approaches the topic from the positive side was added, apparently after the fact, to the design of the Johns Hopkins investigation (Hoehn-Saric et al., 1964) of the effects of role induction procedures on the outcomes of psychotherapy. On the basis of six 3-minute samples of their interviews, therapists were rated for social influence or potency. Truax and his associates (Truax et al., 1968) found significant differences attributable to potency for two out of the five outcome criteria used. The clearest effect was registered in the therapist's rating of global improvement; a less clear but significant effect was also shown in the patient's self-rating of improvement. When ratings for presenting the therapeutically facilitative conditions (empathy, respect, genuineness) were partialed out, only effects just short of significance remained. In view of the vagueness of the definition of potency and the borderline results, it is not clear that a new factor in outcome was demonstrated. If one attributes positive power to the role of the therapist as a model, then part of the results that Farson (1961) obtained might be interpreted as mixed. Setting aside his finding that, in general, clients in client-centered therapy display no greater resemblance to their own therapists than to other ones at the close of therapy, we turn to the fact that peer judgments of the therapists's adjustment were negatively correlated with the likelihood that a client will show increased resemblance to his therapist.

As has been mentioned, most of the research done clusters around countertransference. Cutler's (1958) research, already cited with regard to the working alliance, also showed that therapist's interventions were more likely to be ego (defensively) oriented than task oriented when the patient was displaying behavior which represented a mode that was conflict laden for the therapist. Yulis and Kiesler (1968), in an analogue-type study, found supporting evidence. A group of therapists, classified as high and low anxious on the basis of oral responses in a standard situation, were given forced choices between two interpretive responses to recorded communications in simulated psychotherapy. The high-anxious therapists were shown to select the interpretive response representing low personal involvement, whereas the low-anxious therapists tended toward the more personal choice involving alternative interpretations. Since the latter was regarded as more representative of the communication situation, selection of the interpretation excluding personal involvement of the therapist was taken as evidence of countertransference.

One strategy for examining the role of therapist conflicts is to study the behaviors of patients that arouse anxiety. Research by Russell and Snyder (1963) and by Heller, Meyers, and Kline (1963) has demonstrated that therapist hostility and anxiety are provoked by patient hostility. Cain (1962) found that, when patient resistance took the form of oppositional responses (hostility), the therapist, though he showed no signs of speech disruption, was more likely than in the case of other forms of resistance to respond by avoidance rather than approach behavior. Bandura, Lipsher, and Miller (1960) sought to relate therapist anxiety over the expression of hostility to his methods of responding on encountering it and the consequences of this response. They found that therapists rated as expressing their own hostility in direct terms were more likely to respond with approach reactions when patients expressed hostility toward extratherapeutic objects than were therapists rated low on direct hostility, but the two groups did not differ when the therapist himself was the object of hostility. Therapists who displayed a high need for approval were more likely to avoid patient hostility, whether displayed toward them or others, than therapists who rated low on approval need. In general, therapists were less likely to approach the patient's hostility when they were the object than when the patient directed his hostility toward others. Finally Bandura et al. found that approach responses were almost certain to be followed by continuing expression of hostile feelings and avoidance reactions by cessation of such expression, thereby establishing a direct link between therapist anxieties and the course of therapy.

Munson (1960) applied propositions regarding personality factors in vocational choice to the therapeutic enterprise. The general argument (Bordin, Nachmann, & Segal, 1963) is that part of the intrinsic attractiveness of an occupation resides in the opportunities it affords for specific preferred ways for seeking gratification and for reducing anxieties. In earlier research, which paid particular attention to the therapeutic responsibilities of the clinical psychologist, Galinsky (1962) found predicted differences between reports of childhood experiences by graduate students in physics and those in clinical psychology. Some of the predictions were founded on the expectation that clinical psychologists will have had more formative experience with the free exchange of emotion, and that direct expression of their curiosity about persons and their relations to each other will have been permitted and even fostered. Munson chose to examine how a therapist's response to client restiveness is influenced by the interaction between the client's behavior and those therapist personality patterns which are presumed to be intimately related to his choice of occupation. Munson's review of the growing literature on therapist's motivations supported her conclusion that nurturance and inquisitiveness are two needs importantly served by therapeutic work and that the choice of doing psychotherapy is, in part, an attempt to gratify these needs. This presupposes that there are legitimate, noninterfering gratifications to be obtained by the therapist from his work. The work of the therapist affords him realistic opportunities to gratify these two needs: nurturance, the need to help and to be needed by another; and inquisitiveness, the need to learn the innermost secrets of others.

Munson went on to assume that unresolved conflicts around achieving either or both of these gratifications would become a source of difficulty for the therapist when he encountered a client whose own behavior blocked one or another of these satisfactions. Using an adaptation of Cutler's (1958) methods, she selected three moderately experienced male counselors who were approximately equal in number of conflicts but differed with regard to nurturance and inquisitiveness. One counselor was without conflict with respect to either need; the other two showed conflict for both, but differed in that one was oversensitized to his nurturing behavior and undersensitized to his inquisitiveness, whereas the other showed the reverse. On the basis of ratings of brief intake interviews and behavior in the initial interview, clients were identified as high or low in willingness to explore themselves and to accept the counselor's help. Self-exploration was seen as a gratification of inquisitiveness, and receptiveness to help as a gratification of nurturance. Gratifying and nongratifying clients were assigned to all three counselors to examine the influences of resistiveness on counselor responses in these initial interviews. Immediatley after the interview, each counselor rated his satisfaction with it and the suitability of the client for counseling. Several months later, after completion of counseling, each counselor rated his enjoyment of his work with each client. Munson found that conflicted counselors were less likely to respond in a manner to facilitate client expression when the client was a highly resistant one, whereas the nonconflicted counselor's responses were unaffected. The conflicted counselors' expressions of satisfaction with the first interview, their judgments of the client's suitability for counseling, and their enjoyment of the working relationship, retrospectively reported, were similarly influenced. The nonconflicted counselor was influenced only in his judgment of enjoyment. Most of the effects seemed attributable to client expressions of opposition to help, and it seemed to make no difference whether the conflicted counselor was under- or oversensitized to his conflicts. Unfortunately, there were insufficient observations to reach a firm conclusion about these differentiated phenomena.

If we consider that Bandura found that all of his therapists showed avoidance responses to hostility directed toward them, as compared to hostility directed toward others, and that the nongratification of nurturance in Munson's investigation was defined by oppositional responses directed primarily toward the counselor and his methods, it suggests that a therapist's conflict over his need to nurture rather than anxiety over the expression of hostility may be an important source of his response to hostility directed toward him. Williams (1962) tried to pursue this question further in terms of the therapist's willingness to offer commitments of his own resources as one expression of nurturance. He reasoned that, since the need to nurture grows out of identification with a nurturing figure and since conflict over nurturing is likely to induce conflict over dependency in the child, a therapist who has conflict over dependency will also have conflicts over nurturance, and these will affect differentially his response to patients presenting dependency problems. Using an actress to role-play three patient roles: one an overtly dependent person, a second a counterdependent person, and the third a person whose problem did not involve dependency, Williams obtained only scattered confirmations of his hypothesis.

The potential usefulness of Williams' strategy of using persons trained to enact particular client or patient roles is supported by two demonstrations that therapists' behaviors can by influenced in such analogue situations. Alexik and Carkhuff (1967) trained a "client" to try for high levels of self-exploration during the initial and late periods of an hour and to try for a low level of self-exploration during the middle period. Counselors of 8 or more years of experience were differentiated before the experiment into those high and those low in their usual levels of presenting the therapeutically facilitating conditions of empathy, respect, and genuineness. They found that, unlike the lows, whose levels of functioning dropped during the middle period of low client self-exploration, without recovery in the final period, the highs maintained their levels during the middle period and actually showed higher levels of functioning during the final one. Dustin (1971) trained students to recognize counselor's efforts to understand them and to reinforce these efforts through acquiescent responses or statements of praise. With counselors in the beginning stages of training, he showed that such differential reinforcement over a period of five interviews was marked by an increase in the frequency of the counselor's efforts to understand.

PERSONALITY AND THEORETICAL COMMITMENTS

The thought that the choice of psychotherapy as a vocation and the capacity to respond appropriately to particular personality types may reflect the personality makeup of the therapist leads naturally to the question of whether the choice of a particular theoretical orientation, accompanied as it must be by prescribed modes of responding, is also conditioned by factors in the personality makeup of the therapist. Strupp (1962) has made the most extensive studies of the reactions representing different persuasions, professional training, and levels of experience, with or without personal psychotherapy. Since his data do not include personality characteristics, he cannot contribute evidence bearing directly on the question. He did find that client-centered therapists, as compared to psychoanalytic ones, were more optimistic about outcomes, more reluctant to attach diagnostic labels of the dire sort or to give differentiated descriptions of defense mechanisms, and more hesitant to state specific therapeutic goals (Strupp, 1958). Comparing reactions in a simulated therapeutic situation, he found, as expected, that client-centered therapists responded preponderantly with reflections, whereas psychoanalytically oriented therapists were more willing to answer direct questions, to use exploratory questions, and to respond in a mode involving greater inference and initiative. Williams (1959), comparing three psychoanalytically oriented and three client-centered psychotherapists, all psychologists, found that the former were more willing to offer commitments, that is, to make their resources available for those that the patient lacks or is momentarily unable to use.

Thus there is good reason to believe that theoretical orientation influences not only how a psychotherapist thinks about psychotherapy and how he views his patients, but also how he acts in psychotherapy. There are lacking, however, direct studies of personality correlates of such preferences. The closest evidence is the contradictory results obtained by studies relating dominance to directiveness, which were reviewed in this chapter (Bohn, 1965; Hardy, 1948; Parker, 1967).

MATCHING THERAPIST AND PATIENT

The influence of the therapist's personality on psychotherapy may depend on the personality of the patient. Are certain kinds of persons better able to encounter without disabling anxiety the unusual sensitivity, bizarre thinking, and behavior so characteristic of schizophrenic patients? Does similarity or complementarity influence the development of an effective working alliance? To the degree that modeling plays a part in psychotherapy, its effect would seem to be limited by the nature of the match between therapist and patient. If one assumes that there are many successful patterns of living and that the one chosen is influenced by the realities of individual differences, it is by no means certain that every therapist's pattern will be compatible with what is workable for his patient. If the measure of compatibility becomes, as it did in a number of related studies, a reflection of the individual's current functioning, the preceding clear statement becomes difficult to translate into predictions. Presumably, a patient is not functioning successfully either interpersonally or intrapersonally at certain important times or in important areas of his life. Is requiring compatibility, in the sense of similarity to the therapist, a way of saying that a person who is himself similarly unsuccessful is better able to help another become successful? What seems more likely is that a person who has overcome his own difficulties may be more sensitive to the issues and therefore more helpful to another person in overcoming similar difficulties. If one further assumes that underlying character style is not changed but is made more viable by successful psychotherapy, then the similarity and the difference between patient and therapist involves subtle distinctions that are likely to strain the crude measures of personality now available.

Therapist-Patient Similarity

Carson and Heine (1962) responded to the complexities of these issues by suggesting that the relationship between therapist-patient similarity and effectiveness of treatment should be curvilinear; that is, moderate similarity would be most closely related to success of treatment. If the therapist was too much like the patient (they were thinking in terms of empathy), his personal involvement would become an obstacle. If the therapist and patient were too dissimilar, there might be an interfering lack of involvement or an incompatibility of style or both. Using senior medical students in short-term outpatient treatment, Carson and Heine found a curvilinear relationship between similarity on the MMPI and supervisor's rating of the success of treatment. Pairs who were neither very dissimilar nor very similar received the highest average ratings for success. Unfortunately, two efforts at replicating these data failed (Carson & Llewellyn, 1966; Lichtenstein, 1966).

Most other investigations of similarity have used measures bearing on personality style or personal needs without regard to pathology and with different kinds of outcome measures. For the most part, curvilinearity of relationships was either not evident or, in some instances, not even tested. Mendelsohn (1968), in summarizing a series of studies (Mendelsohn & Geller, 1963, 1965), found evidence for a curvilinear relationship for one sample of clients in short-term counseling but failed to replicate this result in the other sample. In one sample, middle similarity on the Myers-Briggs Type Indicator, a reflector of cognitive and perceptual orientation based on

Jungian theory, was most favorably related to client evaluation of outcome, but this was not replicated in the second sample. Moreover, in neither sample was there a relation to the counselor's evaluation of outcome. There was a complex relationship between similarity and duration of counseling. High dissimilarity almost invariably led to short counseling, while high similiarity led as often to short and to long counseling; that is, there was greater variability of duration for high- than for low-similarity pairs. High similarity was also associated with failure of clients to appear for scheduled interviews, and such failures usually occur early in counseling. If the client returns, he is likely to remain for a relatively large number of interviews.

Snyder (1961), reporting on himself as therapist, found a positive relationship between his patients' similarity to him in terms of the Edwards Personal Preference Schedule, a measure of needs, and the readiness of each to express positive attitudes toward the other. Cannon (1964), adopting Snyder's therapist and patient report forms but using the Autonomy, Schizoid Functioning, and Repression-Suppression Scales of the Omnibus Personality Inventory as the bases for similarity, found small effects, in no very clear pattern. A similar finding of small relationship without clear pattern was reported by Bare (1967), using the Edwards inventory and two others. To muddy the waters further, Lesser (1961), using shift in correlation between self and ideal Q sorts as evidence of progress, found a negative correlation with similarity of therapist and patient self-sorts.

A special kind of similarity, perhaps akin to that tapped by using the Myers-Briggs Type Indicator, is envisaged when, for example in using Kelly's framework, one examines the influence of a similar cognitive structure or frame of reference on the process and the outcome of therapy. One might expect that the major influence would be on the level of mutual understanding attained. Three investigations clustered around Kelly's Role Construct Repertory Test as a technique for examining the degree to which patient. and therapist share constructual systems. Landfield and Nawas (1964) found evidence that patients rated improved by external judges were more likely to share constructual dimensions with their therapists than those rated as less improved. Ourth and Landfield (1965) converted the therapist and client conceptual dimensions to a semantic differential format on which therapist and client rated each other, themselves, and their ideal selves, but only the ratings of the other person were utilized in differentiating premature from nonpremature terminators, defined in terms of dyadic agreement. As expected, the premature terminators were marked by evidence of less meaningfulness of the members of the dyad for each other. Carr (1970) looked at similarity in terms of the level of discrimination displayed in separating a number of stimulus persons along one's own

conceptual dimensions. Patients whose differentiation scores approxi
those of their therapists showed more improvement in terms of their
ratings and reported more symptom reduction than patients whose diff
entiation scores were more discrepant.

Therapist-Patient Complementarity

The possibility that a therapist-patient dyad works best when the personalities of the two are complementary rather than similar has not been
thoroughly investigated. The Fundamental Interpersonal Relations Orientation Scale (FIRO-B) developed by Schutz (1958) has provided a vehicle
for three studies. Its scores reflect how a person treats others and how he
wants to be treated by others in three need areas (inclusion, control, and
affection). An index of compatibility is derived for each of the three need
areas, two of them, reciprocal and originator compatibility, corresponding
to complementarity. Reciprocal compatibility reflects the degree to which
each person's expressed behavior matches the other person's wished-for
behavior. Originator compatibility is an index of how well each person's
interest in initiating behavior matches the other person's desire to receive
such behavior. Interchange compatibility, indicating the amount of agreement on how involved the members of the dyad wish to become in each
of the three need areas, is more of an index of similarity than of
complementarity.

In the first effort to apply this instrument, Sapolsky (1965) presented
data on only the sum of the three indices for a population of hospitalized
women patients seen by psychiatric residents. The major finding was a
correlation of .45 with supervisor's rating for improvement. In addition, he
found that, although there were no significant relations to patients' attitudes at 4 weeks, at the time of discharge there were significant signs that
the greater the compatibility the more the patient felt similar to her
therapist and understood by him. In data based on briefer counseling
involving about four weekly interviews, Mendelsohn and Rankin (1969)
found no relation between overall compatibility and client's evaluation of
the relationship. Moreover, in the case of women clients, their data showed
that only for control needs was there a positive relationshp; the relationships for inclusion and affection were negative, and the significant compatibility index varied according to the need area: reciprocal and interchange for inclusion, originator and interchange for control, and reciprocal
for affection. No significant relations were evident for male clients. Unfortunately, the third investigator (Gassner, 1970) did not address the question of sex differences or of the interaction of need areas and indices. With
a population of chaplains in training and of state hospital patients of both

sexes, Gassner paired "therapists" and patients to form equal numbers of high- and low-compatibility groups, balanced for sex of patients. There were no analyses for sex or for need area. Patients in the high-compatibility group gave higher interpersonal attraction ratings than those in the low-compatibility group at both 3 and 11 weeks. When Gassner compared the three indices entering into the composite, reciprocal compatibility and interchange compatibility were the contributors to the positive relationship. Observations of behavior change were confined to 3 weeks with no significant differences obtained.

Thus we can conclude that, although further examination of a complementarity factor in therapeutic dyads is encouraged, the influence of sex differences and other population differences and of the needs and indices chosen is unclear.

A-B Scale and Schizophrenic Versus Neurotic Diagnosis

Working at the Phipps Clinic at Johns Hopkins Hospital, Whitehorn and Betz carried out a series of studies of the therapeutic work of successive samples of psychiatric residents with schizophrenic patients. They were able to identify groups of therapists differing markedly in rates of success (Betz & Whitehorn, 1956; Whitehorn & Betz, 1954, 1957) and to differentiate the therapists in terms of vocational interests and in style of treatment (Whitehorn & Betz, 1957, 1960; Betz, 1962, 1963). The successful therapists, designated as "A therapists," were characterized by high scores on lawyer, author-journalist, and advertising man scales; the unsuccessful therapists, designated as "B therapists," by high scores on mathematics-physical science teacher, printer, and personnel director scales on the Strong Vocational Interest Blank. Later a set of items was drawn to represent the A-B scale. Examining categories of therapeutic approach based on case notes, Whitehorn and Betz found the two types of therapists to differ in the kind of relationship (As were better able to gain the confidence of their patients); type of understanding (As tended to understand the motivation and meaning of patent behavior, whereas Bs tended to formulate their understanding solely in narrative, biographical terms; strategic goals selected (As sought to facilitate the patient's understanding of his capabilities and potentialities for constructive conflict resolution through the development of a dependable meaningful relationship, whereas Bs set goals in terms of supervised living, symptom decrease, socialization, and insight into pathology); and, finally, tactical patterns used (As were actively, personally involved and characterized by initiative, honest disagreement, challenging of self-depreciation, and setting realistic limits, whereas Bs adopted passive, interpretive, and/or instructional or practical care patterns).

When McNair, Callahan, and Lorr (1962) adduced evidence that *B* therapists were more effective than *A* therapists in working with outpatient neurotics, this created an accumulation of provocative findings, which stimulated a near avalanche of clinical, quasi-clinical, and analogue research. The data of McNair et al. represented a contradiction of the Phipps research, in that the original groups of *A* and *B* therapists were shown to have exhibited similar rates of success with neurotic patients. This ambiguity survives after three other investigations, which sought only roughly comparable outcome measures. Uhlenhuth and Duncan (1968) and Berzins, Ross, and Friedman (1972) used outpatient samples, more roughly differentiated as neurotic and schizoid. Much more experienced therapists were employed in the latter study; in fact, senior medical students composed the therapist group in the former. The Uhlenhuth-Duncan investigation used a total weighted score on a symptom checklist as the criterion for the results of treatment, which consisted of from 6 to 10 weekly interviews, with negative results for the *A-B* scale or for matching with patients. Berzins et al. relied on a criterion based on a combination of therapist and patient ratings. With regard to the therapist's appraisal of his own effectiveness, there was slight support for the interactional hypothesis, but the results in terms of the patient's rating of his improvement were ambiguous. Neurotic patients of *B* therapists rated themselves more improved than did schizoid patients of these therapists. Both types of patients of the *A* therapists, however, rated themselves as more improved than did the corresponding patients of the *B* therapists, albeit only the schizoid patients were significantly different. Moreover, there was no significant difference between the two types of patients of the *A* therapists.

This study also considered the possibility that the interaction effect was attributable to differential reactions of the two types of therapists to patients with "poorer" and "better" prognoses. As a test of this possibility, data from two other groups of patients, adjustment reactions and passive-aggressive personalities, were thrown into the analysis. Assuming the former group to represent the most favorable prognosis and the latter group to fall between the neurotic and schizoid groups, Berzins et al. tested for this ordering of outcome and obtained slight support with regard to therapist's appraisals, but none whatsoever with regard to patient ratings. Beutler et al. (1972) obtained clear-cut negative results with inpatients. Using therapist posttreatment evaluation and length of hospitalization as criteria, they found no difference when favorable matchings (i.e., *A* with schizophrenic patients and *B* with neurotic patients) were compared with unfavorable ones.

Bedmar and Mobley (1971) summarized briefly their unpublished study in which no interaction effect was obtained, using a wide variety of outcome measures, except that the neurotic and schizophrenic patients responded differentially in terms of depth of self-exploration.

Apart from removing the ambiguity as whether there is in fact an interaction effect between therapist type and patient type, there is a clear need for direct observation of the two kinds of therapists conducting therapy with both neurotic or schizophrenic patients. Do they differ in therapeutic style regardless of patient? Is one affected by the difference in patients more than the other? The results thus far are once more not clearly supportive of the interaction hypothesis and not much more supportive of the claim for any differences between A and B therapists. Several investigators compared the two kinds of therapists in terms of all or part of the facilitating conditions of empathy, respect, and genuineness. Bednar (1970) identified 20 A therapists and 27 B therapists in a large national sample and compared their patient's responses on a relationship questionnaire with negative results. Schizophrenic and neurotic patients were identified by application of the Spitzer Psychiatric Status Schedule. Similarly, Bednar and Mobley (1971) reported that their unpublished study (possibly involving the same data) found no differences attributable to facilitating conditions. On the other hand, though Berzins et al. (1972) found no differences in outcome, their A therapists were rated higher in accurate empathy in interviews with schizophrenic as compared with neurotic patients, and B therapists showed the opposite trend. In this study, however, empathy did not relate to improvement. In another analysis of data from their national sample, Bednar and Mobley (1971) examined various expressions of attitudes toward their patients and found only one instance of an interaction effect, in that As increased their liking of neurotic patients over the course of therapy and Bs increased their liking for schizophrenic patients over the same period. In other respects there were no differences in the esteem in which the therapists held their patients or in the warmth that they felt toward them.

Two other inquiries compared the two kinds of therapists in work with neurotic patients. Both of these were done in the same medical center, but one (Scott & Kemp, 1971) observed the first interviews of medical students, whereas the other (Segal, 1970) obtained two interviews in on-going psychotherapy from advanced clinical psychology interns. In results reminiscent of the unpublished study by Bednar and Mobley (1971), Scott and Kemp found that, although there were no differences between As and Bs in ratings of empathy, warmth, and genuineness, the patients of the B therapists were rated higher on depth of self-exploration. Segal concerned himself with somewhat different therapist response patterns, drawing on three ratings systems (Bales, 1950; Lennard & Bernstein, 1960; Strupp,

1960). Although the two groups of therapists did not differ in overall activity, he found that *B*s were more likely than *A*s to ask for orientation, to respond in a facilitating rather than an influencing manner, and to encourage the patient to talk. With differences of borderline significance, *A*s were more prone to respond sarcastically or cynically and to offer direct interpretations. For 11 other categories of response, no reliable differences were displayed.

Most of the support for the interaction hypothesis is adduced from analogue-type studies in which *A*s other than actual psychotherapists, most often college undergraduate students, classified on the *A-B* scale, encounter either pseudo patients or protocols designed to represent the avoidance of others and turning against the self, sets of symptoms taken to represent schizophrenic and neurotic patients, respectively. In addition, the *A-B* scale has been linked, using psychotherapists or others, sometimes both, as *A*s, to measures of field dependence (*A*s being more field dependent) and to a number of personality inventories (with a general tendency for *A*s to emerge as more emotional, vulnerable, and feminine, meaning more intuitive and less physically active and aggressive) .[3]

Stimulated by the research on the *A-B* scale, Bron (1971) took a more general look at the potentialities of the Strong Vocational Interest Blank for assessing the therapist's capacity to respond to the needs of different kinds of clients. His review of relevant data and his own preliminary analyses of data contributed by 36 psychologists and graduate student interns led him to identify three types, labeled "teachers," "guides," and "analysts," on the basis of three sets of occupational scales. One set contained abstract-theoretical occupations within the biological-scientific grouping (artist, architect, psychologist, physician); the second set consisted of the welfare grouping (YMCA physical director, YMCA secretary, personnel director, public administrator, social science teacher, city school superintendent, social worker, minister); and the final group consisted of the verbal occupations (lawyer, author-journalist, advertising man). The "analysts" were defined as being above the average for this population in the abstract-theoretical and verbal groupings, the "guides" as above the average in the welfare grouping, and the "teachers" as above the average in all three groupings.

Bron tested the usefulness of this typing of counselors in a college counseling center with three types of clients: (1) those presenting personal concerns and upsets, (2) those seeking help with curricular and/or vocational choices, and (3) those simply desiring information about themselves. The second and third types of clients are typically not oriented toward

---

[3] Razin (1971) and Chartier (1971) offer excellent critiques of the research.

psychotherapy and are usually seen very briefly, whereas the former group is usually found to be more ready to engage in a more extended effort. Using duration of counseling and evaluations by both client and counselor as criteria, Bron found consistent though not dramatic effects for counselor types, with some differences according to the sex of the client. Though there were no differences in the type 2 clients' evaluations of their counseling, "teachers" saw these clients longer than the other two types of counselors and rated their levels of understanding of these clients higher than did the other counselor types. Of the three types of counselors, "guides" were most satisfied with their work with the information-seeking clients, and "analysts" were least satisfied, but no differences in duration were obvious. The duration of counseling by "analysts" for clients presenting personal problems was dramatically longer than by either of the other two types. Except that female clients were generally more satisfied than males, there were no differences in how the clients of the three types of counselors evaluated their counseling, and the "teachers" again rated themselves higher in understanding these clients than either of the other two types. Although the numbers involved (20 counselors and 658 clients) are impressively large and probably unbiased for the agency in question, the generalizability of these results to psychotherapy in general is uncertain. Nevertheless, this is an interesting and promising approach.

SUMMARY

This chapter has been concerned with the question of the degree to which the process of psychotherapy and/or its results are products of the personal characteristics of the therapist beyond the specific actions flowing from his training and associated theoretical commitments. While direct evidence of variance attributable to the person of the therapist, separate from his training and theoretical convictions, is hard to come by and thus far inconclusive, the review has shown a body of supporting evidence large enough to mark this as a serious question. Although the evidence is by no means clear cut, the contention that the personal characteristics of the psychotherapist influence the nature and effectiveness of his working alliances, the patterns of the working situation he adopts and maintains, and his choice and effectiveness of interventions seems tenable. Clearly much effort is needed to remove the ambiguity created by conflicting results and to bring as yet untouched areas under systematic observation.

Although there may have been an overconcentration on the A-B scale, it has served the useful purpose of emphasizing the positive contributions of personality factors to balance against an earlier oversensitivity to the therapist's personality (i.e., his conflicts) as an obstacle in therapy. We need to extend Henry's (Henry, Sims, & Spray, 1971) exploration into what makes a therapist to the specifics of the therapeutic process, the therapist's strategic choices, and his choice of theoretical commitment.

CHAPTER 8

The Personality of the Patient
as an Influence on Psychotherapy

I believe that the patient as a factor in psychotherapy provides the key to understanding and reconciling the conflicting claims which arise around methods of treatment. In Chapter 6, I concluded my review of research on therapeutic interventions by finding encouraging signs of movement toward direct empirical confrontations among alternative approaches, albeit few, if any, approaches have been ruled out. I suggested that more definitive knowledge would enable us to understand what varieties of therapies will be most effective using particular methods with specific types of persons presenting specific kinds of problems. In Chapter 7 we examined research bearing on the role of the therapist as a person in treatment. In this chapter we shall consider the influence of the patient on the therapeutic process.

Stating it badly, I advance the proposition that commitments in regard to contradictory methods in psychotherapy are founded in differences in the persons served and, perhaps, linked to differences in the kinds of changes sought. This assertion should not be read as an effort to reconcile all differences over method. It suggests merely that, when individual differences among clients or patients are systematically introduced as factors, observation will completely invalidate only some of the extant methods and their associated beliefs. Systematic empirical evidence will also result in the elimination of contradictions by further specification of the conditions conducive to the effectiveness of alternative methods. This is not a neutral position with respect to theory. On the contrary, my review of theories in Chapter 1 pointed to psychoanalytic theory as the source of the most differentiated statements regarding the applicability of treatment according to the patient's personality. Many psychoanalytic writers have followed Eissler's (1953) lead in relating ego psychology to required modifications in the parameters of psychoanalytic technique.

RELEVANT PATIENT PERSONALITY DIMENSIONS

Implementation of the proposition that the patient's personality will determine the relevance of alternative methods of treatment requires a theory and a technology of measurement sufficiently developed to permit the designation and measurement of the features of personality that are crucial to the valid treatment response. To anticipate the research to be reviewed later in this chapter, such a review reveals that, although my proposition is already in the public domain, relatively little research has been directed toward it. I believe that this is so because investigators have been discouraged by the relatively primitive state of personality theory and measurement.[1] A contributing factor is that proponents of various conceptions of treatment other than psychoanalytic either propose a method applicable to all, thereby denying the relevance of individual differences, or, as in the case of most behavior therapists, deny the very relevance of personality as a construct. On the other hand, clinicians and therapists have not been able to agree in their characterizations of abnormal persons or their significance for treatment. One result has been the decreasing prominence given to psychodiagnostic procedures, especially of the projective variety, in connection with both psychotherapy and the clinical training of psychologists (Jackson & Wohl, 1966; Shemberg & Keeley, 1970; Thelan, Varble, & Johnson, 1968). Post-World War II optimism about projective testing has been replaced, under the pressure of strong debunking data, by a pessimistic, largely atheoretical empiricism on the part of personalogists, increasingly divorced from any close tie to clinical observation. I believe that in the rubbish pile of discarded methods and beliefs lie techniques which can be developed for valuable uses. Their reclamation will require painstaking sifting through mistaken, even illogical claims which good research has exposed. We need to mine through poorly conceived, badly executed, often trivial studies to uncover the veins of gold.

So much for prophecy. Where do we turn in looking for the dimensions of the patient's personality on which choice of treatment methods or partial modifications of them can be based? Not only must we define such indications, but also we must be able to specify the formal or informal methods by which such discriminations are to be made. For the most part, most efforts have been in terms of common psychiatric terminology. There are, of course, the broad separation by Freud of neuroses as the prime targets of psychoanalysis and the later modifications introduced to apply to the psychoanalytic treatment of schizophrenics (e.g., Federn, 1952; Wexler,

---

[1] For example, Fulkerson and Barry (1961) comment on the absence at that time of a definitive taxonomy of tests. This condition persists.

1953) and of borderline and narcissistic personalities (e.g., Hollon, 1966; Kernberg, 1970), and to the treatment of depressives (e.g., Jacobson, 1971).

Hammer (1968) provides a very useful distillation of psychoanalytically oriented suggestions for varying treatment technique according to diagnosis. With regard to obsessive patients, he proposes to counteract their extreme reliance on isolation, intellectualization, and ritual by an emphasis on emotional encounters, in which he advises the therapist to permit himself greater expressiveness than he would with other neurotics, especially of the more hysterical variety. In addition, Hammer advocates varying the length of sessions. With depressed persons, he supports other breaks from neutrality, suggesting that the therapeutic relationship should be marked by concrete acts of giving as a medium for expressions of warmth that can communicate to such patients. He advocates other forms of personal expressiveness, such as the use of humor as a relaxant (e.g., the Groucho Marxian, "I will not join any country club that would have me as a member") or the active elicitation designed to aid the person to get in touch with his rage. Since Hammer is primarily concerned with the interpretive parameter, he refers to the danger with paranoid and masochistic personalities that inferential interpretive activity will precipitate—a feeling that one's mind is being read—and that will block treatment. He favors also more indirect forms of interpretation as less likely to be experienced as accusations or as narcissistic injuries. He cautions that the therapist of schizoid personalities must be prepared to endure long periods of loss of communicative contact and emphasizes the need for simple and direct interpretations.

Other methods seem to have been oriented toward a particular kind of person. The Gestalt emphasis on sensory and sensual experience and its playing down, even contempt for, talking and analyzing seem to be directed toward the obsessive and intellectualizing components of personality. Similarly, desensitization was developed with phobias as the original target. Some practitioners (Marks & Gelder, 1966) have differentiated simple from complex phobias as a basis for deciding on the appropriateness of behavior therapy or psychodynamically oriented methods. Lewinsohn (Lewinsohn & Atwood, 1969; Lewinsohn & Shaw, 1969) illustrates the application of reinforcement theory to the treatment of depressives.

The limitations of diagnostic categorizations as bases for differential treatment are not confined to the sketchiness of our knowledge and the roughness of our methods. Typing or any other form of categorizing persons, though convenient and dramatic, suffers from oversimplification of human complexity. By superimposing discontinuities, it obscures the continuities between persons we call psychotic and those labeled neurotic and normal.[2] Reliance on personality dimensions rather than diagnostic categories conjures up a mechanical-analytic reductionism repugnant to both the psychodynamically and the humanistically oriented. Many psychotherapists are turned off by the idea that the validity of psychotherapeutic methods on the nature of the persons being treated because it connotes a mechanically functioning psychotherapist. To them it converts a necessarily genuinely spontaneous relationship into one dominated by prior calculation. But such need not be the case. The definition and isolation of particular personality attributes need not be unaccompanied by conceptions of their dynamic association in functioning persons. Moreover, the validation of such notions need not result only in the facilitation of prior treatment plans rigidly adhered to. It can also contribute toward a more sensitized therapist who is quicker to sense the inappropriateness of his responses and to modify his reactions in accord with this new awareness. In other words, if further observation demonstrates that the usefulness of various patterns of therapeutic response is conditional on particular characteristics of the patient, this is a reality with which therapists will have to come to grips in order to include it in their functioning as persons and professionals.

NEEDED RESEARCH DESIGNS

Pursuing questions about the influence of the patient on the process and outcome of psychotherapy requires research designs in which a particular kind of person, defined in replicable terms, is given alternative treatments, or a specific treatment is tried with two kinds of persons and/or presenting problems. One can hardly overlook the complexities of fulfilling the requirements of such designs. For example, how adequately do we define a person when we record his presenting problem? Any sophisticated clinician is aware that the way in which a patient initially states his problem or even how the problem appears by the end of the first interview may be far different from how it will appear on further examination. Moreover, there can be a considerable difference between what is conveyed by the patient's "complaint" and the total impact of his communications and behavior in the first session. Ultimately, we will need to look at persons and therapeutic processes in terms of what connections there are, both in theory and in observation, between therapeutic events and the changes sought and achieved.

[2] See Menninger, Mayman, and Pruyser (1963) for a psychoanalytic attempt to deal with this complexity.

The point made in Chapter 7 is that for the purposes of research it is worthwhile to assume that all therapists cannot achieve equal effectiveness with all methods, or, in other words, that the same methods will not have the same impact when mediated by two different kinds of person-therapists, even though both are equally well trained. In this chapter, these complexities are magnified by the suggestion that the characteristics of the patient will influence the effect of the method and the relation of the therapist to the method. A particular therapist may be able to be usefully passive with most of his patients except particular types, even though responding in the same way to these types would contribute to therapeutic progress. We need to work toward complex research designs in which method differences, therapist-person differences, patient-person differences, and their first- and second-order interactions are systematically analyzed.

PERSONALITY AND COLLABORATION

One source of the interaction between patient personality and method of treatment could be the differences in what is demanded of the patient in the treatment process. As was suggested in Chapter 5, methods of psychotherapy differ in the degree to which they require the patient to pay attention to his inner experience as well as his overt response and the amount of instigation to control that experience. Hence, it appears tenable and therefore worth testing empirically whether patients differ in predictable ways in how well they can satisfy the demands of different treatment methods.

Situational Requirements

The amount of time, money, and physical or psychic energy required by a particular method appears to constitute one set of factors that should be taken into account. Persons already depleted in these respects or any of them might be expected to be unable to meet the requirments of very demanding treatments. To the extent that the more experienced therapists are to be found in private practice, the poor, who are largely synonomous with the lower class, are less able to command the help of expert psychotherapists. But equally important are the time and energy required. A person whose economic circumstances are marginal is more likely to suffer ill health and undernourishment and to be less protected from crime and other social vicissitudes. His daily life is dominated by real, immediate threats to his well being and even his very existence or that of his loved ones. He lives in a continual state of emergency. It should be no surprise that treatments which require turning attention to himself and his inner experience to the momentary exclusion of the external forces impinging upon him, even were he to accept the necessity to do so, would in such circumstances be very difficult to comply with.

As discussed in Chapter 5, the differential access of lower-class patients to psychotherapy has been well documented. Lorion's (1973) review of relevant research finds that low-income patients display higher attrition rates than middle- or upper-class ones, but that some of this difference may be attributable to the greater tendency of the therapist to initiate termination with lower-class patients. Lerner (1972) is emphatic in her belief that therapist attitude and commitment are the major determiners of social class factors in the effects of treatment. Her investigation was designed to demonstrate that traditional psychotherapy, when conducted by therapists dedicated to the belief that this technique is applicable to lower-class patients and capable of relating to them, could be effective. She did, in fact, find that lower-class patients did better than higher-class ones with this group of therapists, albeit the results were not very robust. A number of other investigators failed to find any significant relationship between socioeconomic class and success or improvement (Brill & Storrow, 1960; Coles, Branch, & Allison, 1962; Katz, Lorr, & Rubenstein, 1958; Rosenthal & Frank, 1958).

The possibility that class differences have consequences for rates of attrition, but not for success for those who stay, pinpoints the issues in the working alliance. It seems credible, as has been suggested, that largely middle-class therapists are willing to offer less of themselves to lower-class patients, and particularly less willing to accept the necessity of concerning themselves with their patients' real-life problems to the point of intervening in their behalf. In Lerner's study social workers dominated the agency and made up an important core of her therapists. They were a particular subset of social workers who owed as much to Jane Addams as to Freud. To accept this proposition—that with such patients the therapist must concern himself with the real economic and social pressures—is to say that a person must be free of the extremes of such pressures before being able to devote more than a passing effort to an introspective self-examination and to trust his companion on such a journey.

The results obtained by Love, Kaswan, and Bugental (1972) are more difficult to fit into this paradigm. They compared the effectiveness of child psychotherapy, parental counseling, and didactic feedback to parents of observations of their own and their child's interactions within the family and with peers. Although this brief child psychotherapy was uniformly ineffective, lower-class parents responded best to parental counseling, while middle- and upper-class parents responded best to didactic feedback. The investigators attribute this difference to the greater readiness of lower-class parents to rely on an expert and the more receptive response of higher-class parents to a situation in which their own autonomy and problem-solving abilities are employed. They point out, moreover, that higher-class fathers were more likely to be involved in the treatment. If the former of these explanations is to be accepted, it would be evidence that there are class-linked/psychological differences relevant to the form of the working alliance, which will be discussed below. The fact, however, that the didactic feedback therapists were largely (three-fourths) male and the other two sets of therapists were largely (also three-fourths) female offers room for other possible explanations.

The imperiousness of immediate threats and demands on the individual is not tied solely to socioeconomic circumstances. Acute physical conditions accompanied by threats of death or emotionally disorganizing psychological states may have the same effect in at least temporarily limiting the amount of attention or energy a person has to devote elsewhere. To obtain a working alliance, the therapist does well to temper his concern with his treatment process with measures designed to aid the patient in coping with his immediate emergency and, when these emergency states can be only slightly ameliorated, to tailor his treatment to curtailed energies. Consistent with this perspective is May's (1968) demonstration that psychotherapy alone was less likely to be helpful to acute schizophrenics than psychotherapy accompanied by chemotherapy or even chemotherapy alone.

Pain and Hope

Even if not crucially depleted, a patient must be sufficiently motivated to expend the effort required for collaboration. Such motivation might be expected to be a function of the amount of stress being experienced and the faith and hope that treatment will relieve it. In testing the tenability of this hypothesis, as with the others related to psychotherapeutic collaboration, we are hampered by the paucity of studies directed specifically to these questions. A definitive answer requires research designs in which therapeutic collaboration in the first contact, in early contacts, or as a separate continuing feature of the treatment process is the dependent variable. Instead, we are, at present, forced to rely on more fallible inferences drawn from studies of attributes associated with early attrition or with improvement or success. Of the two, attrition is the more direct reflector of failures in collaboration; while collaboration may be necessary, it may not be sufficient for improvement or success. Even with regard to attrition, the patient's inability or unwillingness to enter into collaboration may be only one contributing factor. Moreover, the dividing point in terms of number of interviews between withdrawal as attrition and withdrawal as appropriate termination, while generally involving a therapist's judgment, may vary widely among studies. Incidentally, Cartwright (1955) found evidence to support the existence of a "failure zone" in client-centered therapy between the thirteenth and twenty-first interviews, which Taylor (1956) replicated in a psychoanalytically oriented clinic. In light of such findings, the fact that the definition of "terminator" or "attritor" in investigations varied from a few interviews to 16 makes the results very difficult to interpret.

There have been only initial exploratory efforts at focusing on quality of therapeutic collaboration as the dependent variable.[3] None has yet taken the additional needed step of comparing the collaborative demands of two different treatment modalities. In one of the earliest investigations, White, Fichtenbaum, and Dollard (1964) examined first interviews for indices which forecast dropping out in less than three sessions. The successful indices included favorable attitudes toward therapy and the therapist, expressions of anxiety, and ambivalent feelings and intimate associates, accompanied by citing of instances or possibilities of well being and achievement. In recently completed doctoral research, Ryan (1973) related a variety of indices of the personal characteristics of the patient, including indicators of pain and hope, to personal freedom and willingness to ally with the therapist, as manifested during the first interview with psychodynamically oriented therapists. After reviewing psychoanalytic, client-centered, and Sullivanian writings, Ryan concluded that two features, personal freedom and quality of alliance, were critical features of collaboration in all of these treatment modalities. The results obtained underline several methodological difficulties and some substantive complexities. First, though personal freedom and quality of the alliance were seen as two distinct, albeit functionally related characteristics, they were found to correlate with each other at a level uncomfortably close to the top permitted by their respective reliabilities. Moreover, the definition of personal freedom in terms of the flexibility and integration with which the patient expresses himself in the first interview clearly marks it as a possible measure of the outcome, in addition to its presumed instrumental role in therapeutic collaboration. Second, Ryan found that hope was not just a momentary state descriptive of the patient as he enters therapy, but is reflective of presumably more enduring personal characteristics[4] embedded in the level of development

---

[3] Studies of the sources of expectations about required roles and the effects of psychotherapy were reviewed in Chapter 5 and will not be discussed further here.
[4] Perhaps Rose's and Elton's (1972) finding that students who seek personal counseling show a higher and more aggressive intellectual disposition and more risk-taking inclination than those who do not is supportive of this conclusion.

of object relations, inferred from early memories (Mayman & Faris, 1960). Hence, in hope we may have a characteristic which not only is significant for collaboration, as Ryan found, but also is likely to bear directly, not just through collaboration, on the effectiveness of treatment. Although pain might be conceived as a motivator toward collaboration, when it is overwhelming or arises from an absolute poverty of personal resources, high levels of it can be seen as indicators of obstacles toward collaboration. Ryan found that, when hope was high, pain correlated not at all with the quality of the alliance (if anything, slightly positively), whereas, when hope was low, pain correlated significantly negatively with this index of therapeutic collaboration.

This evidence for a complex relationship between pain (and degree of disturbance and pathology) and collaboration is further confirmed by the data on a specific collaboration: that demanded in free association and the ambiguous conditions that prevail in formal psychoanalysis (Bordin, 1955). For this kind of collaboration, I (Bordin, 1966) found that hospitalized psychiatric patients responded as adequately as college students who were free of overt signs of psychiatric difficulties. Heller (1968a) reported that when subjects were selected as primed for self-disclosure greater ambiguity was associated with more self-disclosure. Yet Kaplan (1966) found that high-anxiety subjects, when ambiguity was pushed to an extreme level (they were asked to free associate when placed in a room by themselves), were unable to respond as adequately as their comparable fellows operating under the less ambiguous instruction to "talk about the things you would talk about if you were a patient who comes to a therapist."

Perhaps indicative of the positive effects of pain on collaboration were differences obtained by Bron (1971), incidentally to his study of the Strong Vocational Interest Blank as a source of relevant personality differences in therapists. He found that college counseling center clients presenting personal concerns and upsets established a dramatically longer-enduring working relationship than those either seeking help with curricular and/or vocational choice or simply seeking information about themselves. Another bit of evidence of the positive relationship between distress and collaboration comes from Eisenman (1966), who found that high-anxious patients, in terms of either the Taylor Manifest Anxiety Scale (MA) or the Cornell Index, displayed longer speaking time in group therapy than low-anxious ones. Following Schacter's (1959) linking of birth order and anxiety, he found similar effects for first borns. Moreover, there was an interaction effect with anxiety.

Much of the literature on personality characteristics associated with early termination stems from research on psychiatric patients in Veterans

Administration hospitals and outpatient clinics during the 1950s. As Fulkerson and Barry (1961) so well documented, the interpretability of these studies is marred by differences in the definition of "terminator," the problems of the "failure zone," and the fact that termination may be partly an artifact of the kind of personality problems in which the staff is interested and which it is skilled in handling. These factors may account for their observation that the results obtained, particularly through use of the Rorschach, have been inconsistent. Yet, despite this overall inconsistency, there is an enduring thread of evidence that people are more likely to stay in therapy if they feel distressed or uncomfortable (e.g., Gallagher, 1954; Taulbee, 1958; Lorr, Katz, & Rubinstein, 1958). The largest and most thoroughgoing series of studies was done by Lorr and his collaborators on data gathered from nationally dispersed VA outpatient clinics. A preliminary investigation (Rubinstein & Lorr, 1956) found evidence that self-dissatisfaction, as reflected in discrepancies in ratings of self and ideal, and higher educational and occupational achievement characterized the stayers to a greater degree than the terminators. A larger followup study (Lorr et al., 1958) found further evidence that self-dissatisfaction was associated with persistence and added evidence that anxiety, as indicated by MA, was also so associated. But the data on social achievement were more ambiguous. Yet these characteristics did not forecast improvement within the sample that stayed (Katz, Lorr, & Rubinstein, 1958). In a subsequent new sample (McNair, Lorr, & Callahan, 1963), MA and self-dissatisfaction once more differentiated, along with the therapist's rating of motivation for treatment and education.[5]

As mentioned earlier, evidence bearing on the connection of pain and hope with ultimate outcome of psychotherapy is difficult to interpret. Negative results could obtain because these two factors are not, in truth, intimately related to the quality of therapeutic collaboration, or it could be that they are relevant but that this particular form of treatment is either generally ineffective or ineffective in this sample of patients and/or therapists. We have already seen instances (e.g., Katz et al., 1958; Gallagher, 1954) where anxiety was found to be related to early termination but not to improvement ratings. One investigation, however, did report similar relations to ratings of improvement. Using MMPI and Rorschach indices, Taulbee (1958) found that "continuers are more anxious, sensitive, dependent, self-doubting, and have increased awareness of feelings of inadequacy, inferiority, and depression" (p. 87). He refers to unpublished data

---

[5] The possibility that such findings apply only to this specialized population is negated by the data of Terwilliger and Fiedler (1958) showing similar differences between college students who sought personal counseling and those who did not.

on 56 of his 85 cases in which these characteristics were shown to be related to therapists' ratings of improvement. Strupp et al. (1963) found a correlation of .63 between degree of initial disturbance and therapists' ratings of improvement. Yet, when Prager and Garfield (1972) assessed client initial disturbance by three means: average elevation on the MMPI, score on the Q Disturbance Scale, and ratings by therapist and supervisor and by judges using a tape recording of the second interview, the measures of felt disturbance were found to relate negatively to client, therapist, and supervisor ratings of change.

That these discrepancies may be due to the technical factors pinpointed by Fiske, Cartwright, and Kirtner (1964) is suggested by the finding that, when change in disturbance is used as the criterion, essentially zero correlations are obtained. On the other hand, severity of disturbance and degree of distress, although related, may not be identical, and this difference may account for some of the discrepant results. Within University of Chicago Counseling Center cases, Cartwright and Lerner (1963) found that ratings of need for change based on self-ideal discrepancies related positively to improvement. Within the same treatment setting, an earlier study (Kirtner & Cartwright, 1958a) showed that those rated successful and those whose treatment persisted longer than 21 interviews were rated as highest in discomfort and dissatisfaction on the basis of TAT plus first interview, whereas those rated failures and falling into the 13- to 21-interview zone were rated most comfortable and satisfied. The short (less than 13 interviews) success and failure groups ranked in between in both comfort and satisfaction. Using the Rorschach with students seeking university health service psychiatric treatment, Whitely and Blaine (1967) found little if any differentiation between short and long term, but that composite Rorschach index, whose components include signs of free-floating anxiety and awareness of conflict, differentiated no change from symptomatic improvement and more basic change groups.

Thus we see that, though a great deal of research has been accumulated, little of it provides clear answers to the tenability of pain and hope as characteristics that contribute or detract from the patient's willingness and ability to enter into therapeutic collaboration. There is certainly a heavy weight of evidence that anxiety and distress contribute positively to collaboration. Yet it is clear that too little effort has been aimed directly at this question, with the result that we must rely on very indirect evidence. Moreover, attention must be given to the possibility that pain or distress is curvilinear in its relation to collaboration, namely, that too little or too much is detrimental, and that this function may vary with the different forms of collaboration demanded by varieties of treatment. Finally, under certain conditions, pain and distress may signify a general poverty of resources or an absence of those required in a particular form of collaboration. With regard to hope, even less is known. Here future research will need to distinguish between situational determinants of hope (e.g., expectations) and determinants that are reflections of the enduring character of the individual, such as his faith in the future.

Dependence, Independence, and Other Relationship Orientations

As suggested by Ryan's (1973) finding that hope and level of object relations are related to each other and to the quality of the therapeutic alliance, there is reason to expect that a patient's ability to enter into any kind of therapeutic collaboration or into particular kinds will be influenced by general personality trends in this regard. Elsewhere (Raush & Bordin, 1957; Bordin, 1965b) I have suggested that the pattern of commitment offered by the therapist must be adapted to the degree and type of anxiety about dependence. When anxiety is expressed in the form of overt dependence, the development of an effective working alliance will be furthered by sufficient evidence that the therapist can be trusted to offer his resources in support of the patient at times when the patient lacks the needed ones or is momentarily unable to use them. Conversely, when anxiety is expressed in the form of counterdependence, the therapist must be careful to offer the patient the assurance that he will be permitted to use his own resources to the fullest; the patient must build his trust in himself before he can trust the therapist. The importance of such considerations in forging a working alliance will be a function of the amount of anxiety surrounding the need to rely on others.

Other than Ryan's work, there is little direct research evidence bearing on the above suppositions. Williams (1959) compared three patients, classified as overtly dependent on the basis of their first interviews with three others classified as counterdependent. Analyzing five subsequent interviews, drawn mainly from the early phases of psychotherapy, she found that for this population, characterized by high anxiety about dependency, regardless of the form of response to it, Speisman's (1959) demonstration of the sequential relation between resistance and depth of interpretation could not be duplicated. The fact that this finding had been replicated suggests the possibility, consistent with the above formulations, that anxiety about dependency must be attended to and may require a longer time before interpretive intervention can be used constructively. When Williams analyzed the degree of commitment of his own resources offered by the therapist, she found that oppositional forms of resistance were positively correlated with degree of commitment, a result expected only for counterdependents. Somewhat in accord with expectations, counterdependents were more prone to exhibit the oppositional form of resistance. Also in keeping with expectation, counterdependent patients were less likely to proceed with the therapeutic work of self-exploration after greater commitment from the therapist.

Since dependency may play a part in the social reinforcing functions of the therapist, emphasized in some forms of behavior therapy, there has been some research in that direction, which at the same time may contribute data bearing on the function of anxiety about dependency on the formation of the working alliance. Most relevant were results obtained by Cairns and Lewis (1962) in an analogue situation. Although their procedures were designed solely to identify high- and low-dependency groups through self-report and a behavioral test, they comment that the low-dependent subjects "tended to deny any form of dependency behavior" (p. 6). They were moved to offer this observation by the most striking aspect of their results, namely, that low-dependent subjects responded obversely to reinforcement procedures—in other words, they conditioned negatively. Babladelis' (1961) demonstration of a −60 correlation between score on the autonomy scale of the Edwards Personal Preference Schedule and increase in self-reference in a verbal conditioning experiment offers further evidence of the relevance of anxiety about dependence for the working alliance in behavior therapy. Other work has shown that delinquents reject dependency behavior (Cairns, 1961) and are less amenable to conditioning for the emission of dependency-expressing verbs than are nondelinquents (Steuart & Resnick, 1970).

Relevant to the general proposition that dependency and the working alliance are intimately related, but less directly related to my assumptions regarding the role of anxiety about dependence, is the work of Heilbrun on the relation between measures of "counseling readiness," based on need scales developed for the Adjective Checklist (Heilbrun, 1958, 1959), and early defection in counseling and psychotherapy. This measure of counseling readiness is different from that contained in an early note by the Grants (Grant & Grant, 1950) in which they called attention to the potential fruitfulness of such a variable and reported high agreement in independent ratings based on listening to first interviews. As defined by Marguerite Grant, the rating seemed to be an amalgam of estimates of anxiety and other indicators of felt desire and hope for change, along with evidence of the capacity to express and grapple with conflicting feelings reminiscent of the work of Rice and her collaborators (Rice & Wagstaff, 1967).

Heilbrun, from the very first of his studies (1961), found a sex linkage between needs for achievement, deference, autonomy, dominance, and abasement and early defection from counseling or psychotherapy. Female defectors exhibited lower achievement needs and were more deferent, less autonomous, less dominant, and more abasing than their counterparts who stayed. Conversely, male defectors showed higher achievement needs, less deference, more autonomy, more dominance, and less abasement than their counterparts. These results, supported in other samples (Heilbrun & Sullivan, 1962; Heilbrun, 1964) and extended in analogue studies (Heilbrun, 1968, 1970, 1971, 1973), suggest that the client who conforms most closely to the expected cultural stereotype of masculinity or femininity for his or her own sex tends to terminate early. Moreover, these stereotypes are intimately connected to dependence and independence, as shown by linkage of these interaction effects to problem-solving behavior (Heilbrun, 1970, 1971). Confidence in the generalizability of Heilbrun's work is somewhat undermined by Van Atta's (1968) report that when needs were assessed by the Edwards Personal Preference Schedule a different set—heterosexuality, exhibitionism, order, and endurance—constituted the differentiating ones. Stayers were higher on the first two and lower on the latter ones. In addition to the difference in methods of assessing needs, Heilbrun's defectors left somewhat earlier (they were selected as staying for less than 6 interviews—mean of 1.8 or 1.9, as compared to being selected as staying for less than 10 interviews—mean of 2.4). In light of Heilbrun's work, it is remarkable that Van Atta did not analyze for sex differences. His failure to refer to Heilbrun suggests that he was unaware of the latter's research.

Since there were almost equal numbers of males and females in the stayer and nonstayer groups, following Heilbrun's findings of opposite relationships, one might have expected the pooled groups to yield negative results due to a canceling effect. On the other hand, supporting Heilbrun, Taulbee (1958), studying male veterans, found that continuers exhibited stronger feminine interests or less adequate identification with cultural norms of masculinity. Similarly, Alexander and Abeles (1969) showed that male clients who met the criteria of stayers (were in therapy for five or more interviews) averaged higher in the feminine direction than the norms on the Masculinity-Femininity Scale of the MMPI, but, contrary to Heilbrun's results, the female clients did not differ from their sex norms and the two client groups did not differ in the dependency behavior displayed during therapeutic interviews.

Schroeder's (1960) investigation of the relation between client acceptance of responsibility and difficulty with therapy also presents results which offer problems in relation to Heilbrun's views. Via content coding of client discussion of his or her problems in a self-interview technique administered before therapy, Schroeder measured the extent to which a client viewed his own behavior as a source of his problems or disclaimed agency and attributed the source to something outside himself. It does not seem farfetched to equate this emphasis on self-agency with the assumption of an independent posture, which, according to Heilbrun, would forecast a greater likelihood of fitting in to psychotherapy for women but not for men. Unfortunately, Schroeder defined difficulty in therapy as terminating early (less than 10 interviews) or taking a long time (staying for more than 30 interviews) and did not analyze by sex. Her sample included 34 men and 14 women. Despite confounding for sex and for early defection, she found that high responsibility went with high difficulty. Moreover, those high in responsibility were judged by their therapists at the close of therapy to have displayed greater movement. If the women in Schroeder's sample had outnumbered the men rather than the opposite, one might have suggested that this preponderance accounted for the results and have thus found further support for Heilbrun. As it is, it remains a finding difficult to integrate unless one argues that Schroeder's "responsibility" has less to do with dependency than with an external focus à la Rice, a not unlikely possibility.

The work of Cairns and of Steuart and Resnick, cited above, points up some communalities between the influence of patient anxiety about dependency and working alliances in either psychodynamic or behavior therapeutic relationships. Although their results are marred by the failure of another set of investigators to replicate them, Timmons and Noblin demonstrated conditioning effects similar to those found by Cairns for oral and anal character types identified on the basis of the Blacky test. In their original investigation (Timmons & Noblin, 1963), they showed that the orals, who can be expected to be overtly dependent, could be readily conditioned to select personal pronouns in a Taffel-type situation with mild affirmatory response as the reinforcement and could just as readily be extinguished for that behavior. Not only did the anals not condition, but also they actually made the reinforced choice less frequently than they had during the operant period. Moreover, the frequency of choice returned to the operant level during the extinction period. Thus the anals responded in the counterdependent fashion expected of this kind of person. These results were then replicated and extended to the use of negative reinforcements (Noblin, Timmons, & Kail, 1966), but Cooperman and Child (1971) failed to confirm. Although the slight variations in experimental conditions cited by the latter investigators as possible causes of the failure to replicate may account for it, the explanation does not appear compelling.

There are other ways of viewing the relationship-oriented characteristics of persons which may have close connections to anxieties about dependence, but still represent an appreciably different tack. One of these is the proposition that one factor in the susceptibility to personal influence is a motive to seek the approval of others (Crowne & Marlowe, 1964). Strickland and Crowne (1963) believed that high need for approval would be accompanied by a defensiveness in self-disclosure which would interfere with the working alliance, leading to premature termination. Unfortunately, their investigation did not include direct measures of either the working alliance or the inappropriateness of termination. They did find a negative correlation with length of therapy and therapist ratings of defensiveness. In fact, therapists' ratings of the patient (patient's liking/respect for therapist, therapist's liking/respect for patient, patient's satisfaction and improvement) all tended to correlate negatively with need for approval. A later analogue study (Doster & Strickland, 1971) found no relationship to directly observed level of personal disclosure.

Another related direction is to assume that previous history or relationships, especially with parents, will influence the working alliance. Mueller (1968) found connections between clients' reports on their relationships in their families and observed relationships to therapists. In an experiment, Baugh, Pascol, and Cottrell (1971) found that subjects who reported positive early experiences with parents talked more and avoided eye contact less than those who reported negative experiences. Finally, Horton and Kriauciunas (1970) found that adolescent clients who fell more toward the love than the hate end of a scale of interpersonal relations, derived from the MMPI, were less likely to terminate inappropriately. Clearly, these different, sometimes contradictory concepts, observational methods, and results need to be integrated conceptually and empirically. My formulations regarding anxieties about dependence, as well as differences in modes of response to such anxiety and their consequences for the effects of commitment, represent one beginning.

In summary, then, there is a sound basis in common sense, in theory, and in research data for believing that dependency and other associated relationship variables are significant patient factors in the formation of working alliances, whether in psychodynamically or behavior-oriented psychotherapy. Unfortunately, too little of the past research has been specifically oriented to the concept of the working alliance. This is the direction in which we must go, however, if we are to convert the general knowledge toward making psychotherapy more incisive.

Character and Other Personality Demands

In the preceding discussion I singled out dependence-independence and similar characteristics as likely to be functionally implicated in collaboration. As we turn to other possible functional relationships, there are even fewer formal data, either direct or indirect, and opinion is confusing and contradictory. For example, I have already suggested that Gestalt therapy methods, specifically the great emphasis on attention to body movements accompanying verbal communication (Fagan & Shepherd, 1970; Polster & Polster, 1973), may have a greater impact on intellectualizing and obsessively oriented persons. Yet Braatøy (1954, pp. 169–175), summarizing his own and others' clinical observations, concludes that hysterical patients and others related to hysterics will enter quickly into a therapeutic alliance in which attention is directed toward somatic manifestations, whereas the compulsive neurotic can enter into such collaboration only after a long period of trust building in which a regular time schedule and the basic agreement, "This is going to take a long time," establish for the patient that quick change is not intended. Virtually no direct evidence is available on how personality and attention to body movements interact. Freedman et al. (1972) provide tangential data growing out of their interest in personality factors related to the readiness to accompany oral communication with bodily movement. They found that field-dependent volunteer women accompanied their speech in personal interviews with more movements oriented toward the body than field independents, especially in response to "cold" interviewers.

I have already spoken of the possible curvilinear relationship between anxiety and ability to collaborate in a free associative therapeutic task. The task itself and accompanying conditions of low responsiveness of the therapist may be anxiety provoking, and specific kinds of persons more susceptible. Moreover, as Bellak (1961) suggests, some kinds of persons will find the regressive aspects of the task difficult to perform (obsessive personalities), whereas others will have difficulty with the observing (hysterics) or the synthesizing (schizoid) aspects. Here again direct data are sparse. Temerlin (1956) compared performance in the autokinetic situation of patients who had been rated as good and as poor free associaters by their psychotherapist and his supervisor. On the ground that productive free association is marked by flexibility and variability, Temerlin expected that his good free associators would be more variable in judging the extent of autokinetic movement on successive trials, and this expectation was confirmed. Schneider (1953) chose to relate Rorschach performance to therapists' ratings of free associative performance during psychotherapy. Using a score based mainly on various indices of balance (e.g., movement and color, form and color), he found significant positive relationships to therapists' ratings. Using an experimental free associative interview with performance rated for involvement, freedom, and spontaneity, in addition to a general rating (Bordin, 1966b), I found no confirmation of Temerlin's results, but some support for Schneider in two separate samples of male college student volunteers. In this study and related exploratory observations there was some evidence that number of reversals reported during fixation on a reversible figure is positively related to performance, and that score on an ego control scale[6] derived from the MMPI is negatively related.

Mann (1965) devised MMPI and Rorschach indices of hysteric, obsessive, and borderline personality trends, inspired by a culling of research and theory. When she identified individuals in my two samples of student volunteers high on one of these three indices and compared the three groups for performance in free association, she found some differences that conformed to Bellak's expectation and others that did not. As expected, obsessive personality types displayed more self-observation than did hysterics and were less overtly inhibited; borderlines showed more primary process responses than either of the other groups. Contrary to expectations, obsessives displayed greater involvement (i.e., energy investment) and as much spontaneity as did hysterics. The borderlines were generally more similar to obsessives than to hysterics, a result about which no clear expectations existed, especially in view of the ambiguities created by the fact that all subjects were free of any known psychiatric history.

If one roughly equates the Epstein-Fenz (1967) repression-sensitization scale to the hysteric-obsessive distinction, Stein's (1971) results on the effects of forewarning on the task to free associate to emotionally laden word stimuli represent further confirmation of Mann's findings. Using GSR/basal conductance range scores as an index of arousal, Stein found that repressors displayed more arousal when the associative task was unexpected and that sensitizers were more aroused when notified in advance of the task. The confirmatory interpretation requires complex assumptions. If we take the indications of arousal as reflecting interfering anxiety, we find a correspondence to Mann's observation that obsessives were better able to perform the self-observing aspects, but the anomaly that obsessives also displayed greater affective involvement remains. For example, Stein found that the repressors (hysterics) were also higher in an immediate repetition of the task designed to tap spontaneous recovery. If the arousal index can reflect affective involvement as well as interfering anxiety, Stein's data contradict these latter aspects of Mann's results and are more in accord with general lore about the greater amenability of hysterics to psychoanalysis. Holt's system of rating the management of primary process, which seems a close relative to Schneider's balance indices, was shown to be positively correlated with a positive response syndrome in a sensory deprivation situation (Goldberger & Holt, 1961). Finally, Stollak et al. (1967) reported that subjects expressing the most satisfaction with themselves spoke more about themselves in the present tense and used more

---

[6] The high end of this scale appears to suggest conventionality, inhibition, and narrow or slow expressiveness.

feeling words during a 15-minute period of solitary free association than those expressing dissatisfaction with themselves.

It is to be hoped that the further use of the free association analogue will lead to studies clarifying questions regarding personality differences in initial responses to the free associative task.

Whenever methods of psychotherapy feature a working situation in which the patient takes the lead in struggling with himself, his problems, and his experiences, even when free association per se is not the rule, it would appear that certain qualities associated with introspection, thinking, and communicating are demanded of him. Intelligence and verbal facility, imaginative and cognitive flexibility may all be involved. A great deal of work has centered around voice quality as an index of the degree to which the client is entering into a psychodynamically oriented working alliance. The earliest of this series of studies of client-centered therapy, by Kirtner and Cartwright (1958), suggested that those who terminated in 12 or fewer interviews and were judged unsuccessful could be differentiated from failures in the 12- to 21-interview zone in terms of their first interview behavior. The former were more frequently characterized by an externalized approach to their problems, whereas the latter, although also externalized, were less blatantly so and were more able to discuss feelings, even though in a distant style. Successful cases were marked by much more immediacy, especially of feeling.

Rice has pursued this line of investigation, concentrating on paralinguistic indices of expressiveness, possibly reflective of the individual's capacity to enter deeply and fully into an experience of self. In the first study (Rice & Wagstaff, 1967), voice quality displayed in the first interview was found to identify early terminators and to differentiate those who improved from those who were unimproved at completion of treatment. Using the same cases in collaboration with Gaylin (1973), Rice found that those who were judged to respond to psychotherapy with a turning inward of attention and energy and who directed it toward self-exploration were marked by such indices of flexibility and creativity as the total number of Rorschach responses, the proportion devoted to responses featured by determinants other than form, and the number of responses featuring complex organizations. The MMPI failed to show any differentiations. It is not clear whether the third study (Rice, 1973) involved a further analysis applied to essentially the same population (48 of an original 52); all data were from the University of Chicago Counseling Center. In any case, this was a complex analysis seeking to examine the full therapy career and the interactions between therapist and patient influences. A striking feature of the results was that client style (i.e., voice quality) does not change over the course of therapy, yet is the sole predictor of outcome. These last results suggest that this index of voice quality reflects some capacity of the individual which bears on his ability to collaborate, but does not itself change in company with improvement. The Balanced against the evidence that voice quality reflects an enduring personality feature (Rice & Gaylin, 1973) and is unchanged in therapy is Warren's and Rice's (1972) demonstration that voice quality could be changed by extratherapy sessions designed to make the client aware of differences in voice quality and to practice the desired one. The generalizability of these results is yet to be established.

Ryan (1973) sought without success to relate Gaylin's measure and other Rorschach indices to ratings of personal freedom as exhibited in the first interview. He did find a suggestion that readiness to perceive human movement is positively related. Without further data, it is not possible to conclude that this represents a failure to confirm the results of Rice and Gaylin, since it may reflect either the difference between client-centered and psychoanalytically oriented psychotherapy or the difference between the ratings of personal freedom and the Rice-Wagstaff voice quality measure or both.

To the extent that psychotherapy attrition studies tap factors bearing on the patient's capacity to conform to the requirements of the situation, their results support the belief that intelligence, verbal facility, and cognitive flexibility are implicated. Studies of wide-ranging samples of male veterans utilizing Veterans Administration outpatient clinics have consistently shown that early-attrition groups were marked by lower vocabulary scores (Lorr, Katz, & Rubinstein, 1958; McNair, Lorr, & Callahan, 1963; Rubinstein & Lorr, 1956) or lower verbal intelligence (Affleck & Mednick, 1959). Moreover, Auld and Eron (1953) obtained the same results in terms of verbal intelligence in a nonveteran adult outpatient sample. With regard to Rorschach indices of cognitive flexibility, the results are marked by much greater inconsistency. There is, however, a marked consistency in finding that early attrition is associated with much less productivity (R) (Affleck & Mednick, 1959; Auld & Eron, 1953; Gibby et al., 1953, 1954; Koltov & Meadow, 1953; Taulbee, 1958). When it comes to the perception of human movement or closely allied responses, failures to confirm abound.

We might expect that collaboration in behavior therapy would be less demanding of those qualities of psychological mindedness, verbal facility, and cognitive flexibility which are thought to be required by therapy from a psychodynamic orientation. Ryan and Gizynski (1971), after interviewing a group of patients at varying periods of time after completion of behavior therapy, thought that they saw evidence that persons who are drawn to this type of treatment are marked by an externalizing style of dealing with themselves and their problems. That cognitive flexibility and a stance toward exploring and confronting one's feelings may represent obstacles toward collaboration in this pattern of psychotherapy is suggested by their observations of dissatisfactions by some with the tedium, artificiality, and mechanical qualities of the treatment process. Obviously, more systematic and direct observation is needed to confirm such impressions.

A pair of investigations by Hekmat examines a question which cuts across psychodynamic and behavior therapies, namely, what personality characteristics influence the conditionability of self-disclosure. Both of these studies relied on experimental analogues with recruited subjects. In one, Hekmat (1971b), starting from demonstrations by Eysenck and others that introverts are more conditionable than extroverts, tested the extension of this phenomenon to affective self-disclosure in response to colored pictures of people, objects, and places, with positive results. The second experimental design (Hekmat & Theiss, 1971) used the Personal Orientation Inventory, a measure of self-actualizing potential, to test the idea that those high in this quality would be oriented to draw on themselves as the basis of action and therefore resist external influences such as conditioning. Once again, affective self-disclosure in response to colored pictures was the dependent variable, but whereas the earlier study used expressions of approval as the reinforcing stimuli, this one relied on reflective statements that were merely paraphrases of the subject's preceding response. The group high in self-actualizing potential exhibited a higher rate of self-disclosure during preconditioning trials, but no significant effects of conditioning, and maintained its level of response in the face of extinction. Although this result would seem to fulfill expectation, it may not represent an adequate test. Since the high group seems to have already established the desired response pattern, as shown by its preconditioning response rate being higher than the rates of the other groups after conditioning, a test of its susceptibility to a specifically designed deconditioning process is required. In addition, since, to my knowledge, data on the connection between introversion and self-actualization are not available, the results of the two experiments cannot be related to each other.

Sarason (1958) provides suggestive evidence that some of the patient's personality characteristics may have the same consequences for collaboration in either behavior or psychodynamically oriented therapy. He selected anxiety, defensiveness, and hostility, measured by personality inventories, in a sample of neurotic and psychotic patients in intensive treatment. He found that two measures of anxiety and the measure of defensiveness differentiated levels of conditioning in a relatively impersonal verbal reinforcement situation. Anxiety correlated positively and defensiveness negatively with level of conditioning. On this basis of their therapists' ratings, those low on complicance were also lower on anxiety, but not significantly different on defensiveness. They did, however, condition least. Sarason interpreted his findings in terms of the greater feeling of vulnerability of the anxious person influencing this need to accept direction from an authoritative person in a strange situation.

To the extent that behavior approaches, with their emphasis on setting the patient a series of specific tasks, may tap attitudes toward authority, this feature of the patient's personality can be expected to influence the nature and course of treatment, especially the collaborative aspects of it. But the setting of specific tasks and other related collaborative aspects may be included also in other therapies. In fact, Dana (1954), using ratings of the adequacy of responses to Card IV of the Rorschach as indices of attitudes toward authority, found that those rated as giving inadequate responses were more likely to be rated as unimproved in short-term (less than 20 interviews) psychotherapy. This same index was the only Rorschach differentiation that Whitely and Blaine (1967) were able to find between long- and short-term (less than 24 interviews) therapy samples. The long-term therapy sample gave more adequate responses. Studies of early terminators at Veterans Administration outpatient clinics (Lorr et al., 1958; McNair et al., 1963; Rubinstein & Lorr, 1956) found them higher than continuers on a measure of antisocial behavior and psychopathic tendencies, but they were also higher on the F scale, which is interpreted to reflect authoritarian attitudes and conventionality. Whether the latter observation is contradictory to the former depends on how much one attributes the F scale to attitudes toward authority or to rigidity.

Two other investigations may have a bearing, but they vary widely in conceptual perspective and in methods, providing little basis for convergence of the results. In the first of these, Horton and Kriauciunas (1970) compared adolescent clients of a community youth counseling service who were judged by their counselors as having left counseling before it was completed with those who completed it (median number of interviews 6 vs. 13). Examining differences between the two groups on the MMPI, they found support for the idea that teenagers who displayed evidences of marked rebellion toward authority were poor prospects for counseling, but little support for the idea that continuers would be characterized as help seekers. The other experiment is relevant if one turns to Rotter's (1966) notion about locus of control as a source of understanding reactions to collaboration with an intervening therapist. Nowicki, Bonner, and Feather et al., (1972) administered two kinds of interviews to college student subjects, one consisting of training for relaxation and the other being a semistructured exploration of family and personal background and present-day activities. Two clinically trained interviewers alternated in conducting the two types of interviews. After each interview, subjects filled out Leary's Interpersonal Checklist as a rating of the interviewer. The results showed an interaction between procedure and locus of control. Those who perceived their loci of control as internal rated the interviewers in the relaxation condition more dominant than did the externals, and the latter rated them more loving. Obviously, these results are only tenuously related to issues of collaboration.

Other than possible embeddedness in studies relating them to improvement, there has been no evidence relating such global measures as ego strength, based on the MMPI, and the Rorschach Prognostic Rating Scale to collaboration. As the review by Luborsky et al. (1971) shows, the results relating these two measures to improvement are highly mixed and basically discouraging. It suggests to me that such global approaches are to be avoided in favor of relating much more specific features of functioning to particular phases of the therapeutic process.

Diagnosis

Embedded in many clinical discussions of the treatment process for a particular diagnostic class are specifications relevant to the kind of working alliance required and to its vicissitudes. Mention was made earlier of Braatøy's (1954) distinction between the ready response of hysterical patients to attention to body movements, and the attitude of compulsive neurotics, who require a long period of trust building as a preliminary to a positive use of such attention. Kernberg (1970) summarizes accumulated clinical impressions that the narcissistic personality on entering treatment gives a pseudo appearance of dependence as a function of the satisfactions of closeness, but that his fear of dependence makes for shallowness in the relationship and for subtle efforts to devaluate the therapist and to use him as an audience for his own independent but unavailing "analytic" work. Drawing on a range of approaches to therapy for phobias, behavior as well as psychodynamic, Andrews (1966) proposes that phobics are marked by an exaggerated dependency, to which the therapist must respond by partially reciprocating these demands for protection and guidance as a preliminary toward urging the steps which entail confrontation of the phobic stimuli and a movement toward self-reliance.

Greenson (1967, p. 207) summarizes the clinical experience of psychoanalysts that psychotic or borderline patients, impulse-ridden persons, and young children, all of whom dare not give up their reality testing even temporarily or partially, will require modifications in the regression-facilitating features of the working relationship. The implication is, of course, that, without such modifications or even in spite of them, these patients, as contrasted with those of greater ego strength and flexibility, primarily neurotics, will experience greater difficulty in the wide range of collaborations demanded in the psychoanalytic process. Similarly, Arieti (1961), in discussing psychoanalytic therapy of schizophrenics, stresses the long process entailed in developing an effective working alliance and the remission of the acute phase as preliminary to a treatment phase directed toward more lasting fundamental change. The extended initial period demanded by the schizophrenic's devastatingly pervasive fear of relatedness requires active, sensitive intervention directed toward the building of basic trust. Weigert (1961) warns that, whereas the psychotherapist may expect a gradual melting of the schizophrenic patient's armor of distrustful withdrawal and seemingly resigned hopelessness, the manic-depressive patient is frequently carried away by spurious hopes and gullibility. She offers no simply formulated solutions to this type of patient's parodoxically urgent demand for the help that he desperately refuses.

Research designs directed toward the interaction of diagnosis and treatment methods are few and far between; virtually none of them has been addressed to specific questions regarding the working alliance. Truax and his associates (Truax & Carkhuff, 1965b; Truax & Wargo, 1969; Truax, Wargo, & Voeksdorf, 1970) in a series of investigations of group therapy found that role induction training was useful to the therapy of hospitalized, largely psychotic patients, and with outpatients, largely neurotic, but had no influence on the therapy of institutionalized delinquents. The differences in therapy were defined in outcome terms rather than in terms of the working alliance. Since these investigators had obtained measures of group depth of self-exploration, it is unfortunate that their only use of this observation was as an independent variable, relating it to outcome; they did not address the question of whether role training influenced depth of self-exploration, one index of the working alliance, or whether these two influences on outcome operated independently of each other.

Other data certainly suggest that the development of a working alliance with delinquents and criminals, more specifically psychopaths, may have a different course and fate from that involving other patient groups. Earlier in this chapter mention was made of Cairns' (1961) demonstration that delinquents reject dependency behavior and of Steuart's and Resnick's (1970) evidence that delinquents are less amenable than nondelinquents to conditioning of the emission of dependency-expressing verbs. Starting from Heider's balance theory of interpersonal perception, Harari (1971) showed that, in an experimental situation far removed from psychotherapy, delinquent, as compared to nondelinquent adolescents, were much more balance seeking (led to like another person) when that person had power as compared to moral obligation to bring about a desired change; non-delinquents exhibited the opposite tendency. Speaking of the attainment of affection and trust for the therapist by the patient, Harari concludes: "In the case of the delinquent adolescent who indicates that he needs help, the message to the therapist is clear: he must be directive, structured, limit setting, perhaps even 'omnipotent.' Failing to do so, he will lose the patient's affection and thus jeopardize the entire therapeutic process" (p. 133). If the aforementioned evidence of the psychopath's counterdependent stance is to be taken seriously, the application of Harari's prescription must be tempered with a concern for the delinquent's sensitivity about accepting dependence. Giving even greater pause are the conflicting results obtained regarding the responsiveness of psychopaths to social reinforcers in conditioning situations.

Doctor and Craine (1971) sought to resolve contradictory findings by distinguishing between "primary" and "neurotic" psychopaths among a sample of postnarcotic male addicts. Although they obtained differences in ease of conditioning drug language usage, these differences were opposite from the expected direction, namely, the primary psychopaths conditioned better than the neurotic ones, thereby only adding to the confusion. How Di Caprio's (1970) proposed method of verbal satiation as a means of getting rid of such unwanted positive emotion-ladden responses as over-eating or drug addiction would work with psychopaths is at this date untested.

In a report which gives only brief attention to describing the complex methodology, Tourney et al. (1966) compared psychotherapeutic processes in samples of psychoneurotic and schizophrenic patients in therapy with psychiatric residents. Some inferences about the collaborative process may be made from such findings as the following: therapist errors of commission interfere more with the schizophrenic patient's verbal productivity and are more likely to arouse his anxiety and to provoke negative reactions toward the therapist, whereas the neurotic patient is more likely to manifest resistance and hostility toward the therapist; the two groups are differentiated in their response to errors of commission only in that greater anxiety is exhibited by the neurotics; in addition to such differences, anxious and depressed therapist reactions elicit greater manifestation of thought disorders in schizophrenics, and hostile therapist responses, although provoking anxiety, are accompanied by schizophrenics' manifesting more positive feelings to the therapist. Similar support for general notions about the differences in the collaborative styles of neurotic and schizophrenic patients may be inferred from the results obtained by Howard, Orlinsky, and Trattner (1970) in their study of the psychotherapy of female outpatients.

Their data derived from therapist self-reports on therapeutic style (Therapy Orientation Questionnaire) and from patient's reports on their therapeutic experiences at the end of consecutive sessions through a considerable period of their therapy. The biggest differentiating effect was found for an impersonal-personal dimension of the therapist's technique. The impersonal emphasis showed a big effect on schizophrenics in promoting greater involvement with the therapist, including both attraction, seeking to dominate or to obtain support, and a greater concern with reality in seeking orientation and talking about fantasy. In contrast, the only effect on patients presenting anxiety reactions was to foster a greater experience of self-rejection, and in depressive reactions and personality disorders the impersonal technique inhibited the development of personal involvement with the therapist.

To the extent that patient level of experiencing as defined in client-centered research is an index of collaboration in therapy similar to compliance with the task of free association in psychoanalytic therepy, there are possible contradictions between my results (Bordin, 1966b) and those of Kiesler (1971). I found that hospitalized psychiatric patients responded as well to the task of free association as did college student subjects free of overt signs of psychiatric difficulty. Comparing process data from individual psychotherapy with schizophrenics with those obtained in work with outpatient college student neurotics, Kiesler found that neurotic patients, regardless of ultimate success, manifested a higher level of experiencing in the first five interviews than did the schizophrenics. More successful cases do score higher in level of experiencing over the whole course of the therapy. If one assumes that a great overlap exists between experiencing and free associative response, as was suggested in Chapter 5, and that my sample of college students should be expected to respond as well as neurotic college students or better, these two sets of findings would appear contradictory. Other than invalidating one or both of these assumptions, it might be possible to resolve the contradiction by pointing out that my college student sample was participating not in therapy but in an experimental procedure analogous to psychotherapy and as subjects rather than patients. The lower level of personal involvement to be expected under these conditions may have accounted for the discrepancy.

One of the most meaningful research designs would be the comparison of contrasting methods of treatment with a given diagnostic group. Although a number of such investigations have been reported, none of them has directed sufficient attention to the question of the working alliance to warrant reviewing it here. Instead these studies will be considered below as we turn to the influence of patient personality on the effect of interventions.

PERSONALITY AND INTERVENTION EFFECTS

On reviewing the work bearing on the dependence of the effects of various kinds of interventions on the personality of the patient, I am left with a dismaying sense of not being able to draw clear issues or conclusions. Apart from my own limitations, as we shall see, research has simply not been definitive enough. Moreover, as I developed my ideas and delved into the research from the point of view of the collaboration between patient and therapist, a suspicion began to form that the personality of the patient has the greatest differential effect on the kind of collaboration into which he can enter and in which therapy can be carried out to a conclusion. Particularly, as I looked at prescriptions for differential treatment according to diagnosis (e.g., Federn, 1952; Wexler, 1953; Kernberg, 1970; Hammer, 1968; Marks and Gelder, 1966), I found most of the differences to be concentrated on the working alliance. This finding suggests that, if the patient can enter the required alliance, the intervention will work. This point is well illustrated by the finding by Katz, Lorr, and Rubinstein (1958) that those characteristics which predicted with reasonable accuracy whether a patient would prematurely terminate his therapy had no predictive value for subsequent improvement for those who stayed the course. Yet there are reports which encourage a belief that therapeutic effectiveness and efficiency can be enhanced by the proper selective application of treatment methods. Kennedy (1965), for example, by establishing criteria for separating school phobias into two groups, one marked by a sudden acute onset in a basically sound parental relationship and the other by more chronic, continuing difficulties in a basically disharmonious parental relationship, was able to devise a quick treatment for the first group which achieved complete remission in all 50 cases in his sample. Since his clinic accepted only a few of the other type of phobia for teaching purposes, he confines his report to the simple statement that its success in treating the second type "has not been remarkable."

Although there have been many investigations of outcome of psychotherapy for particular diagnostic groups or in relation to specific personality attributes (see Luborsky et al., 1971), very few of them provide cross-study bases for comparisons of rates of improvement, so that no conclusions can be drawn about the effectiveness of different types of interventions or intervention patterns. One of the few reports which approaches this goal was offered by an individual practitioner (Yaskin, 1936), summarizing his experience in the treatment of 100 cases seen in private outpatient practice. Using his own estimates as the criteria, he reports high rates of recovery or improvement with conversion and anxiety hysterics when treated by relatively short-term (less than 6 months) partially psychoanalytic techniques. With compulsive-obsessive patients treated by similar methods a much lower rate was obtained. Many other methods of treatment were used (e.g., suggestion, persuasion, sedatives, physical therapy), always, in the case of the obsessive-compulsives, with partial analysis. With the hysterics, partial analysis was not always employed, but recovery or improvement was observed only in instances into which this treatment entered. One research group examining the treatment of ulcerative colitis by psychoanalytic methods (Karush et al., 1968) reported that with borderline or psychotic patients there was nearly double the likelihood of a poor result, as compared to the treatment of nonpsychotic patients. One investigation focused on group therapy with college students who displayed marked underachievement (Mandel, Roth, & Berenbaum, et al., 1968). Using a psychoanalytic framework, Mandel et al. identified three subgroups: neurotic difficulty, traced to the oedipal period and marked by gross, unsophisticated defenses in maintaining dependence on parental figures; behavior disorder, also designated as nonachievement syndrome (NAS), seen as fixated at preadolescent latency and marked by excellence at "game relationships" designed to continue dependence and to avoid being confronted with the developmental issues of adolescence; and adolescent reaction, seen as the most mature—the need is for attaining an integrated self-involving acceptance as a person and support for decision making. Only the NAS group showed a significant relationship between personality change in response to therapy and increase in academic achievement.

A few studies have used such broad categories as to offer little basis for definitive conclusion apart from the statistical significance of the results. When Johnson (1965) differentiated between college student clients presenting emotional and those with vocational problems, he found a positive relationship between number of interviews and outcome for the former, but not for the latter. This difference might reflect differences in the level of collaboration, influenced by the greater pain of those presenting emotional problems. Two investigations (Berenson, Mitchell, & Laney, 1968; Mitchell & Namenek, 1972) examined confrontations in first interviews with college student clients as compared with inpatients, largely schizophrenic. Although confrontations represent interventions susceptible of analysis as factors independent of the working alliance (but of course not uninfluenced by it), the fact that observations were drawn from the first hour suggests the highly special circumstance in which the working alliance is only just being formed. In any case the effects of differences between clients and patients were barely noticeable. Mitchell and Namenek found that the clients, unlike the patients, increased their levels of self-exploration in response to confrontations from therapists rated low in therapy facilitating characteristics, a result difficult to comprehend.

The phobias have been a particularly fruitful area for the application of research designs directed toward comparing methods of treatment with a particular kind of person. Andrews' (1966) review is particularly useful in pointing up features that might distinguish major approaches to psychotherapy of phobias and also in pinpointing possible interaction between treatment of choice and presenting problem. Andrews finds avoidance and dependence as the main elements in phobias, leading him to the conclusion that the treatment process must necessarily include the building of an attachment to the therapist, which can provide him with the leverage to exert pressure on the patient to confront the phobic situation and to learn new ways of responding. With the support and encouragement of the therapist, the phobic patient learns new ways of responding and also acquires a new conception of himself. Andrews suggests that this description of the treatment process is in accord with the beliefs and procedures of all types of therapists except those adhering to a behavior orientation. Furthermore, he believes that the latter group's more specific and more limited treatment may be in order in instances where the phobia represents a relatively isolated difficulty in an otherwise satisfactory life pattern.

Despite the specificity of Andrews' propositions, and the fact that more definitive research is available on phobias than other pathological states, it is still not possible to test their tenability with the data at hand. Paul's (1966) classic study of speech anxiety does not differentiate the subjects with regard to dependence, nor is the comparison of systematic desensitization with "insight"-oriented treatment analyzed further with regard to the dependency and confrontation issues as they operated in the latter treatment. Hence we are left only with evidence that in a heterogeneous group of college students, who had sought help only after a specific invitation to volunteer, desensitization was more effective in reducing the symptom than insight-oriented therapy. It is of interest that Kennedy's (1965) brief treatment of phobic children involved advising parents to gently but firmly push their children to attend school. Unfortunately, an otherwise well controlled investigation of the comparative effects of desensitization and psychotherapy with phobic children (Miller et al., 1972), over two thirds of whom were school phobic, did not appear to include such procedures with parents and did not apply Kennedy's criteria for identifying phobias susceptible of that treatment. No differences in effectiveness of desensitization and psychotherapy were discernible.

A number of investigators have examined the role of thought and other mediating processes in the treatment of phobias (Karst & Trexler, 1970;

Nolan, Mattis, & Holliday, 1970; Trexler & Karst, 1972), but offer us no basis for accepting or rejecting Andrews' assumptions regarding the influence of changed conceptions of self. Nolan and his associates do report that college women subjects presenting fears of both rats and snakes, after being treated by desensitization for the rat fear, could apply the treatment themselves for the snake fear, but with only slight results of little duration. Rational treatment, patterned after Ellis, however, produced distinct results, though they did not appear as enduring as those obtained by desensitization. The two studies by Karst and Trexler were concerned solely with cognitive therapies applied to public speaking anxiety. In the first (Karst & Trexler, 1970), therapies based on Ellis versus Kelly were compared and no difference was obtained, but both produced significant improvement by the close of treatment. The finding of improvement was replicated for rational emotive therapy in the later study, as compared to attention-placebo and no-treatment controls.

Earlier in this chapter, while discussing how patient personality differences can influence the working alliance into which the patient can enter, I suggested the possibility that collaboration might be less demanding in behavior therapy than in psychodynamically oriented therapy in one respect, namely, the patient's willingness and ability to engage in self-observation and in the flexibility and range of his cognitive skills. There is the further possibility that differences in dynamic organization will make some persons more responsive than others to a treatment which focuses on a specific segment of their response repertoire, as does behavior therapy. The empirical possibilities are best illustrated by Novick's (1966) examination of the results of symptomatic treatment of enuresis. He selected for treatment two sets of enuretic boys; in one the symptom had been present since birth, and in the other it had appeared after at least a 6-month period of continence. The treatment procedure consisted of 10 days of supportive therapy, relieving the child's guilt, increasing his confidence, and allying with him by dissuading his mother from the employment of harshly punitive measures, followed, if no positive effects were visible, by installing a wetting alarm apparatus. Those with acquired enuresis (previously continent) responded more favorably to routine supportive treatment alone and took less time to reach the criterion of 14 consecutive symptom-free nights, but wet more frequently after cure in a 10-month followup period and exhibited significantly more new symptoms after treatment. Unfortunately, though Baker (1969) employed the wetting alarm apparatus, he did not address the question of patient differences.[7]

In considering the treatment of depressive patients, Lewinsohn and his

---

[7] Since he does not cite Novick, he may have been unaware of this previous study.

associates (Lewinsohn, Weinstein, & Alper, 1970; Lewinsohn & Shaffer, 1971) have suggested that the depressed person suffers from a reduced rate of positive reinforcement and propose that he be treated by teaching him the social skills needed for eliciting such reinforcements from others. They tried to buttress this position by demonstrating that depressed individuals were more vulnerable to aversive stimuli than less depressed normal or psychiatric controls (Lewinsohn, Lobitz, & Wilson, 1973). Although such greater vulnerability might lead to being less skilled in social situations because of avoiding them, it suggests also that, social skill or not, the depressed person's attention and experience will be captured by aversive elements in situations. Evidence (Miller & Seligman, 1973) that depressed individuals do not change their expectancies for success in a test of skill in response to positive reinforcements to trials would seem to support this alternative. Another, wider-ranging study of predictors of response to differential treatments of depression (Weckowitz et al., 1971) gives little information for our purpose, since the psychotherapy of these hospitalized patients, which was compared with drugs and shock, is left undefined. From a large body of measures the investigators found evidence that neurotic-depressives are more responsive to psychotherapy than to either of the other two kinds of treatment, but that therapy is longer and the prognosis is not good.

SUMMARY

Review of the evidence seems to support the belief that the patient's personality has a bearing on the outcome of particular methods of psychotherapy. I find most of the data pointing to the conclusion that personality differences affect the form of collaboration successfully established, rather than the usefulness of the interventions for which collaboration is required. However, the evidence also indicates that we do not have available as yet a definitive basis for distinguishing the influence which a specific working alliance in a particular kind of treatment produces from the effects of treatment when good collaboration has been established. These two sets of factors have not been separated thoroughly enough in research designs. It is quite possible for different therapists looking at the same sets of investigations to arrive at different conclusions. Differentiation and refinement of the effects of patient personality are the challenge for future investigators.

CHAPTER 9

Postscript

This book evolved over a period of years. I began with a sense of the scattered quality of research in psychotherapy. What we need more than anything else, I thought, is a shared, greater sense of direction with regard to substantive questions and the instrumental definitions and methods required to put them to test. Then the desired result would be achieved, namely, an acceleration in the degree to which research can participate in the dialogue of ideas, whereby the tenability of conflicting ideas (and associated procedures) can be tested against observation and the paradoxes of conflicting results pursued more deeply, often to new insights. Now, at the completion of my task, I have a somewhat different view, perhaps because I know the field better, but also because the field itself may have already begun to change in the direction to which I had hoped to move it. If I make any contribution, as I trust I will, it will be in aiding in the acceleration of that motion.

My changed notions of the state of our knowledge of change in psychotherapy are founded in my reviews of research in the preceding four chapters. Although, for the most part, still very rough and loose, there is much more convergence to be found than was suggested by the remark, made about 1950, that "psychotherapy is an undefined technique applied to unspecified problems with unpredictable outcome" (e.g., Raimy, 1950, p. 93), echos of which persist to this day, or by the commonly heard prefacing clause, "since no effects of psychotherapy have been established. . . ." As I have shown, there is respectable evidence of short- or long-term effects of various aspects of the psychotherapeutic situation and of the functional relations among various components of it. True, these items of evidence are still a great distance from fostering a highly advanced level of precision in theoretical propositions and in procedural specifications, but nevertheless contradict the position of the nihilistic skeptic.

I believe that we are entering a period with potential for great progress. The past decade has seen an explosion of ideas about psychotherapeutic procedures. Flights of creativity carry with them the seeds of their own destruction if their creators are unwilling to subject them to the disciplined reworking that either high art or science requires. Adherence to new procedures must not be allowed to wax and wane in response to fads and fashions, or, more importantly, to be kept alive by human misery and the hope for relief in the absence of verification of their underlying ideas and effects. The tools for carrying forward these necessary processes of verification are appearing. As I write these closing words on my contribution to these tasks, there lies on my desk the recently issued compilation and critical analysis by Kiesler (1973) of direct and indirect measures applied to psychotherapeutic process, a magnificent aid to the convergence of data from research. It adds materially to the resources offered by Strupp and Bergin (1969) and by the report of the workshop on research planning (Fiske et al., 1970). All these will lead to even greater movement away from a fascination with the politics of ideology toward a more finely honed examination of specific processes within their social and interpersonal contexts, such as London (1972), within the framework of behavior modification, has recently advocated with eloquence and clarity.

The reader will perforce draw his own conclusions about the areas needing the most research attention and those that are most ready for further progress. My own completion needs require articulation of my views from the perspective of the review just completed.

The biggest methodological issue, that of the criterion or of criteria, lies beyond the narrow scope of research on psychotherapy in the broader area of personology and abnormal psychology. We seem to be on a 20- to 30-year plateau in the evolution of concepts and measurements applicable to the enduring features of human behavior and experience. More than additional gross evaluative studies, we need new ideas and investigations directed toward the criterion in change-oriented investigations. While we await such developments, hopefully not too long delayed, I see a special need for two kinds of more restricted methodologically oriented investigations. One of these is a more thorough examination of the relations among different channels of observation of the process of psychotherapy, with particular emphasis on the cost/benefit of making available the full range of sensory channels (visual, auditory, etc.) versus different degrees of restriction. The other need is for fuller investigation of the generalizability of various analogues through bridging research. Under the impetus of the behavior therapists, reliance on data from analogues has far outstripped demonstration that they are in fact relevant to the naturalistic events to which they are intended to apply. We need such research not only to prevent us from diverting energies off into blind alleys and to avoid becoming prisoners of false facts, but also to stimulate the development of valid analogues which can be instrumental to a rapid surge in productive research.

Exploitation of the impressive research on the conditions offered by the therapist that facilitate psychotherapy and the influence of expectations requires utilization of the concept of a working alliance. We need to examine the different kinds of working alliances built into the different genres of psychotherapy and behavior change, with the aim of ascertaining the personal demands on therapist and/or patient that each makes and the consequences of one or the other participant being unable to meet one or more of these demands.

My review uncovers the fact there have been few critical empirical confrontations between competing theories and practices of psychotherapy. One reason for such a lack is the unevenness of empirical investigations from within each framework. Client-centered therapy and behavior therapy have been the most thoroughly investigated. Although there have been almost as many studies of psychoanalytically oriented ideas, they are relatively scarce when viewed against the range and complexities of the theory. Research has concentrated on a few aspects (e.g., interpretative interventions and patient response—even these rather incompletely); such areas as transference and countertransference, especially as process phenomena, are hardly touched. Neopsychoanalytic, Gestalt and existentially oriented psychotherapies are virtually untouched by empirical examination. Incidentally, I find myself watching with great anticipation the growing preoccupation of behavior therapists with ideas and research on self-control. At present they are most concerned with, in effect, the transfer of the selection and control for reinforcements from the therapist to the patient. Before long, I anticipate, not without some glee engendered from old scars, that this attention to self-control will sensitize them to the self-defeating self-controls that human beings are capable of developing. Moreover, they will begin to see these self-controls as the source of some of the human phenomena that are most resistant to change. If and when such a point is reached, the most meaningful and constructive research critical to the choice between psychodynamic and behavior views will evolve.

References

Abeles, N. Liking for clients—its relationship to therapist's personality and empathic understanding. *American Psychologist*, 1964, **19**, 572–573.

Adler, A. *The practice and theory of individual psychology.* New York: Harcourt Brace, 1924.

Adler, A. *Superiority and social interest.* H. and Rowena Ansbacher (Eds.). Evanston, Ill.: Northwestern University Press, 1964.

Affleck, D. C., & Mednick, S. A. The use of the Rorschach test in the prediction of the abrupt terminator in individual psychotherapy. *Journal of Consulting Psychology*, 1959, **23**, 125–128.

Alexander, F., & French, T. M. *Psychoanalytic therapy.* New York: Ronald Press, 1946.

Alexander, J. F., & Abeles, N. Dependency changes in psychotherapy as related to interpersonal relationships. *Journal of Consulting & Clinical Psychology*, 1968, **32**, 237–242.

Alexander, J. F., & Abeles, N. Psychotherapy process: sex differences and dependency. *Journal of Counseling Psychology*, 1969, **16**, 191–196.

Alexander, J. M., & Isaacs, K. M. The function of affect. *British Journal of Medical Psychology*, 1964, **37**, 231.

Alexik, Mae, & Carkhuff, R. R. The effects of the manipulation of client depth of self-exploration upon high and low functioning counselors. *Journal of Clinical Psychology*, 1967, **23**, 210–212.

Allen, F. H. *Psychotherapy with children.* New York: Norton, 1942.

Allen, G. J. Effectiveness of study counseling and desensitization in alleviating test anxiety in college students. *Journal of Abnormal Psychology*, 1971, **77**, 282–289.

Allen, T. W. Effectiveness of counselor trainees as a function of psychological openness. *Journal of Counseling Psychology*, 1967, **14**, 35–40.

American Psychological Association, Committee on Test Standards. Technical recommendations for psychological tests and diagnostic techniques. *Psychological Bulletin*, 1954, **51**, Supplement No. 2.

Anderson, Susan C. Effects of confrontation by high- and low-functioning therapists. *Journal of Counseling Psychology*, 1965, **15**, 411–416.

Anderson, Susan C. Effects of confrontation by high- and low-functioning therapists on high- and low-functioning clients. *Journal of Counseling Psychology*, 1969, **16**, 299–302.

Andrews, J. D. W. Psychotherapy of phobias. *Psychological Bulletin*, 1966, **66**, 455–480.

Angyal, A. *Foundations for a science of personality.* New York: Commonwealth Fund, 1941.

Apfelbaum, B. *Dimensions of transference in psychotherapy.* Berkeley: University of California Press, 1958.

Appel, V. H. Client expectancies about counseling in a university counseling center. Paper read at Western Psychological Association, San Jose, California, April 1960.

Arieti, S. Introductory notes on the psychoanalytic therapy of schizophrenics. In A. Burton (Ed.), *Psychotherapy of the psychoses.* New York: Basic Books, 1961.

Ashby, J. D., Ford, D. H., Guerney, B. B., Jr. & Guerney, Louise F. Effects on clients of a reflective and a leading type of psychotherapy. *Psychological Monographs,* 1957, **71** (24, whole No. 453).

Astin, A. W. The functional autonomy of psychotherapy. *American Psychologist,* 1961, **16**, 75–78.

Auld, F., Jr. Vicissitudes of communication in psychotherapy. In J. M. Shlien (Ed.), *Research in psychotherapy.* Vol. III. Washington, D.C.: American Psychological Association, 1968.

Auld, F., Jr., & Dollard, J. Measurement of motivational variables in psychotherapy. In L. A. Gottschalk and A. H. Auerbach (Eds.), *Methods of research in psychotherapy.* New York: Appleton-Century-Crofts, 1966.

Auld, F., Jr., & Eron, L. D. The use of Rorschach scores to predict whether patients will continue psychotherapy. *Journal of Consulting Psychology,* 1953, **17**, 104–109.

Auld, F., Jr., & Murray, E. J. Content-analysis studies of psychotherapy. *Psychological Bulletin,* 1955, **52**, 377–395.

Auld, F., Jr., & White, Alice M. Sequential dependencies in psychotherapy. *Journal of Abnormal & Social Psychology,* 1959, **58**, 100–104.

Ayllon, T., & Azrin, N. H. *The token economy: A motivational system for therapy and rehabilitation.* New York: Appleton-Century-Crofts, 1968.

Ayllon, T., & Haughton, E. Control of the behavior of schizophrenic patients by food. *Journal of Experimental Analysis of Behavior,* 1962, **5**, 343–352.

Azima, H., Vispo, R., & Azima, Fern J. Observations on anaclitic therapy during sensory deprivation. In P. Solomon et al. (Eds.), *Sensory deprivation.* Cambridge, Mass: Harvard University Press, 1961.

Babladelis, Georgia. Personality and verbal conditioning effects. *Journal of Abnormal Social Psychology,* 1961, **62**, 41–43.

Baehr, G. O. The comparative effectiveness of individual psychotherapy, group psychotherapy, and combinations of these methods. *Journal of Consulting Psychology,* 1954, **18**, 179–183.

Baer, D. M. Some remedial uses of the reinforcement contingency. In J. M. Shlien (Ed.), *Research in psychotherapy.* Vol. III. Washington, D.C.: American Psychological Association, 1968.

Baker, B. L. Symptom treatment and symptom substitution in enuresis. *Journal of Abnormal Psychology,* 1969, **74**, 42–49.

Bales, R. F. *Interaction process analysis.* Reading, Mass.: Addison-Wesley, 1950.

Bandura, A. Psychotherapists' anxiety level, self-insight and psychotherapeutic competence. *Journal of Abnormal & Social Psychology,* 1956, **52**, 333–337.

Bandura, A. Modelling approaches to the modification of phobic disorders. In R. Porter (Ed.), *Ciba Foundation symposium: The role of learning in psychotherapy.* London: Churchill, 1968.

Bandura, A. Psychotherapy based upon modeling principles. In A. E. Bergin & S. L. Garfield (Eds.), *Handbook of psychotherapy and behavior change.* New York: John Wiley, 1971.

Bandura, A., Blanchard, E. B., & Ritter, B. The relative efficacy of desensitization and modeling approaches for inducing behavioral, affective, and attitudinal changes. *Journal of Personality & Social Psychology,* 1969, **13**, 173–199.

Bandura, A., Lipshur, D., & Miller, P. E. Psychotherapists' approach-avoidance reactions to patient's expressions of hostility. *Journal of Consulting Psychology,* 1960, **24**, 1–8.

Bare, Carole E. Relationships of counselor personality and counselor-client personality similarity to selected success criteria. *Journal of Counseling Psychology,* 1967, **14**, 419–425.

Barrett-Lennard, G. T. Dimensions of therapist response as causal factors in therapeutic change. *Psychological Monographs,* 1962, **76** (43, whole No. 562).

Baugh, J. R. Pascol, G. R., & Cottrell, T. B. Relationship of reported memories of early experiences with parents on interview behavior. *Journal of Consulting & Clinical Psychology,* 1971, **37**, 187–194.

Beck, S. J. The Rorschach test, communication and psychotherapy. In L. A. Gottschalk and A. H. Auerbach (Eds.), *Methods of research in psychotherapy.* New York: Appleton-Century-Crofts, 1966.

Bednar, R. L. Therapeutic relationship of A-B therapists as perceived by client and therapist. *Journal of Counseling Psychology,* 1970, **17**, 119–122.

Bednar, R. L., & Mobley, M. J. A-B therapist perception and preferences for schizophrenic and psychoneurotic clients. *Journal of Abnormal Psychology,* 1971, **78**, 192–197.

Beery, Judith W. Therapists' responses as a function of level of therapist experience and attitude of the patient. *Journal of Consulting & Clinical Psychology,* 1970, **34**, 239–243.

Begley, C. E., & Liberman, L. R. Patient expectations of therapists' techniques. *Journal of Clinical Psychology,* 1970, **26**, 112–116.

Bellak, L. Free association: Conceptual and clinical aspects. *International Journal of Psychoanalysis,* 1961, **42**, 9–20.

Berdach, Elsie, & Bakan, P. Body position and the free recall of early memories. *Psychotherapy: Theory, research, and practice,* 1967, **4**, 101–102.

Berenson, B. G., Carkhuff, R. R. & Myrus, Pamela. The interpersonal functioning and training of college students. *Journal of Counseling Psychology,* 1966, **13**, 441–446.

Berenson, B. G., Mitchell, K. M., & Laney, R. C. Level of therapist functioning, types of confrontation and type of patient. *Journal of Clinical Psychology,* 1968, **24**, 111–113.

Berenson, B. G., Mitchell, K. M., & Moravec, J. A. Level of therapist functioning, patient depth of self-exploration, and type of confrontation. *Journal of Counseling Psychology,* 1968, **15**, 136–139.

Bergin, A. E. The effects of psychotherapy: Negative results revisited. *Journal of Counseling Psychology,* 1963, **10**, 244–250.

Bergin, A. E. The evaluation of therapeutic outcomes. In A. E. Bergin & S. L. Garfield (Eds.), *Handbook of psychotherapy and behavior change*. New York: John Wiley, 1971.

Bergin, A. E., & Jasper, L. G. Correlates of empathy in psychotherapy: A replication. *Journal of Abnormal Psychology*, 1969, **74**, 477–481.

Bergin, A. E., & Solomon, B. Personality and performance correlates of empathic understanding in psychotherapy. In T. Tamlinson & J. Hart (Eds.), *New directions in client-centered therapy*. Boston: Houghton-Mifflin, 1970.

Bergman, D. V. Counseling method and client response. *Journal of Consulting Psychology*, 1951, **15**, 216–224.

Bergman, P. An experiment in filmed psychotherapy. In L. A. Gottschalk and A. H. Auerbach (Eds.), *Methods of research in psychotherapy*. New York: Appleton-Century-Crofts, 1966.

Bernstein, D. A. Modification of smoking behavior: An evaluative review. *Psychological Bulletin*, 1969, **71**, 418–440.

Berzins, J. I., Friedman, W. H., & Seidman, E. Relationship of the A-B variable to patient symptomatology and psychotherapeutic expectancies. *Journal of Abnormal Psychology*, 1968, **74**, 119–125.

Berzins, J. I., Ross, W. F., & Friedman, W. H. A-B therapist distinction, patient diagnosis, and outcome of brief psychotherapy in a college clinic. *Journal of Consulting & Clinical Psychology*, 1972, **38**, 231–237.

Betz, Barbara J. Experience in research in psychotherapy with schizophrenic patients. In H. H. Strupp & L. Luborsky (Eds.), *Research in psychotherapy*. Vol. VI. Washington, D.C.: American Psychological Association, 1962.

Betz, Barbara. Bases of therapeutic leadership in psychotherapy with the schizophrenic patient. *American Journal of Psychotherapy*, 1963, **17**, 196–212.

Betz, Barbara J. Studies of the therapist's role in the treatment of the schizophrenic patient. *American Journal of Psychiatry*, 1967, **123**, 963–971.

Betz, Barbara, & Whitehorn, J. C. The relationship of the therapist to the outcome of therapy in schizophrenia. *Psychiatric Research Reports*, 1956, No. 5, 89–105.

Beutler, L. E. Attitude similarity in marital therapy. *Journal of Consulting & Clinical Psychology*, 1971, **37**, 298–301.

Beutler, L. E., Johnson, D. T., Neville, E. W. Jr., & Workman, S. N. "Accurate Empathy" and the A-B dichotomy. *Journal of Consulting & Clinical Psychology*, 1972, **38**, 372–375.

Bixler, R. H. Limits are therapy. *Journal of Consulting Psychology*, 1949, **13**, 1–11.

Blanchard, E. B. Relative contributions of modeling, informational influences, and physical contact in extinction of phobic behavior. *Journal of Abnormal Psychology*, 1970, **76**, 55–61.

Block, J., & Thomas, H. Is satifaction with self a measure of adjustment? *Journal of Abnormal & Social Psychology*, 1955, **51**, 254–259.

Bohn, M. J., Jr. Counselor behavior as a function of counselor dominance, counselor experience and client types. *Journal of Counseling Psychology*, 1965, **12**, 346–352.

Bohn, M. J., Jr. Therapist response to hostility and dependency as a function of training. *Journal of Consulting Psychology*, 1967, **31**, 195–198.

Bolgar, Hedda. The case study method. In B. B. Wolman (Ed.), *Handbook of clinical psychology*. New York: McGraw-Hill, 1965.

Boomer, D. S., & Dittmann, A. T. Speech, rate, filled pause, and bodily movement in interviews. *Journal of Nervous & Mental Diseases,* 1964, **139,** 324–327.

Bordin, E. S. Ambiguity as a therapeutic variable. *Journal of Consulting Psychology,* 1955, **19,** 9–15.

Bordin, E. S. Response to free association as a reflection of personality. *Acta Psychologica,* 1964, **23,** 120–121.

Bordin, E. S. Simplification as a strategy for research in psychotherapy. *Journal of Consulting Psychology,* 1965, **29,** 493–503. (a)

Bordin, E. S. The ambivalent quest for independence. *Journal of Counseling Psychology,* 1965, **12,** 339–345 (b)

Bordin, E. S. Curiosity, compassion, and doubt: The dilemma of the psychologist. *American Psychologist,* 1966, **21,** 116–121. (a)

Bordin, E. S. Personality and free association. *Journal of Consulting Psychology,* 1966, **30,** 30–38. (b)

Bordin, E. S. Free association: An experimental analogue of the psychoanalytic situation. In L. A. Gottschalk and A. H. Auerbach (Eds.), *Methods of research in psychotherapy.* New York: Appleton-Century-Crofts, 1966. (c)

Bordin, E. S. The personality of the therapist as an influence in psychotherapy. In M. J. Feldman (Ed.), *Studies in psychotherapy and behavioral change: Research in individual psychotherapy.* Buffalo Studies Vol. IV. Buffalo: State University of New York at Buffalo, 1968.

Bordin, E. S., Cutler, R. L., Dittmann, A. T., Harway, N. I., Raush, H. L., & Rigler, D. Measurement problems in process research on psychotherapy. *Journal of Consulting Psychology,* 1954, **18,** 79–82.

Bordin, E. S., Nachmann, Barbara, & Segal, S. J. An articulated framework for vocational development. *Journal of Counseling Psychology* 1963, **10,** 107–118.

Boudewyns, P. A., & Wilson, A. E. Implosive therapy and desensitization therapy using free association in the treatment of inpatients. *Journal of Abnormal Psychology,* 1972, **79,** 259–268.

Bozarth, J. D., & Grace, D. P. Objective ratings and client perceptions of therapeutic conditions with university counseling center clients. *Journal of Clinical Psychology,* 1970, **26,** 117–118.

Braatøy, T. *Fundamentals of psychoanalytic technique.* New York: John Wiley, 1954.

Brams, J. M. Counselor characteristics and effective communication in counseling. *Journal of Counseling Psychology,* 1961, **8,** 25–30.

Breedlove, J. L., & Krause, M. S. Evaluative research design: A social casework illustration. In L. A. Gottschalk and A. H. Auerbach (Eds.), *Methods of research in psychotherapy.* New York: Appleton-Century-Crofts, 1966.

Breger, L., & McGaugh, J. L. Critique and reformulation of "learning-theory" approaches to psychotherapy and neurosis. *Psychological Bulletin,* 1965, **63,** 338–358.

Brill, N. Q., & Storrow, H. A. Social class and psychiatric treatment. *Archives of General Psychiatry,* 1960, **3,** 340–344.

Bron, G. D. Client-counselor compatibility and the outcome of counseling. Unpublished thesis, University of California, Berkeley, 1971.

Bugental, J. F. T. *The search for authenticity.* New York: Holt, Rinehart and Winston, 1965.

Burdock, E. I., Cheek, F., & Zubin, J. Predicting success in psychoanalytic training. In P. Hoch & J. Zubin (Eds.), *Current approaches to psychoanalysis*. New York: Grune & Stratton, 1960.

Burstein, J. W., & Carkhuff, R. R. Objective, therapist and client ratings of therapist-offered facilitative conditions of moderate to low functioning therapists. *Journal of Clinical Psychology*, 1968, **24**, 240–241.

Butler, J. M., & Haigh, G. V. Changes in the relation between self-concepts and ideal concepts consequent upon client-centered counseling. In C. R. Rogers and R. F. Dymond (Eds.), *Psychotherapy and personality change*. Chicago: University of Chicago Press, 1954.

Butler, J. M., Rice, Laura N., & Wagstaff, Alice K. *Quantitative naturalistic research*. Englewood Cliffs, N.J. Prentice-Hall, 1963.

Cain, A. C. Therapist response to client resistance. Unpublished doctoral thesis, University of Michigan, 1962.

Cairns, R. B. The influence of dependency inhibition on the effectiveness of social reinforcements. *Journal of Personality*, 1961, **29**, 466–488.

Cairns, R. B., & Lewis, M. Dependency and the reinforcement value of a verbal stimulus. *Journal of Consulting & Clinical Psychology*, 1962, **26**, 1–8.

Calvin, A. D. Some misuses of the experimental method in evaluating the effect of client-centered counseling. *Journal of Counseling Psychology*, 1954, **1**, 249–251.

Campbell, D. T. Factors relevant to the validity of experiments in social settings. *Psychological Bulletin*, 1957, **54**, 297–312.

Campbell, D. T., & Fiske, D. W. Convergent and discriminative validation by the multitrait-multimethod matrix. *Psychological Bulletin*, 1959, **56**, 81–105.

Campbell, R. E. Counselor personality and background and his interview sub-role behavior. *Journal of Counseling Psychology*, 1962, **9**, 329–334.

Cannon, H. J. Personality variables and counselor-client affect. *Journal of Counseling Psychology*, 1964, **11**, 35–41.

Cannon, J. R., & Carkhuff, R. R. Effects of rater level of functioning and experience upon the discrimination of facilitative conditions. *Journal of Consulting & Clinical Psychology*, 1969, **33**, 189–195.

Caracena, P. F. Elicitation of dependency expressions in the initial stage of psychotherapy. *Journal of Counseling Psychology*, 1965, **12**, 268–274.

Caracena, P. F., & Vicory, J. R. Correlates of phenomenological and judged empathy. *Journal of Counseling Psychology*, 1969, **16**, 510–515.

Carkhuff, R. R. Training in the counseling and therapeutic practices: Requiem or reveille? *Journal of Counseling Psychology*, 1968, **15**, 68–74.

Carkhuff, R. R., Kratochvil, D., & Friel, T. Effects of professional training: Communication and discrimination of facilitative conditions. *Journal of Counseling Psychology*, 1968, **15**, 68–74.

Carkhuff, R. R., & Truax, C. B. Training in counseling and psychotherapy: An evaluation of an integrated didactic and experiential approach. *Journal of Consulting Psychology*, 1965, **29**, 333–336.

Carr, J. E. Differentiation similarity of patients and therapist and the outcome of psychotherapy. *Journal of Abnormal Psychology*, 1970, **76**, 361–369.

Carson, R. C., & Heine, R. W. Similarity and success in therapeutic dyads. *Journal of Consulting Psychology*, 1962, **26**, 38–43.

Carson, R. C., & Llewellyn, C. E., Jr. Similarity in therapeutic dyads: A reevaluation. *Journal of Consulting Psychology*, 1966, 30, 458.

Cartwright, D. S. Success in psychotherapy as a function of certain actuarial variables. *Journal of Consulting Psychology*, 1955, 19, 357–363.

Cartwright, D. S. Note on changes in psychoneurotic patients with and without psychotherapy. *Journal of Consulting Psychology*, 1956, 20, 403–404.

Cartwright, D. S., Kirtner, W. L., & Fiske, D. W. Method factors in changes associated with psychotherapy. *Journal of Abnormal and Social Psychology*, 1963, 66, 164–175.

Cartwright, Rosalind D., & Lerner, Barbara. Empathy, need to change, and improvement within psychotherapy. *Journal of Consulting Psychology*, 1963, 27, 138–144.

Cautella, J. R. Treatment of compulsive disorders by covert sensitization. *Psychological Record*, 1966, 16, 33–41.

Cautella, J. R. Covert sensitization. *Psychological Reports*, 1967, 20, 459–468.

Chance, Erika. *Families in treatment.* New York: Basic Books, 1959.

Chartier, G. M. A-B variable: Real or imagined? *Psychological Bulletin*, 1971, 75, 22–33.

Chinsky, J. M., & Rappaport, J. Brief critique of the meaning and reliability of "accurate empathy" ratings. *Psychological Bulletin*, 1970, 73, 379–381.

Chordorkoff, B. Self-perception, perceptual defense, and adjustment. *Journal of Abnormal & Social Psychology*, 1954, 49, 508–512. (a)

Chordorkoff, B. Adjustment and the discrepancy between perceived and ideal self. *Journal of Clinical Psychology*, 1954, 10, 266–268. (b)

Clemes, S. R., & D'Andrea, V. J. Patient's anxiety as a function of expectation and degree of initial interview ambiguity. *Journal of Consulting Psychology*, 1965, 29, 397–404.

Cochrane, Carolyn T. Effects of diagnostic information on empathic understanding by the therapist in a psychotherapy analogue. *Journal of Consulting & Clinical Psychology*, 1972, 38, 359–365.

Cohen, H. L. Educational therapy: The design of learning environments. In J. M. Shlien (Ed.), *Research in psychotherapy.* Vol. III. Washington, D.C.: American Psychological Association, 1968.

Colby, K. M. Experiment on the effects of an observer's presence on the image system during psychoanalytic free association. *Behavioral Science*, 1960, 5, 197–210.

Colby, K. M. On the greater amplifying power of causal correlative over interrogative inputs on free association in an experimental psychoanalytic situation. *Journal of Nervous & Mental Diseases*, 1961, 133, 233–239.

Colby, K. M. Causal correlations in clinical interpretations. In Loriss Paul (Ed.), *Psychoanalytic clinical interpretation.* London: Free Press of Glencoe, 1963.

Cole, C. W. Effects of verbal stimuli in a counseling analogue. *Journal of Counseling Psychology*, 1965, 12, 408–413.

Coles, N. J., Branch, C. H. H., & Allison, R. B. Some relationships between social class and the practice of dynamic psychiatry. *American Journal of Psychiatry*, 1962, 118, 1004–1012.

Cook, J. J. Silence in psychotherapy. *Journal of Counseling Psychology*, 1964, 11, 42–46.

Cooke, G. Evaluation of the efficacy of the components of reciprocal inhibition psychotherapy. *Journal of Abnormal Psychology*, 1968, **73**, 464–467.

Coombs, C. H. *A theory of data*. New York: John Wiley, 1964.

Cooperman, M., & Child, I. L. Differential effects of positive and negative reinforcement on two psychoanalytic character types. *Journal of Consulting & Clinical Psychology*, 1971, **37**, 57–59.

Covner, B. J. Studies in phonographic records of verbal material: Written reports of interviews. *Journal of Applied Psychology*, 1944, **28**, 89–98.   (a)

Covner, B. J. Studies in phonographic records of verbal material: III. The completeness and accuracy of counseling interview reports. *Journal of General Psychology*, 1944, **30**, 181–203.   (b)

Cronbach, L. J., & Meehl, P. E. Construct validity in psychological tests. *Psychological Bulletin*, 1955, **52**, 281–302.

Crowder, J. E. Relationship between therapist and client interpersonal behaviors and psychotherapy outcome. *Journal of Counseling Psychology*, 1972, **19**, 68–75.

Crowne, D. P., & Marlowe, D. *The approval motive*. New York: John Wiley, 1964.

Culbert, S. A. Trainer self-disclosure and therapeutic growth in a T-group. Unpublished doctoral dissertation, University of California, Los Angeles, 1966.

Cutler, R. L. Countertransference effects in psychotherapy. *Journal of Consulting Psychology*, 1958, **22**, 349–356.

Cutler, R. L., Bordin, E. S., Williams, Joan, & Rigler, D. Psychoanalysts as expert observers of the therapy process. *Journal of Consulting Psychology*, 1958, **22**, 335–340.

Dana, R. H. The effect of attitudes toward authority on psychotherapy. *Journal of Clinical Psychology*, 1954, **10**, 350–353.

Davidson, G. C. Systematic desensitization as a counterconditioning process. *Journal of Abnormal Psychology*, 1968, **73**, 91–99.

Davidson, G. C. A procedural critique of "desensitization and the experimental reduction of threat." *Journal of Abnormal Psychology*, 1969, **74**, 86-87.

Davidson, P. O., & Hiebert, S. F. Relaxation training, relaxation instruction, and repeated exposure to a stressor film. *Journal of Abnormal Psychology*, 1971, **78**, 154–159.

Davis, John D. *The interview as arena*. Stanford, Calif.: Stanford University Press, 1971.

Denker, P. G. Results of treatment of psychoneuroses by the general practitioner: A followup study of 500 cases. *Archives of Neurology & Psychiatry*, 1947, **57**, 504–505.

Denner, B. Deception, decision making, and gestalt therapy. *Journal of Consulting Psychology*, 1968, **32**, 527–531.

Dibner, A. S. Ambiguity and anxiety. *Journal of Abnormal & Social Psychology*, 1958, **56**, 165–174.

Dibner, A. S., Palmer, R. D., Cohen, B., & Gofstein, A. G. The use of an open-ended group in the intake procedure of a mental hygiene unit. *Journal of Consulting Psychology*, 1963, **27**, 83–88.

Di Caprio, N. S. Essentials of verbal satiation therapy: A learning-theory-based behavior therapy. *Journal of Counseling Psychology*, 1970, **17**, 419–424.

Dicken, C., & Fordham, M. Effects of reinforcement of self-references in quasi-therapeutic interviews. *Journal of Counseling Psychology*, 1967, 14, 145–152.

Dies, R. R., & Hess, A. K. An experimental investigation of cohesiveness in marathon and conventional group psychotherapy. *Journal of Abnormal Psychology*, 1971, 77, 258–262.

Dittes, J. E. Extinction during psychotherapy of GSR accompanying "embarrassing" statements. *Journal of Abnormal & Social Psychology*, 1957, 54, 187–191.

Dittmann, A. T. The interpersonal process in psychotherapy: Development of a research method. *Journal of Abnormal & Social Psychology*, 1952, 47, 236–244.

Dittmann, A. T. Problems of reliability in observing and coding social interactions. *Journal of Consulting Psychology*, 1958, 22, 430.

Dittmann, A. T., & Wynne, L. Linguistic techniques and the analysis of emotionality in interviews. In L. A. Gottschalk & A. H. Auerback (Eds.), *Methods of research in psychotherapy*. New York: Appleton-Century-Crofts, 1966.

Doctor, R. M., & Craine, W. H. Modification of drug language usage of primary and neurotic psychopaths. *Journal of Abnormal Psychology*, 1971, 77, 174–180.

Dollard, J., & Auld, F., Jr. *Searching human motives: A manual*. New Haven, Conn.: Yale University press, 1959.

Dollard, J., & Miller, N. E. *Personality and psychotherapy*. New York: McGraw-Hill, 1950.

Dollard, J., & Mowrer, O. H. A method of measuring tension in written documents. *Journal of Abnormal & Social Psychology*, 1947, 42, 3–32.

Donnan, H. H., Harlan, G. E., & Thompson, S. A. Counselor personality and level of functioning as perceived by counselees. *Journal of Counseling Psychology*, 1969, 16, 482–485.

Doster, J. A., & Strickland, Bonnie R. Disclosing of verbal material as a function of information requested, information about the interviewer, and interviewer differences. *Journal of Consulting & Clinical Psychology*, 1971, 37, 187–194.

Dreikurs, R. The Adlerian approach to psychodynamics. In M. L. Stein (Ed.), *Contemporary psychotherapies*. New York: Free Press of Glencoe, 1961.

Duncan, S., Jr., Rice, Laura N., & Butler, J. M. Therapists' paralanguage in peak and poor psychotherapy interviews. *Journal of Abnormal Psychology*, 1968, 73, 566–570.

Dustin, R. Trained clients as reinforcers of counselor behavior. *Journal of Consulting & Clinical Psychology*, 1971, 37, 351–354.

Dymond, Rosalind F. Adjustment changes over therapy from self-sorts. In C. R. Rogers and R. F. Dymond (Eds.), *Psychotherapy and personality change*. Chicago: University of Chicago Press, 1954.

Edwards, A. L., & Cronback, L. J. Experimental design for research in psychotherapy. *Journal of Clinical Psychology*, 1952, 8, 51–59.

Eisenman, R. Birth order, anxiety, and verbalization in group psychotherapy. *Journal of Consulting Psychology*, 1966, 30, 521–526.

Eissler, K. R. Remarks on the psychoanalysis of schizophrenia. In E. B. Brody and F. C. Redlich (Eds.), *Psychotherapy with schizophrenics*. New York: International Universities Press, 1952.

Eissler, K. R. The effect of the structure of the ego on psychoanalytic technique. *Journal of the American Psychoanalytic Association*, 1953, **1**, 104–141.

Ekman, P., & Friesen, W. V. Nonverbal behavior in psychotherapy research. In J. M. Shlien (Ed.), *Research in psychotherapy*. Vol. III. Washington, D.C.: American Psychological Association, 1968.

Ellis, A. Outcome of employing three techniques of psychotherapy. *Journal of Clinical Psychology*, 1957, **13**, 344–350.

Ellis, A. *Reason and emotion in psychotherapy*. New York: Lyle Stuart, 1962.

Emery, J. R., & Krumboltz, J. D. Standard versus individualized hierarchies in desensitization to reduce test anxiety. *Journal of Counseling Psychology*, 1967, **14**, 204–209.

Epstein, S., & Fenz, W. The detection of areas of emotional stress through variations in perceptual threshold and psychological arousal. *Journal of Experimental Research in Personality*, 1967, **2**, 191–199.

Eysenck, H. J. The effects of psychotherapy: An evaluation. *Journal of Consulting Psychology*, 1952, **16**, 319–324.

Eysenck, H. J. A reply to Luborsky's note. *British Journal of Psychology*, 1954, **45**, 132–133.

Eysenck, H. J. The effects of psychotherapy: A reply. *Journal of Abnormal & Social Psychology*, 1955, **50**, 147–148.   (a)

Eysenck, H. J. Review of C. R. Rogers and R. F. Dymond, *Psychotherapy and personality change*. *British Journal of Psychology*, 1955, **46**, 237–238.   (b)

Eysenck, H. J. The effects of psychotherapy. In H. J. Eysenck (Ed.), *Handbook of abnormal psychology: An experimental approach*. New York: Basic Books, 1961.

Eysenck, H. J. The outcome problem in psychotherapy: A reply. *Psychotherapy: Theory, Research and Practice*, 1964, **1**, 97–100.

Eysenck, H. J. Extroversion and the acquisition of eyeblink and GSR conditioned responses. *Psychological Bulletin*, 1965, **63**, 258–270.   (a)

Eysenck, H. J. The effects of psychotherapy. *International Journal of Psychiatry*, 1965, **1**, 99–142.   (b)

Fagan, Joen, & Shepherd, Irma L. (Eds.), *Gestalt therapy now*. Palo Alto, Calif.: Science and Behavior Books, 1970.

Farson, R. E. Introjection in the psychotherapeutic relationship. *Journal of Counseling Psychology*, 1961, **8**, 337–342.

Fazio, A. F. Treatment components in implosive therapy. *Journal of Abnormal Psychology*, 1970, **76**, 211–219.

Federn, P. *Ego psychology and the psychoses*. New York: Basic Books, 1952.

Feldman, M. P. Aversion therapy for sexual deviations: A critical review. *Psychological Bulletin*, 1966, **65**, 65–79.

Fenichel, O. *Problems of psychoanalytic technique*. Albany, N.Y.: Psychoanalytic Quarterly, Inc., 1941.

Fey, W. F. Doctrine and experience: Their influence upon the psychotherapist. *Journal of Consulting Psychology*, 1958, **22**, 403–409.

Fiedler, F. E. The concept of the ideal therapeutic relationship. *Journal of Consulting Psychology*, 1950, **14**, 239–245.   (a)

Fiedler, F. E. A comparison of therapeutic relationships in psychoanalytic, nondirective and Adlerian therapy. *Journal of Consulting Psychology,* 1950, **14,** 436–445. (b)

Fiedler, F. E., & Senior, Kate. An exploratory study of unconscious feeling reactions in fifteen patient-therapist pairs. *Journal of Abnormal & Social Psychology,* 1952, **17,** 446–453.

Fish, J. M. Empathy and the reported emotional experiences of beginning psychotherapists. *Journal of Consulting & Clinical Psychology,* 1970, **35,** 64–69.

Fisher, S. Plausibility and depth of interpretation. *Journal of Consulting Psychology,* 1956, **20,** 249–256.

Fiske, D. W., Cartwright, D. S., & Kirtner, W. L. Are psychotherapeutic changes predictable? *Journal of Abnormal & Social Psychology,* 1964, 69, 418–426.

Fiske, D. W., Hunt, H. F., Luborsky, L., Orne, M. T., Parloff, M. B., Heiser, M. F., & Tuma, A. H. Planning of research on effectiveness of psychotherapy. *Archives of General Psychiatry,* 1970, **22,** 22–32.

Folkins, C. H., Lawson, K. D., Opton, E. M., Jr., & Lazarus, R. S. Desensitization and the experimental reduction of threat. *Journal of Abnormal Psychology,* 1968, **73,** 100–113.

Folkins, C. H., Lawson, K. D., Opton, E. M., Jr., & Lazarus, R. S. A reply to Davidson's critique. *Journal of Abnormal Psychology,* 1969, **74,** 88–89.

Forer, B. R., Farberow, N. L., Feifel, H., Meyer, M. M., Sommers, Vita S., & Tolman, Ruth S. Clinical perception of the therapeutic transaction. *Journal of Consulting Psychology,* 1961, **25,** 93–101.

Foulds, M. L. Self-actualization and the communication of facilitative conditions during counseling. *Journal of Counseling Psychology,* 1969, **16,** 132–136.

Frank, G. H., & Sweetland, A. A study of the process of psychotherapy. *Journal of Consulting Psychology,* 1962, **26,** 135–138.

Frank, J. D. Problems of controls in psychotherapy as exemplified by the psychotherapy research project of the Phipps Psychiatric Clinic. In E. A. Rubinstein and M. B. Parloff (Eds.), *Research in psychotherapy.* Vol. I. Washington, D.C.: American Psychological Association, 1959.

Frank, J. D. *Persuasion and healing: A comparative study of psychotherapy.* Baltimore: Johns Hopkins Press, 1961.

Freedman, M. B., Leary, T. F., Ossorio, A. C., & Coffey, H. S. Interpersonal dimensions of personality. *Journal of Personality,* 1951, **20,** 143–161.

Freedman N., O'Hanlon, J., Ottman, P., & Witkin, H. A. The imprint of psychological differentiation in kinetic behavior in varying communicative contexts. *Journal of Abnormal Psychology,* 1972. **79,** 239–258.

Freud, S. The dynamics of the transference (1912). *Collected papers.* Vol. II. London: Hogarth Press, 1949. (a)

Freud, S. *Collected papers.* Vol. III. London: Hogarth Press, 1949. (b)

Fromm-Reichmann, Freda. *Principles of intensive psychotherapy.* Chicago: University of Chicago Press, 1950.

Fulkerson, S. C., & Barry, J. R. Methodology and research on the prognostic use of psychological tests. *Psychological Bulletin,* 1961, **58,** 177–204.

Galinsky, M. D. Personality development and vocational choice of clinical psychologists and physicists. *Journal of Counseling Psychology*, 1962, **9**, 299–305.

Gallagher, J. J. Test indicators of therapy prognosis. *Journal of Consulting Psychology*, 1954, **18**, 409–413.

Garduk, Edith L., & Haggard, E. A. The immediate effects on patients of psychoanalytic interpretations. *Psychological Issues*, 1972, **7**, No. 4 (Monograph 28).

Garfield, S. L., & Affleck, D. C. Therapists' judgments concerning patients considered for psychotherapy. *Journal of Consulting Psychology*, 1961, **25**, 505–509.

Garfield, S. L., & Bergin, A. E. Therapeutic conditions and outcome. *Journal of Abnormal Psychology*, 1971, **77**, 108–114.

Gassner, Suzanne M. Relationship between patient-therapist compatibility and treatment effectiveness. *Journal of Consulting & Clinical Psychology*, 1970, **34**, 408–414.

Gaylin, N. L. Psychotherapy and psychological health: A Rorschach function and structure analysis. *Journal of Consulting Psychology*, 1966, **30**, 494–500.

Geer, J. H., & Katkin, E. S. Treatment of insomnia using a variant of systematic desensitization. *Journal of Abnormal Psychology*, 1966, **71**, 161–164.

Geer, J. H., & Turtletaub, A. Fear reduction following observation of a model. *Journal of Personality & Social Psychology*, 1967, **6**, 327–331.

Gendlin, E. Experiencing: A variable in the process of therapeutic change. Report to the American Psychological Association Convention, Washington, D. C., 1958.

Gendlin, E. T. Experiencing: A variable in the process of therapeutic change. *American Journal of Psychotherapy*, 1961, **15**, 233–245.

Gendlin, E. T., Beebe, J., III, Cassens, J., Klein, Marjorie, & Oberlander, M. Focusing ability in psychotherapy, personality and creativity. In J. M. Shlien (Ed.), *Research in psychotherapy*. Vol. III. Washington, D.C.: American Psychological Association, 1968.

Gendlin, E. T., & Zimring, F. M. The qualities of dimensions of experiencing and their change. *Counseling Center Discussion Papers*, 1955, **1** (University of Chicago Library).

Gibby, R. G., Adams, H. B., & Carrera, R. N. Therapeutic changes in psychiatric patients following partial sensory deprivation. *Archives of General Psychiatry*, 1960, **3**, 33–42.

Gibby, R., Stotsky, B., Hiler, E. W., & Miller, D. Validation of Rorschach criteria for predicting duration of therapy. *Journal of Consulting Psychology*, 1954, **18**, 185–191.

Gibby, R., Stotsky, B., Miller, D., & Hiler, E. W. Prediction of duration of therapy from the Rorschach test. *Journal of Consulting Psychology*, 1953, **17**, 348–354.

Ginott, H. G. The theory and practice of "therapeutic intervention" in child treatment. *Journal of Consulting Psychology*, 1959, **23**, 160–166.

Gliedman, L. H., Stone, D. R., Frank, J. D., Nash, E. H., Jr., & Imber, S. D. Incentives for treatment related to remaining or improving in psychotherapy. *American Journal of Psychotherapy*, 1957, **11**, 589–598.

Goin, M., Yamamoto, J., & Silverman, J. Therapy congruent with class-linked expectations. *Archives of General Psychiatry*, 1965, **13**, 133–137.

Goldberger, L., & Holt, R. R. Experimental interference with reality contact: Individual differences. In P. Solomon et al. (Ed.), *Sensory deprivation*. Cambridge, Mass.: Harvard University Press, 1961.

Goldfried, M. R. Systematic desensitization as training in self-control. *Journal of Consulting & Clinical Psychology*, 1971, **37**, 228–234.

Goldstein, A. P. Therapist and client expectation of personality change in psychotherapy. *Journal of Counseling Psychology*, 1960, **7**, 180–184.

Goldstein, A. P. *Therapist-patient expectancies in psychotherapy*. New York: Macmillan, 1962.

Goldstein, A. P. Psychotherapy research by extrapolation from social psychology. *Journal of Counseling Psychology*, 1966, **13**, 38–45.

Goldstein, A. P. *Psychotherapeutic attraction*. New York: Pergamon Press, 1971.

Goldstein, A. P., Heller, K., & Sechrest, L. B. *Psychotherapy and the psychology of behavior change*. New York: John Wiley, 1966.

Goldstein, A. P., & Shipman, W. G. Patient's expectancies, symptom reduction, and aspects of the initial psychotherapeutic interview. *Journal of Clinical Psychology*, 1961, **17**, 129–133.

Goldstein, Jeanne A. Investigation of doubling as a technique for involving severely withdrawn patients in group psychotherapy. *Journal of Consulting & Clinical Psychology*, 1971, **37**, 155–162.

Goldstein, S. G. The effects of "doubling" on involvement in group therapy as measured by frequency and duration of patient utterances. *Psychotherapy*, 1967, **4**, 57–60.

Gordon, J. E. Leading and following psychotherapeutic techniques with hypnotically induced repression and hostility. *Journal of Abnormal & Social Psychology*, 1957, **54**, 405–410.

Gottesman, L. E. The relationship of cognitive variables to therapeutic ability and training of client centered therapists. *Journal of Consulting Psychology*, 1962, **26**, 119–125.

Gottschalk, L. A., Winget, Carolyn M., Bleser, Goldine C., & Springer, Kayla J. The measurement of emotional changes during a psychiatric interview: A working model toward quantifying the psychoanalytic concept of affect. In L. A. Gottschalk and A. H. Auerbach (Eds.), *Methods of research in psychotherapy*. New York: Appleton-Century-Crofts, 1966.

Gould, R. E. Dr. Strangeclass: Or how I stopped worrying about the theory and began treating the blue-collar worker. *American Journal of Orthopsychiatry*, 1967, **37**, 78–86.

Graff, R. W., MacLean, G. D., & Loving, A. Group reactive inhibition and reciprocal inhibition therapies with anxious students. *Journal of Counseling Psychology*, 1971, **18**, 431–436.

Grant, J. D., & Grant, Marguerita Q. "Therapy readiness" as a research variable. *Journal of Consulting Psychology*, 1950, **14**, 156–157.

Greenberg, R. P. Effects of presession information on perception of therapist and acceptivity to influence in a psychotherapy analogue. *Journal of Consulting & Clinical Psychology*, 1969, **33**, 425–429.

Greenblatt, M. Discussion of methods of assessment of change. In E. A. Rubinstein and M. B. Parloff (Eds.), *Research in psychotherapy*. Vol. I. Washington, D.C.: American Psychological Association, 1959.

Greenson, R. R. *The technique and practice of psychoanalysis.* Vol. I. New York: International Universities Press, 1967.

Grossman, D. An experimental investigation of a psychotherapeutic technique. *Journal of Consulting Psychology*, 1952, **16**, 325–331.

Grummon, D. L., and Butler, J. M. Another failure to replicate Keet's study, two verbal techniques in a miniature counseling situation. *Journal of Abnormal & Social Psychology*, 1953, **48**, 597.

Gurman, A. S. Therapists' mood patterns and therapeutic facilitativeness. *Journal of Counseling Psychology*, 1972, **19**, 169–170.

Gurman, A. S. Effects of therapist and patient mood on the therapeutic functioning of high- and low-facilitative therapists. *Journal of Consulting & Clinical Psychology*, 1973, **40**, 48–58.

Haase, R. F. The relationship of sex and instructional set to the regulation of interpersonal distance in a counseling analogue. *Journal of Counseling Psychology*, 1970, **17**, 233–236.

Haggard, E. A., and Isaacs, K. S. Micromomentary facial expressions as indicators of ego mechanisms in psychotherapy. In L. A. Gottschalk and A. H. Auerbach (Eds.), *Methods of research in psychotherapy.* New York: Appleton-Century-Crofts, 1966.

Hammer, E. F. Varying techniques in treatment. In E. F. Hammer (Ed.), *Use of interpretation in treatment.* New York: Grune & Stratton, 1968.

Harari, H. Interpersonal models in psychotherapy and counseling: A social-psychological analysis of a clinical problem. *Journal of Abnormal Psychology*, 1971, **78**, 127–133.

Hardy, Virginia. Relation of dominance to non-directiveness in counseling. *Journal of Clinical Psychology*, 1948, **4**, 300–303.

Hartley, D. L. Perceived counselor credibility as a function of the effects of counseling interaction. *Journal of Counseling Psychology*, 1969, **16**, 63–68.

Harway, N. I., Dittmann, A. T., Raush, H. L., Bordin, E. S., & Rigler, D. The measurement of depth of interpretation. *Journal of Consulting Psychology*, 1955, **19**, 247–253.

Harway, N. I., & Iker, H. P. Objective content analysis of psychotherapy by computer. In K. Enstein (Ed.), *Data acquisition and processing in biology and medicine.* New York: Pergamon Press, 1966.

Hathaway, S. R. Some considerations relative to nondirective counseling as therapy. *Journal of Clinical Psychology*, 1948, **4**, 226–231.

Heilbrun, A. B., Jr. Relationships between the Adjective Check List, Personal Preference Schedule, and desirability factors under varying defensiveness conditions. *Journal of Clinical Psychology*, 1958, **3**, 283–287.

Heilbrun, A. B., Jr. Validation of a need scaling technique for the Adjective Check List. *Journal of Consulting Psychology*, 1959, **23**, 347–351.

Heilbrun, A. B., Jr. Male and female personality correlates of early termination in counseling. *Journal of Counseling Psychology*, 1961, **8**, 31–36.

Heilbrun, A. B., Jr. Further validation of a counseling readiness scale. *Journal of Counseling Psychology*, 1964, **1**, 290–292.

Heilbrun, A. B., Jr. Counseling readiness and the problem solving behavior of clients. *Journal of Consulting & Clinical Psychology*, 1968, **32**, 396–399.

Heilbrun, A. B., Jr. Toward resolution of the dependency-premature termination paradox for females in psychotherapy. *Journal of Consulting & Clinical Psychology*, 1970, **34**, 382–386.

Heilbrun, A. B., Jr. Female preferences for therapist initial interview style as a function of "client" and therapist social role variables. *Journal of Counseling Psychology*, 1971, **18**, 285–291.

Heilbrun, A. B., Jr. History of self-disclosure in females and early defection from psychotherapy. *Journal of Counseling Psychology*, 1973, **20**, 250–257.

Heilbrun, A. B., Jr. & Sullivan, J. D. The prediction of counseling readiness. *Personnel & Guidance Journal*, 1962, **41**, 112–117.

Heine, R. W., & Trosman, H. Initial expectations of the doctor-patient interaction as a factor in continuance in psychotherapy. *Psychiatry*, 1960, **23**, 275–278.

Heinicke, C. M. Frequency of psychotherapeutic session as a factor affecting outcome: Analysis of clinical ratings and test results. *Journal of Abnormal Psychology*, 1969, **74**, 553–560.

Heitler, J. B. Preparation of lower class patients for group psychotherapy. Unpublished doctoral dissertation, University of Michigan, 1971.

Hekmat, H. Reinforcing values of interpretations and reflections in a quasi-therapeutic interview. *Journal of Abnormal Psychology*, 1971, **77**, 25–31.   (a)

Hekmat, H. Extraversion, neuroticism, and verbal conditioning of affective self-disclosure. *Journal of Counseling Psychology*, 1971, **18**, 64–69.   (b)

Hekmat, H., & Theiss, M. Self-actualization and modification of affective self-disclosures during a social conditioning interview. *Journal of Counseling Psychology*, 1971, **18**, 101–105.

Hekmat, H., & Varian, D. Behavior modification through covert semantic desensitization. *Journal of Consulting & Clinical Psychology*, 1971, **36**, 248–251.

Heller, K. Ambiguity in the interview situation. In J. M. Shlien (Ed.), *Research in psychotherapy*. Vol. III. Washington, D.C.: American Psychological Association, 1968.   (a)

Heller, K. Interview structure and interviewer style in initial interviews. Paper presented at Research Conference on Interview Behavior, University of Maryland, 1968.   (b)

Heller, K. Effects of modeling procedures on helping relationships. *Journal of Consulting & Clinical Psychology*, 1969, **33**, 522–526.

Heller, K. Laboratory interview research as analogue to treatment. In A. E. Bergin and S. L. Garfield (Eds.), *Handbook of psychotherapy and behavior change*. New York: John Wiley, 1971.

Heller, K., Meyers, R. A., & Kline, Linda V. Interviewer behavior as a function of standardized client roles. *Journal of Consulting Psychology*, 1963, **27**, 117–122.

Henry, W. E., & Shlien, J. M. Affective complexity and psychotherapy. *Journal of Projective Techniques*, 1958, **22**, 153–162.

Henry, W. E., Sims, J. H., & Spray, S. L. *The fifth profession*. San Francisco: Jossey-1971.

Heron, W., Doane, B. K., & Scott, T. H. Visual disturbances after prolonged perceptual isolation. *Canadian Journal of Psychology*, 1956, **10**, 13–18.

Hoehn-Saric, R., Frank, J. D., Imber, S. D., Nash, E. H., Stone, A. R., & Battle, Carolyn C. Systematic preparation of patients for psychotherapy: 1. Effects on therapy behavior and outcome. *Journal of Psychiatric Research*, 1964, **2**, 267–281.

Hogan, R. A., & Kirchner, J. H. Preliminary report of the extinction of learned fears via short-term implosive therapy. *Journal of Abnormal Psychology*, 1967, **72**, 106–109.

Holder, T., Carkhuff, R., & Berenson, B. Differential effects of the manipulation of therapeutic conditions upon high and low functioning clients. *Journal of Counseling*, 1967, **14**, 63–66.

Hollingshead, A. B., & Redlich, F. C. *Social class and mental illness.* New York: John Wiley, 1958.

Hollon, T. H. Ego psychology and the supportive therapy of borderline states. *Psychotherapy*, 1966, **3**, 135–138.

Holsti, O. R. Content analysis. In G. Lindzey and E. Aronson (Eds.), *Handbook of social psychology* (2nd ed.). Vol. 2. Reading, Mass.: Addison-Wesley, 1968.

Holt, R. R., & Luborsky, L. *Personality patterns of psychiatrists.* Vols. I & II. New York: Basic Books, 1958.

Horton, Margaret, & Kriauciunas, Romualdas. Minnesota Multiphasic Personality Inventory differences between terminators and continuers in youth counseling. *Journal of Counseling Psychology*, 1970, **17**, 98–101.

Houts P. S., MacIntosh, Shirley, & Moos, R. H. Patient-therapist interdependence: Cognitive and behavioral. *Journal of Consulting & Clinical Psychology*, 1969, **33**, 40–45.

Hovland, C. I. Reconciling conflicting results derived from experimental and survey studies of attitude change. *American Psychologist*, 1959, **19**, 8–17.

Howard, K. I., Krause, M. S., & Orlinsky, D. E. Direction of affective influence in psychotherapy. *Journal of Consulting & Clinical Psychology*, 1969, **33**, 614–620.

Howard, K. I., Orlinsky, D. E., & Hill, J. A. The therapist's feelings in the therapeutic process. *Journal of Clinical Psychology*, 1969, **25**, 83–93.

Howard, K. I., Orlinsky, D. E., & Hill, J. A. Affective experience in psychotherapy. *Journal of Abnormal Psychology*, 1970, **75**, 267–275.

Howard, K. I., Orlinsky, D. E. & Trattner J. H. Therapist orientation and patient experience in psychotherapy. *Journal of Counseling Psychology*, 1970, **17**, 263–270.

Howe, E. S. Anxiety-arousal and specificity: Rated correlates of the depth of interpretative statements. *Journal of Consulting Psychology*, 1962, **26**, 178–184.   (a)

Howe, E. S. A study of the semantic structure of ratings of interpretative responses. *Journal of Consulting Psychology*, 1962, **26**, 285.   (b)

Howe, E. S., & Pope, B. An empirical scale of therapist verbal activity level in the interview. *Journal of Consulting Psychology*, 1961, **25**, 510–520.

Howe, E. S., & Pope, B. Therapist verbal activity level and diagnostic utility of patient verbal responses. *Journal of Consulting Psychology*, 1962, **26**, 149–155.

Imber, S. D., Frank, J. F., Nash, E. H., Stone, A. R., & Gleidman, L. H. Improvement and amount of therapeutic contact: An alternative to the use of no-treatment controls in psychotherapy. *Journal of Consulting Psychology*, 1957, **21**, 309–315.

Imber, S. D., et al. A ten-year follow-up study of treated psychiatric outpatients. In S. Lesese (Ed.), *An evaluation of the results of the psychotherapies*. Springfield, Ill.: Charles C Thomas, 1968.

Isaacs, K. S., & Haggard, E. A. Some methods used in the study of affect in psychotherapy. In L. A. Gottschalk & A. H. Auerbach (Eds.), *Methods of research in psychotherapy*. New York: Appleton-Century-Crofts, 1966.

Iscoe, I., & Spielberger, C. D. (Eds.). *Training and research in community mental health*. New York: Appleton-Century-Crofts, 1970.

Jackson, C. W., Jr., & Wohl, J. A survey of Rorschach teaching in the university. *Journal of Projective Techniques & Personality Assessment*, 1966, **30**, 115–134.

Jackson, M., & Thompson, C. L. Effective counselor: Characteristics and attitudes. *Journal of Counseling Psychology*, 1971, **18**, 249–254.

Jacobsen, Edith. *Depression*. New York: International Universities Press, 1971.

Johnson, R. W. Number of interviews, diagnosis and success of counseling. *Journal of Counseling Psychology*, 1965, **12**, 248–251.

Jourard, S. M. *The transparent self*. Princeton, N.J.: Van Nostrand, 1964.

Jouard, S. M., & Jeffee, Peggy E. Influence of an interviewer's disclosures on the self-disclosing behavior of interviewees. *Journal of Counseling Psychology*, 1970, **17**, 252–257.

Kahn, M., & Baker, B. Desensitization with minimal therapist contact. *Journal of Abnormal Psychology*, 1968, **73**, 198–200.

Kahn, M. H., & Rudestam, K. E. The relationship between liking and perceived self-disclosure in small groups. *Journal of Psychology*, 1971, **78**, 81–85.

Kalish, H. J. Behavior therapy. In B. B. Wolman (Ed.), *Handbook of clinical psychology*. New York: McGraw-Hill, 1965.

Kamil, L. J. Psychodynamic changes through systematic desensitization. *Journal of Abnormal Psychology*, 1970, **76**, 199–205.

Kaplan, Frances. Effects of anxiety and defense in a therapy-like situation. *Journal of Abnormal Psychology*, 1966, **71**, 449–458.

Kaplan, M. F. Interview interaction of repressors and sensitizers. *Journal of Consulting Psychology*, 1967, **31**, 513–516.

Karl, N. J., & Abeles, N. Psychotherapy process as a function of the time segment sampled. *Journal of Consulting & Clinical Psychology*, 1969, **33**, 207–212.

Karst, T. O., & Trexler, L. D. Initial study using fixed-role and rational-emotive therapy in treating public-speaking anxiety. *Journal of Consulting & Clinical Psychology*, 1970, **34**, 350–366.

Karush, A., Daniels, G., O'Connor, J., & Stern, L. The response to psychotherapy in chronic ulcerative colitis: I. Pretreatment factors. *Psychosomatic Medicine*, 1968, **30**, 255–276.

Kasmar, Joyce V., Griffin, W. V., & Mauritzen, J. H. Effects of environmental surroundings on outpatients' mood and perception of psychiatrists. *Journal of Consulting & Clinical Psychology*, 1968, **32**, 223–226.

Katz, M. M., Lorr, M., & Rubenstein, E. A. Remainer patient attributes and their relation to subsequent improvement in psychotherapy. *Journal of Consulting Psychology*, 1958, **22**, 411–413.

Katz, M. M., & Lyerly, H. B. Methods of measuring adjustment and social behavior in the community: I. Rationale, description, discriminative validity and scale development. *Psychological Reports*, 1963, **13**, 503–535.

Keet, C. D. Two verbal techniques in a minature counseling situation. *Psychological Monographs*, 1948, **62** (14, Whole No. 287).

Kell, B. L., & Mueller, W. J. *Impact and change: A study of counseling relationships*. New York: Appleton-Century-Crofts, 1966.

Kelly, G. A. *The psychology of personal constructs*. New York: Norton, 1955.

Kennedy, W. A. School phobia: Rapid treatment of fifty cases. *Journal of Abnormal Psychology*, 1965, **70**, 285–289.

Kernberg, O. F. Factors in the psychoanalytic treatment of narcissistic personalities. *Journal of the American Psychoanalytic Association*, 1970, **18**, 51–85.

Kiesler, D. J. Some myths of psychotherapy research and the search for a paradigm. *Psychological Bulletin*, 1966, **65**, 110–136.

Kiesler, D. J. Comparison of Experiencing Scale ratings of naive versus clinically sophisticated judges. *Journal of Consulting & Clinical Psychology*, 1970, **35**, 134.

Kiesler, D. J. Patient experiencing and successful outcome in individual psychotherapy of schizophrenics and neurotics. *Journal of Consulting & Clinical Psychology*, 1971, **37**, 370–385.

Kiesler, D. J. *The process of psychotherapy*. Chicago: Aldine, 1973.

Kiesler, D. J., Klein, Marjorie H., & Mathieu, Phillippa L. Sampling from the recorded therapy interview: The problem of segment location. *Journal of Consulting Psychology*, 1965, **29**, 337–344.

Kiesler, D. J., Mathieu, Phillippa L., & Klein, Marjorie H. Sampling from the recorded therapy interview: A comparative study of different segment lengths. *Journal of Consulting Psychology*, 1964, **28**, 349–357.

Kirtner, W. L., & Cartwright, D. S. Success and failure in client-centered therapy as a function of client personality variables. *Journal of Consulting Psychology*, 1958, **22**, 259–264. (a)

Kirtner, W. L., & Cartwright, D. S. Success and failure in client-centered therapy as a function of initial in-therapy behavior. *Journal of Consulting Psychology*, 1958, **22**, 329–333. (b)

Klein, Marjorie H., Dittmann, A. T., Parloff, M. B., & Gill, M. M. Behavior therapy: Observations and reflections. *Journal of Consulting & Clinical Psychology*, 1969, **33**, 259–266.

Knapp, P. H., Mushatt, C., & Nemetz, S. J. Collection and utilization of data in a psychoanalytic psychosomatic study. In L. A. Gottschalk & A. H. Auerbach (Eds.), *Methods of research in psychotherapy*. New York: Appleton-Century-Crofts, 1966.

Koltov, B., & Meadow, A. Rorschach criteria for predicting continuation in individual psychotherapy. *Journal of Consulting Psychology*, 1953, **17**, 16–20.

Krapfl, J. E., & Nawas, M. M. Client-therapist relationship factor in systematic desensitization. *Journal of Consulting & Clinical Psychology*, 1969, **33**, 435–439.

Kraft, T. Behavior therapy and target symptoms. *Journal of Clinical Psychology*, 1969, **25**, 105–109.

Krasner, L. The therapist as a social reinforcement machine. In H. H. Strupp & L. Luborsky (Eds.), *Research in psychotherapy*. Vol. II. Washington, D.C.: American Psychological Association, 1962.

Krasner, L., & Ullman, L. P. (Eds.). *Research in behavior modification*. New York: Holt, 1965.

Krause, M. S. Behavioral indexes of motivation for treatment. *Journal of Counseling Psychology*, 1967, **14**, 426–435.

Krause, M. S. Clarification of intake and motivation for treatment. *Journal of Counseling Psychology*, 1968, **15**, 576–577.

Krause, M. S., & Pilisuk, M. Anxiety in verbal behavior: A validation study. *Journal of Consulting Psychology*, 1961, **25**, 414–419.

Kreutzer, C. S., Lichtenstein, E., & Mees, H. S. Modification of smoking behavior: A review. *Psychological Bulletin*, 1968, **70**, 520–533.

Lacey, J. I. Psychophysiological approaches to the evaluation of psychotherapeutic process and outcome. In E. A. Rubinstein & M. B. Parloff (Eds.), *Research in psychotherapy*. Vol. I. Washington, D.C.: American Psychological Association, 1959.

Laffal, J. An approach to the total content analysis of speech in psychotherapy. In J. M. Shlien (Ed.), *Research in psychotherapy*. Vol. III. Washington, D.C. American Psychological Association, 1968.

Landfield, A. W., & Nawas, M. M. Psychotherapeutic improvement as a function of communication and adoption of therapist's values. *Journal of Counseling Psychology*, 1964, **11**, 336–341.

Landis, C. A. A statistical evaluation of psychotherapeutic methods. In L. E. Hinsie (Ed.), *Concepts and problems of psychotherapy*. New York: Columbia University Press, 1937.

Lang, P. J. Fear reduction and fear behavior: Problems in treating a construct. In J. M. Shlien (Ed.), *Research in psychotherapy*. Vol. III. Washington, D.C.: American Psychological Association, 1968.

Lang, P. J. The mechanics of desensitization and the laboratory study of fear. In C. M. Franks (Ed.), *Behavior therapy: Appraisal and Status*. New York: McGraw-Hill, 1969.

Lang, P. J., & Lazovik, A. D. Experimental desensitization of a phobia. *Journal of Abnormal & Social Psychology*, 1963, **66**, 519–525.

Lang, P. J., Melamed, B. G., & Hart, J. A physiological analysis of fear modification using an automated desensitization procedure. *Journal of Abnormal Psychology*, 1970, **76**, 220–234.

Lapuc, P. S., & Harmatz, M. G. Verbal conditioning and therapeutic change. *Journal of Consulting & Clinical Psychology*, 1970, **35**, 70–78.

Lazarus, A. A. Behavior therapy In S. B. Shapiro (Ed.), *Six modern therapies* (tape recordings). New York. Scott Foresman, 1964.

Lazarus, A. A. Behavior therapy for sexual problems. *Professional Psychology*, 1971. **2**, 349–353.

Leary, T., & Gill, M. The dimensions and a measure of the process of psychotherapy: A system for the analysis of the content of clinical evaluations and patient-therapist verbalizations. In E. A. Rubinstein and M. B. Parloff (Eds.), *Research in psychotherapy*. Vol. I. Washington, D.C.: American Psychological Association, 1959.

Leitenberg, H., Agras, W. S., Barlow, D. H., & Oliveau, D. C. Contribution of selective positive reinforcement and therapeutic instructions to systematic desensitization therapy. *Journal of Abnormal Psychology*, 1969, **74**, 113–118.

Lennard, H. L. Some aspects of the psychotherapeutic system. In H. H. Strupp and L. Luborsky (Eds.), *Research in psychotherapy*. Vol. II. Washington, D.C.: American Psychological Association, 1962.

Lennard, H. L., & Bernstein, A. *The anatomy of psychotherapy*. New York: Columbia University Press, 1960.

Lerner, Barbara. *Therapy in the ghetto*. Baltimore: Johns Hopkins Press, 1972.

Lesser, W. M. The relationship between counseling progress and empathic understanding. *Journal of Counseling Psychology*, 1961, **8**, 330–336.

Levine, M., & Spivack, G. *The Rorschach index of repressive style*. Springfield, Ill.: Charles C Thomas, 1964.

Levitt, E. E. The results of psychotherapy with children: An evaluation. *Journal of Consulting Psychology*, 1957, **21**, 189–196.

Levy, L. H. *Psychological interpretation*. New York: Holt, Rinehart and Winston, 1963.

Lewin, K. Formalization and progress in psychology. In D. Cartwright (Ed.), *Field theory in social science*. New York: Harper, 1951.

Lewinsohn, P. M., & Atwood, G. E. Depression: A clinical-research approach. *Psychotherapy*, 1969, **6**, 166–171.

Lewinsohn, P. M., Lobitz, W. C., & Wilson, Susan, "Sensitivity" of depressed persons to aversive stimuli. *Journal of Abnormal Psychology*. 1973, **81**, 259–263.

Lewinsohn, P. M., & Schaffer, M. Use of home observations as an integral part of the treatment of depression: Preliminary report and case studies. *Journal of Consulting & Clinical Psychology*, 1971, **37**, 87–94.

Lewinsohn, P. M., & Shaw, D. A. Feedback about interpersonal behavior as an agent in behavior change: A case study in the treatment of depression. *Psychotherapy & Psychosomatics*, 1969, **17**, 82–88.

Lewinsohn, P. M., Weinstein, M. W., & Alper, T. A behavioral approach to the group treatment of depressed persons: A methodological contribution. *Journal of Clinical Psychology*, 1970, **26**, 525–532.

Lichtenstein, E. Personality similarity and therapeutic success: A failure to replicate. *Journal of Consulting Psychology*, 1966, **30**, 287.

Lipkin, S. Clients' feelings and attitudes in relation to the outcome of client-centered therapy. *Psychological Monographs*, 1954, **68**, (Whole No. 372).

Lipman, R., Rickels, K., Covi, L., Derogatis, L., & Uhlenluth, E. Factors of symptom distress. *Archives of General Psychiatry*, 1969, **21**, 328-338.

Loewenstein, R.M. Some thoughts on interpretation in the theory and practice of psychoanalysis. In Louis Paul (Ed.), *Psychoanalytic clinical interpretation*. London: Free Press of Glencoe, 1963.

Lomont, J. F., & Edwards, J. E. The role of relaxation in systematic densensitization. *Behavior Research & Therapy*, 1967, **5**, 11–25.

London, P. *The modes and morals of psychotherapy.* New York: Holt, Reinhart, and Winston, 1964.

London, P. The end of ideology in behavior modification. *American Psychologist*, 1972, **27**, 913–920.

Lorian, R. P. Socioeconomic status and traditional treatment approaches reconsidered. *Psychological Bulltein*, 1973, **79**, 263-270.

Lorr, M. Relation of treatment frequency and duration to psychotherapeutic outcome. In H. H. Strupp and L. Luborsky (Eds.), *Research in psychotherapy.* Vol. II. Washington, D.C.: American Psychological Association, 1962.

Lorr, M. Client perceptions of therapists: A study of the therapeutic relation. *Journal of Consulting Psychology*, 1965, **29**, 140-149.

Lorr, M., Katz, M. M., & Rubinstein, E. A. The prediction of length of stay in psychotherapy. *Journal of Consulting Psychology*, 1958, **22**, 321-327.

Lorr, M., & McNair, D. M. An interpersonal behavior circle. *Journal of Abnormal & Social Psychology*, 1963, **67**, 68–75.

Lorr, M., McNair, D. M., Michaux, W. M., & Raskin, A. Frequency of treatment and change in psychotherapy. *Journal of Abnormal & Social Psychology*, 1962, **64**, 281–292.

Lovaas, O. I. Some studies on the treatment of childhood schizophrenia. In J. M. Shlien (Ed.), *Research in psychotherapy.* Vol. III. Washington, D.C.: American Psychological Association, 1968.

Love, Leonore R., Kaswan, J., & Bugentol, Daphne E. Differential effectiveness of three clinical interventions for different socioeconomic groupings. *Journal of Consulting & Clinical Psychology*, 1972, **39**, 347–360.

Lovitt, R. Comparison of verbal approach-avoidance behavior of trained and untrained therapists. *Journal of Counseling Psychology*, 1970, **17**, 137–140.

Luborsky, L. The patient's personality and psychotherapeutic change. In H. H. Strupp and L. Luborsky (Eds.), *Research in psychotherapy.* Vol. II. Washington, D.C.: American Psychological Association, 1962.

Luborsky, L., Chandler, M., Auerback, A. H., Cohen, J., & Bachrach, H. M. Factors influencing the outcome of psychotherapy: A review of quantitative research. *Psychological Bulletin*, 1971, **75**, 145–185.

MacKinnon, D. W. Fact and fancy in personality research. *American Psychologist*, 1953, **8**, 138–146.

Mahl, G. F. Disturbances and silences in the patient's speech in psychotherapy. *Journal of Abnormal & Social Psychology*, 1956, **53**, 1–15.

Mahl, G. F. Gestures and body movements in interviews. In J. M. Shlien (Ed.), *Research in psychotherapy.* Vol. III. Washington, D.C.: American Psychological Association, 1968.

Mahrer, A. R. *The goals of psychotherapy.* New York: Appleton-Century-Crofts, 1967.

Mandel, H. P., Roth, R. M., & Berenbaum, H. L. Relationship between personality change and achievement change as a function of psychodiagnosis. *Journal of Counseling Psychology*, 1968, **15**, 500–505.

Mann, J. Vicarious desensitization of test anxiety through observation of videotaped treatment. *Journal of Counseling Psychology*, 1972, **19**, 1–7.

Mann, Nancy A. Free association and preferred defenses. Unpublished doctoral thesis, University of Michigan, 1965.

Marcia, J. E., Rubin, B. M., & Efran, J. S. Systematic desensitization: Expectancy change or counter-conditioning? *Journal of Abnormal Psychology*, 1969, **74**, 382-387.

Marks, I. M., & Gelder, M. G. Common ground between behavior therapy and psychodynamic methods. *British Journal of Medical Psychology*, 1966, **39**, 11-23.

Marsden, G. Content-analysis studies of therapeutic interviews: 1954 to 1964. *Psychological Bulletin*, 1965, **63**, 298–321.

Marsden, G. Content-analysis studies of psychotherapy: 1954 through 1968. In A. E. Bergin and S. L. Garfield (Eds.), *Handbook of Psychotherapy and behavior change*. New York: John Wiley, 1971.

Martin, B., Lundy, R. M., & Lewin, M. H. Verbal and GSR responses in experimental interviews as a function of three degrees of "therapist" communication. *Journal of Abnormal & Social Psychology*, 1960, **60**, 234–240.

Martin, J., & Carkhuff, R. R. Changes in personality and interpersonal functioning of counselors-in-training. *Journal of Clinical Psychology*, 1968, **24**, 109-110.

Martin, J. C., Carkhuff, R. R., & Berenson, B. G. Process variables in counseling and psychotherapy: A study of couseling and friendship. *Journal of Counseling Psychology*, 1966, **13**, 356–359.

Matarazzo, J. D., Wiens, A. N., Matarazzo, R. G., & Saslow, G. Speech and silence behavior in clinical psychotherapy and its laboratory correlates. In J. M. Shlien (Ed.), *Research in psychotherapy*. Vol. III. Washington, D.C.: American Psychological Association, 1968.

May, P. R. A. *Treatment of schizophrenia*. New York: Science House, 1968.

Mayeroff, M. *On caring*. New York: Harper & Row, 1971.

Mayman, M., & Faris, M. Early memories as expressions of relationship paradigms. *American Journal of Orthopsychiatry*, 1960, **30**, 507–520.

McCarron, L. T., & Apple, V. H. Categories of therapist verbalizations and patient-therapist autonomic response. *Journal of Consulting & Clinical Psychology*, 1971, **37**, 123–134.

McClain, E. W. Sixteen Personality Factor Questionnaire scores and success in counseling. *Journal of Counseling Psychology*, 1968, **15**, 492–496.

McFall, R. M., & Hammen, Constance L. Motivation, structure, and self-monitoring: Role of non-specific factors in smoking reduction. *Journal of Consulting & Clinical Psychology*, 1971, **37**, 80–86.

McNair, D. M., Callahan, D. M., & Lorr, M. Therapist type and patient response to psychotherapy. *Journal of Consulting Psychology*, 1962, **26**, 425–429.

McNair, D. M., & Lorr, M. An analysis of professed psychotherapeutic techniques. *Journal of Consulting Psychology*, 1964, **28**, 265–271.   (a)

McNair, D. M., & Lorr, M. An analysis of mood in neurotics. *Journal of Abnormal & Social Psychology*, 1964, **69**, 620–627.   (b)

McNair, D. M., Lorr, M., & Callahan, D. M. Patient and therapist influences on quitting psychotherapy. *Journal of Consulting Psychology*, 1963, **27**, 10–17.

McNair, D. M., Lorr, M., Young, H. H., Roth, I., & Boyd, R. W. A three-year follow-up of psychotherapy patients. *Journal of Clinical Psychology*, 1964, **20**, 258–264.

McNemar, Q. A critical examination of the University of Iowa studies of environmental influences upon the IQ. *Psychological Bulletin*, 1940, **37**, 63–92.

Meador, Betty D. Individual process in a brief encounter group. *Journal of Counseling Psychology*, 1971, **18**, 70–76.

Meichenbaum, D. H., & Goodman, J. Training impulsive children to talk to themselves: A means of developing self-control. *Journal of Abnormal Psychology*, 1971, **77**, 115–126.

Meltzoff, J., & Kornreich, M. *Research in psychotherapy*. New York: Atherton Press, 1970.

Mendelsohn, G. A. Effects of client personality and client-counselor similarity on the duration of counseling. *Journal of Counseling Psychology*, 1966, **13**, 228–234.

Mendelsohn, G. A. Client-counselor compatibility and the effectiveness of counseling. Technical report to Vocational Rehabilitation Administration, April 1968.

Mendelsohn, G. A., & Geller, M. H. Effects of counselor-client similarity on the outcome of counseling. *Journal of Counseling Psychology*, 1963, **10**, 71–77.

Mendelsohn, G. A., & Geller, M. H. Structure of client attitudes toward counseling and their relation to client-counselor similarity. *Journal of Consulting Psychology*, 1965, **29**, 63–72.

Mendelsohn, G. A., & Rankin, N. O. Client-counselor compatibilty and the outcome of counseling. *Journal of Abnormal Psychology*, 1969, **74**, 157–163.

Menninger, K. A. *Theory of psychoanalytic technique*. New York: Basic Books, 1958.

Menninger, K., Mayman, M., & Pruyser, P. *The vital balance: The life process in mental health and illness*. New York: Viking Press, 1963.

Merrill, R. M. On Keet's study, "Two verbal techniques in a minature counseling situation." *Journal of Abnormal & Social Psychology*, 1952, **74**, 722.

Meyer, M. M., & Tolman, Ruth S. The reactions of patients to enforced changes of therapists. *Journal of Clinical Psychology*, 1963, **19**, 241–243.

Miller, L. C., Barrett, C. L., Hampe, E., & Noble, Helen. Comparison of reciprocal inhibition, psychotherapy, and waiting list control for phobic children. *Journal of Abnormal Psychology*, 1972, **79**, 269–279.

Miller, W. R., & Seligman, E. P. Depression and the perception of reinforcement. *Journal of Abnormal Psychology*, 1973, **82**, 62–73.

Milliken, R. L., & Kirchner, R., Jr. Counselor's understanding of student's communications as a function of the counselor's perceptual defense. *Journal of Counseling Psychology*, 1971, **18**, 14–18.

Mills, D. H., & Abeles, N. Counselor needs for affiliation and nurturance as related to liking for clients and counseling process. *Journal of Counseling Psychology*, 1965, **12**, 353–358.

Mintz, J., Luborsky, L., & Auerback, A. H. Dimensions of psychotherapy: A factor-analytic study of ratings of psychotherapy sessions. *Journal of Consulting & Clinical Psychology*, 1971, **36**, 106–120.

Mintz, N. L. Patient fees and psychotherapeutic transactions. *Journal of Consulting & Clinical Psychology*, 1971, **36**, 1–8.

Mitchell, K. M., & Berenson, B. G. Differential use of confrontation by high and low facilitative therapists. *Journal of Nervous & Mental Diseases*, 1970, **151**, 303–309.

Mitchell, K. M., & Hall, L. A. Frequency and type of confrontation over time within the first therapy interview. *Journal of Consulting & Clinical Psychology*, 1971, **37**, 437–442.

Mitchell, K. M., & Namenek, Therese M. Effects of therapist confrontation on subsequent client and therapist behavior during first therapy interview. *Journal of Counseling Psychology*, 1972, **19**, 196–201.

Money-Kyrle, R. Normal countertransference and some of its deviations. *International Journal of Psychoanalysis*, 1956, **37**, 360–366.

Moos, R. H., & Clemes, S. R. Multivariate study of the patient-therapist system. *Journal of Consulting Psychology*, 1967, **31**, 119–130.

Moos, R. H., & MacIntosh, Shirley. Multivariate study of patient-therapist system: A replication. *Journal of Consulting & Clinical Psychology*, 1970, **35**, 298–307.

Morgan, R., & Bakan, P. Sensory deprivation hallucinations and other sleep behavior as a function of position, method of report, and anxiety. *Perceptual & Motor Skills*, 1965, **20**, 19–25.

Muehberg, Nancy, Pierce, R., & Drasgow, J. A factor analysis of therapeutically facilitative conditions. *Journal of Clinical Psychology*, 1969, **25**, 93–95.

Mueller, W. J. Patterns of behavior and their reciprocal impact in the family and in psychotherapy. *Journal of Counseling Psychology*, 1968, **16**, Part 2 (monograph).

Mueller, W. J., & Abeles, N. The components of empathy and their relationship to the projection of human movement responses. *Journal of Projective Techniques & Personality Assessments*, 1964, **28**, 322–330.

Mueller, W. J., & Dilling, C. A. Therapist-client interview behavior and personality characteristics of therapists. *Journal of Projective Techniques & Personality Assessments*, 1968, **32**, 281–288.

Muench, G. A. An investigation of the efficacy of time-limited psychotherapy. *Journal of Counseling Psychology*, 1965, **12**, 294–298.

Munson, Joan E. Patterns of client resistiveness and counselor response. Unpublished doctoral thesis, University of Michigan, 1960.

Murray, E. J. A case study in a behavioral analysis of psychotherapy. *Journal of Abnormal & Social Psychology*, 1954, **49**, 305–310.

Murray, E. J. A content-analysis method for studying psychotherapy. *Psychological Monographs*, 1956, **70** (13, Whole No. 420).

Murray, E. J. Verbal reinforcement in psychotherapy. *Journal of Consulting & Clinical Psychology*, 1968, **32**, 243–246.

Murray, E. J., & Jacobson, L. I. The nature of learning in traditional and behavioral psychotherapy. In A. E. Bergin & S. L. Garfield (Eds.), *Handbook of psychotherapy and behavior change*. New York: John Wiley, 1971.

Muthard, J. E. The relative effectiveness of larger units used in interview analysis. *Journal of Consulting Psychology*, 1953, **17**, 184–188.

Myrick, R. D. Effect of a model on verbal behavior in counseling. *Journal of Counseling Psychology*, 1969, **16**, 185–190.

Namenek, A. A., & Schuldt, W. J. Differential effects of experimenter personality and instrumental sets of verbal conditioning. *Journal of Counseling Psychology*, 1971, **18**, 170–172.

Nash, E. H., Hoehn-Saric, R., Battle, Carolyn C., Stone, A. R., Imber, S. D. & Frank,

J. D. Systematic preparation of patients for short-term psychotherapy: II. Relation to characteristics of patient, therapist and the psychotherapeutic process. *Journal of Nervous & Mental Disease*, 1965, **140**, 374–383.

Nawas, M. M., & Pucel, J. C. Relationship factors in desensitization: A persistent trend. *Journal of Counseling Psychology*, 1971, **18**, 239–243.

Noblin, C. D., Timmons, E. O., & Kael, H. C. Differential effects of positive and negative verbal reinforcement on psychoanalytic character types. *Journal of Personality & Social Psychology*, 1966, **4**, 224–228.

Nolan, J. D., Mattis, P. R., & Holliday, W. C. Long-term effects of behavior therapy: A 12-month follow-up. *Journal of Abnormal Psychology*, 1970, **76**, 88–97.

Northrup, F. S. C. *The Logic of the sciences and the humanities.* New York: Macmillan, 1947.

Novick, J. Symptomatic treatment of acquired and persistent enuresis. *Journal of Abnormal Psychology*, 1966, **71**, 363–368.

Nowicki, S., Jr., Bonner, J., & Feather, B. Effects of locus of control and differential interview procedures on perceived therapeutic relationship. *Journal of Consulting & Clinical Psychology*, 1972, **38**, 434–438.

Oppenheimer, R. The growth of science and the structure of culture. *Daedalus*, 1958, **87**, 67–76.

Orlinsky, D. E., & Howard, K. I. The good therapy hour: Experiential correlates of patients' and therapists' evaluations of therapy sessions. *Archives of General Psychiatry*, 1967, **16**, 621–632.

Orne, M. T., & Wender, P. H. Anticipatory socialization for psychotherapy: Method and rationale. *American Journal of Psychiatry*, 1968, **124**, 1202–1212.

Ornston, Patricia S., Cicchetti, D. V., Levine, J., & Fierman, L. B. Some parameters of verbal behavior that reliably differentiate novice from experienced psychotherapists. *Journal of Abnormal Psychology*, 1968, **73**, 240–244.

Ornston, Patricia S., Cicchetti, D. V., & Towbin, A. P. Reliable changes in psychotherapy behavior among first year psychiatric residents. *Journal of Abnormal Psychology*, 1970, **75**, 7–11.

Osburn, H. G. An investigation of the ambiguity of counselor behavior. Unpublished doctoral dissertation, University of Michigan, 1951.

Ourth, Lynn, & Landfield, A. W. Interpersonal meaningfulness and termination in psychotherapy. *Journal of Counseling Psychology*, 1965, 12, 366–371.

Overall, B., & Aronson, H. Expectations of psychotherapy in patients of lower socioeconomic class. *American Journal of Orthopsychiatry*, 1963, **33**, 421.

Pallone, N. J., & Grande, P. P. Counselor verbal mode, problem relevant communication, and client rapport. *Journal of Counseling Psychology*, 1965, **12**, 359–365.

Parker, G. V. Some concomitants of therapist dominance in the psychotherapy interview. *Journal of Consulting Psychology*, 1967, **31**, 313–318.

Parloff, M. B. Communication of value and therapeutic changes. *Archives of General Psychiatry*, 1960, **2**, 300–304.

Parloff, M., Kelman, H., & Frank, J. Comfort, effectiveness, and self-awareness as criteria of improvement in psychotherapy. *American Journal of Psychiatry*, 1954, **111**, 343–351.

Parrino, J. J. Effects of pretherapy information on learning in psychotherapy. *Journal of Abnormal Psychology*, 1971, **77**, 17–24.

Parsons, L. B., & Parker, G. V. C. Personal attitudes, clinical appraisals, and verbal behavior of trained and untrained therapists. *Journal of Consulting & Clinical Psychology*, 1968, **32**, 64–71.

Pascal, G. R., & Zax, M. Psychotherapeutics: Success or failure? *Journal of Consulting Psychology*, 1956, **20**, 325–331.

Passons, W. R., & Olsen, L. C. Relationship of counselor characteristics and empathic sensitivity. *Journal of Counseling Psychology*, 1969, **16**, 440–445.

Paul, G. L. *Insight versus desensitization*. Stanford, Calif.: Stanford University Press, 1966.

Paul, G. L. Behavior modification research: design and tactics. In C. M. Franks (Ed.), *Assessment and status of the behavior therapies and associated developments*. New York: McGraw-Hill, 1968.

Perls, F. S., Hefferline, R. F. & Goodman, P. *Gestalt therapy*. New York: Julian Press, 1951.

Phillips, Jeanne S., Matarazzo, J. D. & Saslow, G. Experimental modification of interviewer content in standardized interviews. *Journal of Consulting Psychology*, 1960, **24**, 528–535.

Pierce, R. M., Carkhuff, R. R., & Berenson, B. G. The differential effect of high and low functioning counselors upon counselors-in-training. *Journal of Clinical Psychology*, 1967, **23**, 212–215.

Polster, E., & Polster, Miriam. *Gestalt therapy integrated*. New York: Brunner/Mazel, 1973.

Popper, K. R. *Conjectures and refutations*. London: Rutledge and Kegan Paul, 1963.

Porter, E. H., Jr. The development and evaluation of a measure of counseling interview procedures: I. The development. *Educational & Psychological Measurement*, 1943, **3**, 105–126.   (a)

Porter, E. H., Jr. The development and evaluation of a measure of counseling interview procedures: II. The evaluation. *Educational & Psychological Measurement*, 1943, **3**, 215–238.   (b)

Powell, W. J., Jr. Differential effectiveness of interviewer interventions in an experimental interview. *Journal of Consulting & Clinical Psychology*, 1968, **32**, 210–215.

Prager, R. A., & Garfield, S. L. Client initial disturbance and outcome in psychotherapy. *Journal of Consulting & Clinical Psychology*, 1972, **38**, 112–117.

Price, Leah Z., & Iverson, M. A. Student's perception of counselors with varying statuses and role behaviors in the initial interview. *Journal of Counseling Psychology*, 1969, **16**, 469–475.

Rachman, S. Aversion therapy: Chemical or electrical? *Behavior Research & Therapy*, 1965, 2, 289–299.

Raimy, V. C. Self-references in counseling interviews. *Journal of Consulting Psychology*, 1948, **12**, 153–163.

Raimy, V. C. (Ed.). *Training in clinical psychology*. Englewood Cliffs, N.J.: Prentice-Hall, 1950.

Rank, O. *Will therapy and truth and reality*. New York: Alfred A. Knopf, 1945.

Rapaport, D. The theory of ego autonomy: A generalization. *Bulletin of the Menninger Clinic*, 1958. **22**, 13–15.

Rapaport, D. The structure of psychoanalytic theory. *Psychological Issues*, 1960, Monograph 6.

Rappaport, J., & Chinsky, J. M. Accurate empathy: Confusion of a construct. *Psychological Bulletin*, 1972, **77**, 400–404.

Raush, H. L. Interaction sequences. *Journal of Personality & Social Psychology*, 1965, **2**, 487–499.

Raush, H. L., & Bordin, E. S. Warmth in personality development and in psychotherapy. *Psychiatry*, 1957, **20**, 351–363.

Raush, H. L., Sperber, Z., Rigler, D., Williams, Joan, Harway, N. I., Bordin, E. S., Dittmann, A. T., & Hays, W. L. A dimensional analysis of depth of interpretation. *Journal of Consulting Psychology*, 1956, **20**, 43–48.

Razin, A. M. A-B variable in psychotherapy: A critical review. *Psychological Bulletin*, 1971, **75**, 1–21.

Rehm, L. P., & Marston, A. R. Reduction of social anxiety through modification of self-reinforcement: An instigation therapy technique. *Journal of Consulting & Clinical Psychology*, 1968, **32**, 565-574.

Reik, T. *Listening with the third ear*. New York: Farrar & Straus, 1949.

Rhoades, J. M., & Feather, B. W. Transference and resistance observed in behavior therapy. *British Journal of Medical Psychology*, 1972, **45**, 99–104.

Rice, Laura N. Therapist's style of participation and case outcome. *Journal of Consulting Psychology*, 1965, **29**, 155–160.

Rice, Laura N. Client behavior as a function of therapist style and client resources. *Journal of Counseling Psychology*, 1973, **20**, 305–311.

Rice, Laura N., & Gaylin, N. I. Personality processes reflected in client vocal style and Rorschach performance. *Journal of Consulting & Clinical Psychology*, 1973, **40**, 133–138.

Rice, Laura N., & Wagstaff, Alice K. Client voice quality and expressive style as indexes of productive psychotherapy. *Journal of Consulting Psychology*, 1967, **31**, 557–563.

Riessman, F., & Scribner, S. The underutilization of mental services by workers and low income groups: Causes and cures. *American Journal of Psychiatry*, 1965, **121**, 798–801.

Rigler, D. Some determinants of therapist behavior. Unpublished doctoral thesis, University of Michigan, 1957.

Ritter, B. The group desensitization of children's snake phobias using vicarious and contact desensitization. *Behavior Research & Therapy*, 1968, **6**, 1–6.

Robbins, L. L., & Wallerstein, R. S. The research strategy and tactics of the psychotherapy research project of the Menninger Foundation and the problem of controls. In E. A. Rubinstein and M. B. Parloff (Eds.), *Reserach in psychotherapy*. Vol. I. Washington: American Psychological Association, 1959.

Rogers, C. R. *Counseling and psychotherapy*. New York: Houghton-Mifflin, 1942.

Rogers, C. R. *Client-centered therapy*. New York: Houghton-Mifflin, 1951.

Rogers, C. R. The necessary and sufficient conditions of therapeutic personality change. *Journal of Consulting Psychology*, 1957, **21**, 95–103.

Rogers, C. R. Therapy, personality, and interpersonal relationships. In S. Koch (Ed.), *Psychology: A study of a science.* Vol. 3. New York: McGraw-Hill, 1959. (a)

Rogers, C. R. A tentative scale for the measurement of process in psychotherapy. In E. A. Rubinstein and M. B. Parloff (Eds.), *Research in psychotherapy.* Vol. I. Washington, D.C.: American Psychological Association, 1959. (b)

Rogers, C. R., & Dymond, Rosalind F. (Eds.). *Psychotherapy and personality change.* Chicago: University of Chicago Press, 1954.

Rogers, C. R., Gendlin, E. T., Kiesler, D., & Truax, C. B. *The therapeutic relationship and its impact: A study of psychotherapy with schizophrenics.* Madison: University of Wisconsin Press, 1967.

Rose, Harriett A., & Elton, C. F. Identification of potential personal problem clients. *Journal of Counseling Psychology,* 1972, **19**, 8–10.

Rosenthal, D. Changes in some moral values following psychotherapy. *Journal of Consulting Psychology,* 1955, **19**, 431–436.

Rosenthal, D., & Frank, J. D. The fate of psychiatric clinic outpatients assigned to psychotherapy. *Journal of Nervous & Mental Disorders,* 1958, **127**, 330–343.

Rosenthal, R. *Experimenter effects in behavioral research.* New York: Appleton-Century-Crofts, 1966.

Rothaus, P., Johnson, D. L., Hansen, P. G., Brown, J. B., & Lyle, F. A. Sentence-completion test prediction of autonomous and therapist-led group behavior. *Journal of Counseling Psychology,* 1967, **14**, 28–32.

Rothaus, P., Johnson, D. L., Hansen, P. G., Lyle, F. A., & Moyer, R. Participation and sociometry in autonomous and trainer-led patient groups. *Journal of Counseling Psychology,* 1966, **13**, 68–76.

Rothaus, P., Johnson, D. L., & Lyle, F. A. Group participation training for psychiatric patients. *Journal of Counseling Psychology,* 1964, **11**, 230–238.

Rothaus, P., Morton, R. B., Johnson, D. L., Cleaveland, S. E., & Lyle, F. A. Human relations training for psychiatric patients. *Archives of General Psychiatry,* 1963, **8**, 572–581.

Rotter, J. R. Generalized expectancies for internal versus external control of reinforcement. *Psychological Monographs,* 1966, **80** (1, Whole No. 609).

Rottschafer, R. N., & Renzaglia, G. A. The relationship of dependent-like verbal behavior to counselor style and induced set. *Journal of Consulting Psychology,* 1962, **26**, 172–177.

Rubinstein, E. A., & Lorr, M. A comparison of terminators and remainers in outpatient psychotherapy. *Journal of Clinical Psychology,* 1956, **12**, 345–349.

Rubinstein, E. A., & Parloff, M. B. (Eds.). *Research in psychotherapy.* Vol. I. Washington, D.C.: American Psychological Association, 1959.

Russell, P. D., & Snyder, W. U. Counselor anxiety in relation to amount of clinical experience and quality of affect demonstrated by clients. *Journal of Consulting Psychology,* 1963, **27**, 358–363.

Ryan, E. R. The capacity of the patient to enter an elementary therapeutic relationship in the initial psychotherapy interview. Unpublished doctoral thesis, University of Michigan, 1973.

Ryan, V. L. The construct validation of psychotherapy outcome. Unpublished thesis, University of Michigan 1970.

Ryan, V. L., & Gizynski, Martha N. Behavior therapy in retrospect: patients' feeling about their behavior therapies. *Journal of Consulting & Clinical Psychology*, 1971, **37**, 1–9.

Salzberg, H. C. Verbal behavior in group psychotherapy with and without a therapist. *Journal of Counseling Psychology*, 1967, **14**, 24–29.

Salzinger, K. The place of operant conditioning of verbal behavior in psychotherapy. In C. M. Franks (Ed.), *Behavior therapy: Appraisal and status*. New York: McGraw-Hill, 1969.

Sapolsky, A. Relationship between patient-doctors compatibility, mutual perception, and outcome of treatment. *Journal of Abnormal Psychology*, 1965, **70**, 70–76.

Sarason, I. G. Interrelationships among individual difference variables, behavior in psychotherapy and verbal conditioning. *Journal of Abnormal & Social Psychology*, 1958, **56**, 339–344.

Sargent, Helen D. Intrapsychic change: Methodological problems in psychotherapy research. *Psychiatry*, 1961, **24**, 93–108.

Saslow, G., & Matarazzo, J. D. A technique for studying changes in interviewer behavior. In E. A. Rubinstein and M. B. Parloff (Eds.), *Research in psychotherapy*. Vol. I. Washington, D.C.: American Psychological Association, 1959.

Schachter, S. *The psychology of affiliation*. Stanford, Calif.: Stanford University Press, 1959.

Schaffer, L., & Myers, J. Psychotherapy and social stratification. *Psychiatry*, 1954, **17**, 83–93.

Schmidt, L. D., & Strong, S. R. Attractiveness and influence in counseling. *Journal of Counseling Psychology*, 1971, **18**, 348–351.

Schneider, S. F. Prediction of psychotherapeutic relationship from Rorschach's test. Unpublished doctoral dissertation, University of Michigan, 1953.

Schoeninger, D. W., Klein, Marjorie H., & Mathieu, Phillipa L. Comparison of two methods for training judges to note psychotherapy recordings. *Journal of Consulting & Clinical Psychology*, 1968, **32**, 499.

Schofield, W. *Psychotherapy: The purchase of friendship*. Englewood Cliffs, N.J. Prentice-Hall, 1964.

Schofield, William. The structured personality inventory in measurement of effects of psychotherapy. In L. A. Gottschalk and A. H. Auerbach (Eds.), *Methods of research in psychotherapy*. New York: Appleton-Century-Crofts, 1966.

Schrier, H. The significance of identification in therapy. *American Journal of Orthopsychiatry*, 1953, **23**, 585–604.

Schroeder, Pearl. Client acceptance of responsibility and difficulty of therapy. *Journal of Consulting Psychology*, 1960, **24**, 467–471.

Schuldt, W. J. Psychotherapists' approach-avoidance responses and clients' expressions of dependency. *Journal of Counseling Psychology*, 1966, **13**, 178–183.

Schutz, W. C. *FIRO: A three-dimensional theory of interpersonal behavior*. New York: Rinehart, 1958.

Scott, R. W., & Kemp, D. E. The A-B scale and empathy, warmth, genuineness, and depth of self-exploration. *Journal of Abnormal Psychology*, 1971, **77**, 49–51.

Seeman, J. A study of the process of nondirective therapy. *Journal of Consulting Psychology*, 1949, **13**, 157–168.

Seeman, J. Psychotherapy. *Annual Review of Psychology*, 1961, **12**, 157–194.

Segal, B. A-B distinction and therapeutic interaction. *Journal of Consulting & Clinical Psychology*, 1970, **34**, 442–446.

Seitz, P. E. D. The consensus problem in psychoanalytic research. In L. A. Gottschalk & A. H. Auerbach (Eds.), *Methods of research in psychotherapy*. New York: Appleton-Century-Crofts, 1966.

Seligman, M., & Sterne, D. M. Verbal behavior in therapist-led, leaderless, and alternating group psychotherapy sessions. *Journal of Counseling Psychology*, 1969, **16**, 325–328.

Shapiro, J. G. Agreement between channels of communication in interviews. *Journal of Consulting Psychology*, 1966, **30**, 535–538.

Shapiro, J. G. Relationships between expert and neophyte ratings of therapeutic conditions. *Journal of Consulting & Clinical Psychology*, 1968, **32**, 87–89.   (a)

Shapiro, J. G. Relationships between visual and auditory cues of therapeutic effectiveness. *Journal of Clinical Psychology*, 1968, **24**, 236–239.   (b)

Shapiro, J. G., Foster, C. P., & Powell, T. Facial and bodily cues of genuineness, empathy and warmth. *Journal of Clinical Psychology*, 1968, **24**, 232–236.

Shemberg, K., & Keeley, S. Psychodiagnostic training in the academic setting: Past and present. *Journal of Consulting & Clinical Psychology*, 1970, **34**, 205–211.

Sherman, A. R. Real-life exposure as a primary therapeutic factor in the desensitization treatment of fear. *Journal of Abnormal Psychology*, 1972, **79**, 19–28.

Sherman, J. A., & Baer, D. M. Appraisal of operant therapy techniques with children and adults. In C. M. Franks (Ed.), *Behavior therapy: Appraisal and status*. New York: McGraw-Hill, 1969.

Shlien, J. M. A client-centered approach to schizophrenia: First approximation. In A. Burton (Ed.), *Psychotherapy of the psychoses*. New York: Basic Books, 1961.

Shlien, J. M. Toward what level of abstraction in criteria? In H. H. Strupp and L. Luborsky (Eds.), *Research in psychotherapy*. Vol. II. Washington, D.C.: American Psychological Association, 1962.

Shlien, J. M. (Ed.) *Research in psychotherapy*. Vol. III. Washington, D.C.: American Psychological Association, 1968.

Shlien, J. M., Mosak, H. H., & Dreikurs, R. Effect of time limits: A comparison of two psychotherapies. *Journal of Counseling Psychology*, 1962, **9**, 31–34.

Shlien, J. M., & Zimring, F. M. Research directives and methods in client-centered therapy. In L. A. Gottschalk and A. H. Auerbach (Eds.), *Methods of research in psychotherapy*. New York: Appleton-Century-Crofts, 1966.

Shostrom, E. L., & Riley, Clara M. D. Parametric analysis of psychotherapy. *Journal of Consulting Psychology*, 1968, **32**, 628–632.

Siegman, A. W., & Pope, B. The effects of ambiguity and anxiety and interviewee verbal behavior. Paper presented at Research Conference on Interview Behavior, University of Maryland, 1968.

Sieveking, N. A., Campbell, M. L., Rileigh, W. J., & Savitsky, J. Mass intervention by mail for an academic impediment. *Journal of Counseling Psychology*, 1971, **18**, 601–602.

Snyder, W. U. An investigation of the nature of nondirective psychotherapy. *Journal of General Psychology*, 1945, **33**, 193–223.

Snyder, W. U. Some investigations of relationhsip in psychotherapy. In E. A. Rubinstein and M. P. Parloff (Eds.), *Research in psychotherapy.* Vol. I. Washington, D.C.: American Psychological Association, 1959.

Snyder, W. U. *The psychotherapy relationship.* New York: Macmillan, 1961.

Snyder, W. U. Comment. *Journal of Counseling Psychology,* 1962, **9,** 29–30.

Solomon, P., Kubzansky, P. E., Leiderman, P. H., Mendelson, J. H., Trumbull, R., & Wexler, D. (Eds.). *Sensory deprivation.* Cambridge, Mass.: Harvard University Press, 1961.

Speisman, J. C. Depth of interpretation and verbal resistance in psychotherapy. *Journal of Consulting Psychology,* 1959, **23,** 93–99.

Spiritas, A. A., & Holmes, D. S. Effects of models on interview-responses. *Journal of Counseling Psychology,* 1971, **18,** 217–220.

Stampfl, T. G., & Levis, D. J. Essentials of implosive therapy: A learning theory based psychodynamic behavioral therapy. *Journal of Abnormal Psychology,* 1967, **72,** 496–503.

Stein, S. H. Arousal level in repressors and sensitizers as a function of response context. *Journal of Consulting & Clinical Psychology,* 1971, **36,** 386–394.

Sterba, R. F. The fate of the ego in analytic therapy. *International Journal of Psychoanalysis,* 1934, **15,** 117–126.

Steuart, D. J., & Resnick, J. H. Verbal conditioning and dependency behavior in delinquents. *Journal of Abnormal Psychology,* 1970, **76,** 375–377.

Stewart, H. Sensory deprivation, personality, and visual imagery. *Journal of General Psychology,* 1965, **72,** 145–150.

Stieper, D. R., & Wiener, D. N. The problem of interminability in outpatient psychotherapy. *Journal of Consulting Psychology,* 1959, **23,** 237–242.

Stoler, N. Client likability: A variable in the study of psychotherapy. *Journal of Consulting Psychology,* 1963, **27,** 175–178.

Stollak, G. E., Denner, B., Jackson, Pamela, & Packard, M. The effects of self-ideal self discrepancies in the content of free association. Paper presented at the Midwestern Psychological Association meeting, Chicago, 1967.

Stone, L. *The psychoanalytic situation.* New York: International Universities Press, 1961.

Strickland, Bonnie R., & Crowne, D. P. Need for approval and the premature termination of psychotherapy. *Journal of Consulting Psychology,* 1963, 27, 95–101.

Strong, S. R. Counseling: An interpersonal influence process. *Journal of Counseling Psychology,* 1968, **15,** 215–224.

Strong, S. R., & Schmidt, L. D. Trustworthiness and influence in counseling. *Journal of Counseling Psychology,* 1970, **17,** 197–204.

Strupp, H. H. A multidimensional comparison of therapist activity in analytic and client-centered therapy. *Journal of Consulting Psychology,* 1957, **21,** 301–308.

Strupp, H. H. The performance of psychoanalytic and client-centered therapists in an initial interview. *Journal of Consulting Psychology,* 1958, **22,** 265–274.

Strupp, H. H. *Psychotherapists in action.* New York: Grune and Stratton, 1960.

Strupp, H. H. The therapist's contribution to the patient's treatment career. In H. H.

Strupp & L. Luborsky (Eds.), *Research in psychotherapy*. Vol. II. Washington, D.C.: American Psychological Association, 1962.

Strupp, H. H., & Bergin, A. E. Some empirical and conceptual bases for coordinated research in psychotherapy: A critical review of issues, trends, and evidence. *International Journal of Psychiatry*, 1969, **7**, 18–20.

Strupp, H. H., Chassan, J. B., & Ewing, J. A. Toward the longitudinal study of the psychotherapeutic process. In L. A. Gottschalk & A. H. Auerback (Eds.), *Methods of research in psychotherapy*. New York: Appleton-Century-Crofts, 1966.

Strupp, H. H., & Luborsky, L. (Eds.). *Research in psychotherapy*. Vol. II. Washington, D.C.: American Psychological Association, 1962.

Strupp, H. H., Wallach, M. S., Jenkins, Joan W., & Wogan, M. Psychotherapists' assessments of former patients. *Journal of Nervous & Mental Disease*, 1963, **137**, 222–230.

Strupp, H. H., Wallach, M. S., & Wogan, M. The psychotherapy experience in retrospect: A questionnaire survey of former patients and their therapists. *Psychological Monographs*, 1964, **78** (11, Whole No. 588).

Strupp, H. H., & Williams, Joan V. Some determinants of clinical evaluations of different psychiatrists. *Archives of General Psychiatry*, 1960, **2**, 434–440.

Suinn, R. M., Jorgensen, G. T., Stewart, S. T., & McGuirk, F. D. Fears as attitudes: Experimental reduction of fear through reinforcement. *Journal of Abnormal Psychology*, 1971, **78**, 272–279.

Sullivan, H. S. *The interpersonal theory of psychiatry*. New York: Norton, 1953.

Sundland, D. M., & Barker, E. N. The orientations of psychotherapists. *Journal of Consulting Psychology*, 1962, **26**, 201–212.

Taulbee, E. S. Relationship between certain personality variables and continuation in psychotherapy. *Journal of Consulting Psychology*, 1958, **22**, 83–89.

Taylor, J. W. Relationship of success and length in psychotherapy. *Journal of Consulting Psychology*, 1956, **20**, 332.

Temerlin, M. K. One determinant of the capacity to free associate in psychotherapy. *Journal of Abnormal & Social Psychology*, 1956, **53**, 16–18.

Terwilliger, J. S., & Fiedler, F. E. An investigation of determinants inducing individuals to seek personal counseling. *Journal of Consulting Psychology*, 1958, **22**, 288.

Thelan, M. H., Varble, D. L., & Johnson, J. Attitudes of academic clinical psychologists toward projective techniques. *American Psychologist*, 1968, **23**, 517–521.

Timmons, E. O. & Noblin, C. D. The differential performance of orals and anals in a verbal conditioning paradigm. *Journal of Consulting Psychology*, 1963, **27**, 383–386.

Toman, W. Pause analysis as a short interviewing technique. *Journal of Consulting Psychology*, 1953, **17**, 1–7.

Tomlinson, T. M., & Hart, J. T., Jr. A validation of the process scale. *Journal of Consulting Psychology*, 1962, **26**, 74–78.

Tourney, G., Bloom, V., Lowinger, P. L., Schoer, C., Auld, F., & Grissell, J. A study of psychotherapeutic process varibales in psychoneurotic and schizophrenic paitents. *American Journal of Psychotherapy*, 1966, **20**, 112–124.

Townsend, A. H. An empirical measure of ambiguity in the context of psychotherapy. *Michigan Academy of Science, Arts and Letters*, 1956, **41**, 349–355.

Trexler, L. D., & Karst, T. O. Rational-emotive therapy, placebo, and no-treatment effects on public-speaking anxiety. *Journal of Abnormal Psychology*, 1972, **79**, 60–67.

Truax, C. B. Therapist empathy, warmth, and genuineness and patient personality change in group psychotherapy: A comparison between interaction unit measures, time sample measures, patient perception measures. *Journal of Clinical Psychology*, 1966, **22**, 225–229.   (a)

Truax, C. B. Influence of patient statements on judgments of therapist statements during psychotherapy. *Journal of Clinical Psychology*, 1966, **22**, 335–337.   (b)

Truax, C. B. Reinforcement and non-reinforcement in Rogerian psychotherapy. *Journal of Abnormal & Social Psychology*, 1966, **71**, 1–9.   (c)

Truax, C. B. Effects of client-centered psychotherapy with schizophrenic patients: nine-year pretherapy and nine-year post-therapy hospitalization. *Journal of Consulting & Clinical Psychology*, 1970, **35**, 417–422.   (a)

Truax, C. B. Length of therapist response, accurate empathy and patient improvement. *Journal of Clinical Psychology*, 1970, **26**, 539–541.   (b)

Truax, C. B. The meaning and reliability of Accurate Empathy ratings: a rejoinder. *Psychological Bulletin*, 1972, **77**, 397–399.

Truax, C. B., & Carkhuff, R. R. Experimental manipulation of therapeutic conditions. *Journal of Consulting Psychology*, 1965, **29**, 119–124.   (a)

Truax, C. B., & Carkhuff, R. R. Personality change in hospitalized mental patients during group therapy as a function of the use of alternative sessions and vicarious therapy pretraining. *Journal of Clinical Psychology*, 1965, **21**, 225–228.   (b)

Truax, C. B., & Carkhuff, R. R. *Toward effective counseling and psychotherapy: Training and practice.* Chicago: Aldine, 1967.

Truax, C. B., Carkhuff, R. R., & Douds, J. Toward an integration of the didactic and experiential approaches to training in counseling and psychotherapy. *Journal of Counseling Psychology*, 1964, **11**, 240–247.

Truax, C. B., Carkhuff, R. R., & Kodman, F., Jr. Relationships between therapist-offered conditions and patient change in group psychotherapy. *Journal of Clinical Psychology*, 1965, **21**, 327–329.

Truax, C. B., Fine, H., Moravec, J., & Millis, W. Effects of therapist persuasive potency in individual psychotherapy. *Journal of Clinical Psychology*, 1968, **24**, 358–362.

Truax, C. B., & Wargo, D. G. Effects of vicarious therapy pretraining and alternate sessions on outcome in group psychotherapy with outpatients. *Journal of Consulting & Clinical Psychology*, 1969, **33**, 440–447.

Truax, C. B., Wargo, D. G., Frank, J. D., Imber, S. D., Battle, Carolyn C., Hoehn-Saric, R., Nash, E. H., & Stone, A. R. Therapist's contribution to accurate, non-possessive warmth and genuineness in psychotherapy. *Journal of Clinical Psychology*, 1966, **22**, 331–334.   (a)

Truax, C. B., Wargo, D. G., Frank, J. D., Imber, S. D., Battle, Carolyn C., Hoehn-Saric, R., Nash, E. H., & Stone, A. R. Therapist empathy genuineness, and warmth and patient therapeutic outcome. *Journal of Consulting Psychology*, 1966, **30**, 395–401.   (b)

Truax, C. B., Wargo, D. G., & Silber, L. D. Effects of group psychotherapy with high accurate empathy and non-possessive warmth with female institutionalized delinquents. *Journal of Abnormal Psychology*, 1966, **71**, 267–274.

Truax, C. B., Wargo, D. G., & Volksdorf, N. R. Antecedants to outcome in group counseling with institutionalized juvenile delinquents: Effects of therapeutic conditions, patient self-exploration, alternate sessions and vicarious therapy pretraining. *Journal of Abnormal Psychology*, 1970, **76**, 235–242.

Uhlenhuth, E. H., & Duncan, D. B. Subjective change with medical student therapists. *Archives of General Psychiatry*, 1968, **18**, 532–540.

Ullmann, L. P., & Krasner, L. *A psychological approach to abnormal behavior.* Englewood Cliffs, N.J.: Prentice-Hall, 1969.

Ullmann, L. P., Krasner, L., & Collins, Beverly J. Modification of behavior through verbal conditioning: Effects in group therapy. *Journal of Abnormal & Social Psychology*, 1961, **62**, 128–132.

Van Atta, R. E. Relationship of personality characteristics to persistence in psychotherapy. *Journal of Consulting & Clinical Psychology*, 1968, **32**, 731–733.

Van Der Veen, F. Effects of the therapist and the patient on each other's therapeutic behavior. *Journal of Consulting Psychology*, 1965, **29**, 19–26.

Van Der Veen, F. Basic elements in process of psychotherapy: A research study. *Journal of Consulting & Clinical Psychology*, 1967, **31**, 295–303.

Varble, D. L. Relationship between the therapists' approach-avoidance reactions to hostility and client behavior in therapy. *Journal of Consulting & Clinical Psychology*, 1968, **32**, 237–242.

Vitalo, R. L. Effects of facilitative interpersonal functioning in a conditioning paradigm. *Journal of Counseling Psychology*, 1970, **17**, 141–144.

Wallach, M. S., & Strupp, H. H. Dimensions of psychotherapists' activity. *Journal of Consulting Psychology*, 1964, **28**, 120–125.

Warren, N. C., & Rice, Laura N. Structuring and stabilizing of psychotherapy for low prognosis clients. *Journal of Consulting & Clinical Psychology*, 1972, **39**, 173–181.

Waskow, Irene E. Reinforcement in a therapy-like situation through selective responding to feelings of content. *Journal of Consulting Psychology*, 1962, **26**, 11–9.

Waskow, Irene E. Counselor attitudes and client behavior. *Journal of Counseling Psychology*, 1963, **27**, 405–512.

Waskow, Irene, & Bergman, P. Does "theoretical orientation" influence ratings of "warmth-acceptance"? *Journal of Consulting Psychology*, 1962, **26**, 484.

Weckowicz, T. E., Yonge, K. A., Cropley, A. J., & Muir, W. Objective therapy predictors in depression. *Journal of Clinical Psychology*, 1971, **27**, 3–27.

Weigel, R. G., Dinges, N., Dyer, R., & Stroumfjord, A. A. Perceived self-disclosure, mental health, and who is liked in group treatment. *Journal of Counseling Psychology*, 1972, **19**, 47–52.

Weigel, R. G., & Warnath, C. F. The effects of group therapy on reported self-disclosure. *International Journal of Group Psychotherapy*, 1968, **18**, 31–41.

Weigert, Edith. The psychotherapy of the affective psychoses. In A. Burton (Ed.), *Psychotherapy of the psychoses.* New York: Basic Books, 1961.

Weitzman, B. Behavior therapy and psychotherapy. *Psychological Review*, 1967, **74**, 300–317.

Welkowitz, Joan, Cohen, J., & Ortmeyer, D. Value system similarity: Investigation of patient-therapist dyads. *Journal of Consulting Psychology*, 1967, **31**, 48–55.

Wexler, M. Psychological distance in the treatment of a schizophrenic patient. In R. Lindner (Ed.), *Explorations in psychoanalysis*. New York: Julian, 1953.

Whalen, Carol. Effects of a model and instructions on group verbal behaviors. *Journal of Consulting & Clinical Psychology*, 1969, **33**, 509–521.

White, Alice M., Fichtenbaum, L., & Dollard, J. Measure for predicting dropping out of psychotherapy. *Journal of Consulting Psychology*, 1964, **28**, 326–332.

Whitehorn, J. C., & Betz, Barbara. A study of psychotherapeutic relationships between physicians and schizophrenic patients. *American Journal of Psychiatry*, 1954, **111**, 321–331.

Whitehorn, J. C., & Betz, Barbara. A comparison of psychotherapeutic relationships between physicians and schizophrenic patients when insulin is combined with psychotherapy and when insulin is used alone. *American Journal of Psychiatry*, 1957, **113**, 901–910.

Whitehorn, J. C., & Betz, Barbara. Further studies of the doctor as a crucial variable in the outcome of treatment of schizophrenic patients. *American Journal of Psychiatry*, 1960, **117**, 215–223.

Whitely, J. M., & Blaine, G. B., Jr. Rorschach in relation to outcome in psychotherapy with college students. *Journal of Consulting Psychology*, 1967, **31**, 595–599.

Whitely, J. M., Sprinthall, N. A., Mosher, R. L., & Donaghy, R. T. Selection and evaluation of counselor effectiveness. *Journal of Counseling Psychology*, 1967, **14**, 226–234.

Williams, Joan V. The influence of therapist commitment on progress in psychotherapy. Unpublished doctoral thesis, University of Michigan, 1959.

Williams, V. G., Jr. The conflicts of the psychotherapist and his commitment to his patient. Unpublished doctoral thesis, University of Michigan, 1962.

Wilson, A. E., & Smith, F. J. Counter-conditioning therapy using free association: A pilot study. *Journal of Abnormal Psychology*, 1968, **73**, 474–478.

Wilson, G. T., Hannon, A. E., & Evans, W. I. M. Behavior therapy and the therapist-patient relationship. *Journal of Consulting & Clinical Psychology*, 1968, **32**, 103–109.

Winborn, B. B., & Rowe, W. Self-actualization and the communication of facilitative conditions: A replication. *Journal of Counseling Psychology*, 1972, **19**, 26–29.

Winder, C. L., Ahmad, Farrukh Z., Bandura, A., & Rau, L. C. Dependency of patients, psychotherapists' responses, and aspects of psychotherapy. *Journal of Consulting Psychology*, 1962, **26**, 129–134.

Wogan, M. Effects of therapist-patient personality variables on therapeutic outcome. *Journal of Consulting & Clinical Psychology*, 1970, **35**, 356–361.

Wolpe, J. *Psychotherapy by reciprocal inhibition*. Stanford, Calif.: Stanford University Press, 1968.

Wolpe, J., & Lazarus, A. A. *Behavior therapy techniques*. New York: Pergamon Press, 1968.

Wylie, Ruth C. *The self concept*. Lincoln: University of Nebraska, 1961.

Yaskin, J. C. The psychoneuroses and neuroses: A review of 100 cases with special reference to treatment and end results. *American Journal of Psychiatry*, 1936, **93**, 107–125.

Yulis, S., & Kiesler, D. J. Countertransference response as a function of therapist anxiety and content of patient talk. *Journal of Consulting & Clinical Psychology*, 1968, **32**, 413–419.

Zeisset, R. M. Desensitization and relaxation in modification of psychiatric patients' interview behavior. *Journal of Abnormal Psychology*, 1968, **73**, 18–24.

Zimmer, J. M., & Pepyne, E. W. A descriptive and comparative study of dimensions of counselor response. *Journal of Counseling Psychology*, 1971, **18**, 441–447

Zuckerman, M. Hallucinations, reported sensations, and images. In J. P. Zubek (Ed.), *Sensory deprivation: fifteen years of research*. New York: Appleton-Century-Crofts, 1969.

Index